Sub-versions of the Archive

Sub-versions of the Archive

Manuel Puig's and Severo Sarduy's Alternative Identities

Carlos Riobó

Lewisburg
BUCKNELL UNIVERSITY PRESS

Published by Bucknell University Press
Co-published with The Rowman & Littlefield Publishing Group, Inc.
4501 Forbes Boulevard, Suite 200, Lanham, Maryland 20706
www.rlpgbooks.com

Estover Road, Plymouth PL6 7PY, United Kingdom

Copyright © 2011 by Carlos Riobó

All rights reserved. No part of this book may be reproduced in any form or by any electronic or mechanical means, including information storage and retrieval systems, without written permission from the publisher, except by a reviewer who may quote passages in a review.

British Library Cataloguing in Publication Information Available

Library of Congress Cataloging-in-Publication Data Available

ISBN: 978-1-61148-036-8 (cloth : alk. paper)
ISBN: 978-1-61148-037-5 (electronic)

∞™ The paper used in this publication meets the minimum requirements of American National Standard for Information Sciences—Permanence of Paper for Printed Library Materials, ANSI/NISO Z39.48-1992.

Printed in the United States of America

Contents

Acknowledgments	7
1. Introduction: Alternative Identities and Aberrant Archives	11
2. Raiding the Archive: An Analysis of an Archival Tradition and Its New Configurations	37
3. Manuel Puig: El "doble irrisorio" de un subgénero: Entering the Archive through *Boquitas pintadas* and *The Buenos Aires Affair*	69
4. Manuel Puig: The Patriarch Betrayed: The Archive's Alternative Voices in *La traición de Rita Hayworth* and *El beso de la mujer araña*	99
5. Severo Sarduy: *Monstrorum Artifex:* Cultural Compendia as Alternative Archives in *De donde son los cantantes* and *Cobra*	124
6. Severo Sarduy: Raiding Archives and Reformulating Narrative Traditions: *Maitreya* and *Colibrí*	163
Notes	189
Bibliography	208
Index	227

Acknowledgments

"When the Labyrinth is Deciphered, it Will Disappear."[1]

WRITING THIS BOOK HAS BEEN AN INDULGENT PLEASURE FOR ME, BUT also a gratification delayed by the effects of the attacks of September 11, 2001 on New York City and on my family. I would like to thank all of those dear friends and relatives who indulged my indulgence with Puig and Sarduy, the enigmatic writers whom I hope never to decipher fully. The labyrinth that I do indeed hope to have deciphered, and, therefore, to have made disappear, is one I entered over a decade ago when I started seeing this project through the lens of my personal aspirations. This is a professional project, and I now know that.[2]

I dedicate this book to my grandmother, Herminia Moreda López de Castiñeiras, whom we lost in 2008 at the age of 105 and to Danny Alter, whom I gained as a husband the same year, after twenty-one years of partnership. They indulged and inspired me, and I love and thank them for it.

I want to express my gratitude here to all those people at Bucknell University Press/AUP who helped my ideas appear in print: Greg Clingham, Nina Forsberg, Julien Yoseloff, Christine A. Retz, and Aníbal González.

To the Office of the Dean of Humanities and Arts at The City College of New York I am grateful for their generous support.

I also want to thank the University of Nebraska Press for giving me permission to reprint parts of my article, "*Heartbreak Tango:* Manuel Puig's Counter-Archive," from *Narrative Beginnings: Theories and Prac-*

---

1. The title of Elizabeth Hellman's collection of poetry is taken from an ancient Egyptian belief.
2. Unless otherwise noted, all translations are my own. All bracketed translations in this book are my own save where otherwise indicated.

tices edited by Brian Richardson. © 2008 by the Board of Regents of the University of Nebraska. I am grateful as well to Koninklijke Brill NV for allowing me to reprint parts of my article, "The Medieval Inheritance of Manuel Puig and Severo Sarduy," from *Medieval Encounters: Jewish, Christian and Muslim Culture in Confluence and Dialogue* 3.2 (1997). To Thomas Colchie, of the Colchie Agency, and to Carlos Puig I am grateful for granting me the nonexclusive rights for using 626 words from the 1989 Seix Barral edition of *Boquitas pintadas*. In addition, I thank the Carmen Balcells Literary Agency for allowing me to use 641 words from Severo Sarduy, *De donde son los cantantes*. © Herederos de Severo Sarduy, 2010. I am also grateful to Lori Nix for her permission to use her photograph, "Library," 2007 on my book's jacket.

Sub-versions of the Archive

1
Introduction: Alternative Identities and Aberrant Archives

THIS IS A BOOK ABOUT MISFITS. MANUEL PUIG AND SEVERO SARDUY are misfits in their societies of origin, their characters are misfits within their novels' plots, and their novels are misfits within Latin American literary history and criticism. This is also, however, a book about fitting in. Novels by Puig and Sarduy are by now considered canonical, and ultimately their characters find ways of inscribing themselves within their social orders. This is a book about negotiating a place at the table, within the canon, or, to be more accurate, within the archive—the site where the origins of both the Latin American literary tradition and Latin America itself are contested.[1]

The theory of the archival origins of the Latin American narrative tradition (of the Latin American novel and Latin America itself) holds that the first discursive and rhetorical models for Latin American literature were those contained in the archive, literally in the Habsburg colonial archives.[2] These models were first the legal template in the colonial era, followed by the natural sciences through the nineteenth century, and anthropology/ethnography after that, in the twentieth century. These so-called master-narratives are nonliterary discourses found in chronicles, historical narratives, petitions to the king, and the like—all deemed to be truth-bearing genres that had bona fides and authenticity, and on which the new literary tradition of Latin America could base itself for enfranchisement. Latin America, as a relatively new entity in world history, had no prestigious antecedents, precursors, or poetics, as Europe did. The earliest Latin American writings were those legal and notarial documents kept in the Habsburg archives.

The archival tradition of Latin American literature maintains that the Latin American novel has pretended to be these types of nonliterary discourse throughout Latin American history. These discourses, despite being nonliterary (or because they are nonliterary), have been deemed authentic, truth-bearing, and prestigious, nonetheless.

I examine in this book how Puig and Sarduy also use the tradition of the archive in their most significant novels. I argue, however, that instead of modeling their novels on nonliterary discourses that are deemed authentic, truth-bearing, and prestigious, they use nonliterary discourses that are nonstandard, unrecognized, and unreliable. They tap into the subliterary genres of the mass media and popular culture. The twist, however, is that Puig's and Sarduy's nonliterary rhetorical models could indeed be authoritative and truth bearing, but to certain segments of society—primarily the underclasses and the marginalized—who are not recognized as prestigious, legitimate, or authoritative by the hegemony. Those subaltern people and voices are configured as "cultured" by the "post-cultural" hegemony, two terms I borrow from Maria Lugones and will apply further to my analysis of specific novels.[3]

Ultimately, when Puig and Sarduy add these discourses and rhetorical models to the archive, as their novels become canonical, they supplement the archive with templates from these subaltern segments of society that future writers may also use as newly legitimized models. In Roberto González Echevarría's theory of the archive, the subaltern disguise themselves rhetorically and formulaically as the hegemonic, but in Puig's and Sarduy's novels, the definitions of the dominant or hegemonic are contingent and relational. People from certain lower social classes would not find literature to be trustworthy or authoritative, for example. They might instead derive truth and power from listening to a tango lyric or from Afro-Cuban slang on the street. Puig's and Sarduy's novels pretend to be nonliterate discourses that are not truth-bearing to the hegemony; these discourses, however, are supposed to be truth-bearing to different segments of the subaltern. Ultimately, neither generic nor social register—whether the high or the low—really proves to be transcendentally truth-bearing in Puig's and Sarduy's novels. The authors consciously exploit their characters' reliance on master-narratives, be these narratives literary or not, and thereby comment on the essence of truth. Truth in these novels is derived from clichés, whether popular truisms or erudite formulas. Nonetheless, Puig and Sarduy add alternative discursive models to the scriptural and prestigious models identified by González Echevarría. They thereby ultimately create an iconography of the marginal, within their novels cum archives, which will be recognizable to writers after them.

In this book, I tell a story of discontinuities, appropriations, and suppressions. The term "alternative identities" in this book's title does not refer to a wholesale rejection of traditional literary characters, or of traditional narrative strategies (formulas) of enfranchisement, in favor of an exclusive focus on the subliterary or marginal.[4] Instead, this book's title refers to a reformulation of dominance. The "dominant," in Puig's and Sarduy's novels, is no longer just what it is purported to have been throughout Latin American literary history: narratives imbued with prestige, people who are literate (or people who mimic the literate, or high culture within a high-low binary definition), and the rhetorical privileges of the patriarchy.[5] For these two writers, dominance, rhetorical privilege, canonicity, and archivization, instead also depend on knowing the codes of popular culture, subaltern people, and the mass media. Dominance for them is situational and fluid and does not have the same standards in every social situation.

The access of Puig's and Sarduy's literary characters to symbolic capital is not always backed by or derived from literature kept in the archive of the lettered. Instead, such access is often dependent on the oral, ephemeral, marginalized, and popular traditions with which the archive is ultimately supplemented by these two writers. They add alternative discursive models, which are not prestigious or officially recognized, to the archive of Latin American literature, while seeming to conform to the traditional archival scheme of pretending to be something other than literature. Puig and Sarduy therefore give these subliterary models and illiterate characters legitimacy and authority, such that they too may serve as truth-bearing and authentic literary templates for future writers.

This book examines texts and discourses that resist easy generic classifications and revel in the friction between literary and nonliterary discourses. Rather than contest the definitions of the literary and the nonliterary, Puig's and Sarduy's novels take advantage of the existence of these categories and the academic and social debates about the nature of these terms. They write from the literary, critical, philosophical, and cultural interstices or gray zone created when academia and popular culture meet or bleed into one another. This book is, therefore, in many ways an exploration of the hybrid— sometimes depicted as pure and other times as impure.[6] It is as much an exploration of the tradition of manipulating the divide between the literary and the nonliterary within Latin American fiction as it is an exploration of how we understand literature in general as an object of study. It is not a direct exploration of the validity of such a divide in the first place. I do not wish to make pronouncements here or to enter into the debate about what is literary and what is nonliterary—the elusive quest for defining what is "literature" indisputably. Instead, I, as Sarduy and Puig do, wish to focus on the use of the historically presumed division as it has influenced Latin American literature from its inception and as it may be subverted by contemporary writers.

Marginal figures in Puig's and Sarduy's novels—the illiterate, the functionally literate, the poor, ethnic and racial minorities, gay people, children, the elderly, women, and other subaltern and disenfranchised members of society—define their environments and often make the rules for their own literary discourses. Their novels, for their literary characters and for readers, hinge on understanding the rules of the disenfranchised world and recognizing its touchstones as much as, if not more than, they hinge on understanding and recognizing the icons and discursive models of erudite, urbane, and academic cultures. Puig and Sarduy's novels benefit from the cultural horizon of the typical Latin American who, unlike his or her European counterpart, lives in a world strongly marked (some would say contaminated) by popular and non-Western cultures.[7] Readers who are unfamiliar with the clichés of subcultures, popular culture, and mass-produced and mass-consumed literary genres, such as the serial novel, are excluded from or alienated by much in Puig's and Sarduy's novels. Their works fashion their own literary models and set up rhetorical antecedents out of the discursive formulas from popular culture and the mass media. Instead of pretending to be narratives of the literate, as novels in the tradition of Latin American fiction do, they subvert the dominant (logocentric) ideology of contemporary Western culture and pretend to be sub- or nonliterary genres. Before Puig and Sarduy, contemporary novelists could not borrow nonliterary discursive models of a popular cultural stripe from the archive of Latin American literature, because these subaltern models were not included *as viable templates* in the archive. Puig and Sarduy endeavor to include them as legitimate models.

The kernel of the idea for this book emerged, some years ago now, in response to two stimuli. The first was a nonchalant remark made in one of my graduate-school classes by a professor of medieval literature. She said "Life is literature and literature is life" as a summation of our discussion of the *Thousand and One Nights*. This did not make sense to me as I thought of all those people who did not read "literature" and of all the many more who also could not read at all. Were they all dead? Thinking that she was waxing metaphoric, I pressed her on the issue. Her automatic response was that even if people did not read, they were still influenced by literature. For me, however, that was the entire nub of the problem, because it is not the same to refer to "literature" as it is to refer to the oral tradition or writing in general—and I mean this descriptively, not prescriptively. Furthermore, I did not think then, and I do not think today, that such a generalization can be made—that life and literature are reciprocally equivalent—except as a metaphor or in reference to specific examples. After all, the illiterate and isolated peasant, for example, knows and cares as much about "literature" as the Ivy League literature professor does about killing and skinning rabbits for dinner.

The second stimulus that sparked the writing of this book was my first job interview at an MLA job convention, in which a very well-known professor asked me if I "really bought into González Echevarría's theory of the archive." As I knew this professor's ideological bent was different from my dissertation advisor's, the aforementioned theorist, and as my interviewer mispronounced the word for "archive" in Spanish—"arquivo" was his version—I was rattled and, therefore, could not answer his question intelligently as I tried to circumvent the correct pronunciation of the word "archivo" altogether. I wanted to avoid correcting him indirectly, thereby jeopardizing my chances of getting the job offer. I did not understand what he could have meant. After all, the theory of the archive had garnered González Echevarría such fame and accolades. And had it not altered the way in which Latin American literature was understood and studied?

I never did find out directly what the interviewer meant; I did not get the job. His question preoccupied me, however, for months. It was not until I had just finished my doctoral dissertation, until after I had studied and thought about the works of Puig and Sarduy deeply and protractedly, that answers started coming to me. The answers are in this book, which is not to say that I have "bought" the premise of my MLA interviewer's question wholesale. This book is a more careful and considered response than I could have given my interlocutors as a graduate student. This book does reevaluate the received knowledge with which I worked at one time. It does question critically the usefulness of the theoretical paradigm of the archive for an all-encompassing understanding of Latin American literature.

In writing this book, I have used different lenses to focus on problems and readings. It was almost inevitable that I use culture as an object of inquiry, given its primary significance in both Puig's and Sarduy's work. I also perform theoretical analyses as well as applied literary readings. To be sure, there have been numerous debates about the nature and limits of "literature" and about how much undivided attention it merits in the academy. The study of culture as an addition to literature, or as an expansion of the definition of text, has inflected Anglo-American academia for decades as well. In his piece entitled "Mentoring Past the Ruins," appearing in the Spring 2008 edition of *LASA Forum*, Alberto Moreiras traces a short history of U.S. Latin American studies, culminating in the ruins of Latin American cultural studies. He sees the 1990s as a watershed period for Hispanists in the U.S. That is when the disciplinary isolation of the 1970s that was bolstered by criticism in digested form contained in the *Latin American Studies Handbook* or in the MLA bibliography for Spanish, followed by the 1980s' "rise of the literature departments of so-called theory," opened up or culminated in legitimacy and recognition.[8]

How and why did Latin American cultural studies attain this exalted reputation at that time? According to Moreiras, it was because the field of engagement was opened up; the literary text was abandoned "as the main horizon of our work."[9] Text in general was included: "the testimonial text, the political text, the visual, the post-dictatorial, the indigenous, the urban, and so forth."[10] Literature, he concludes, "was no longer considered the queen of the humanities; the queen of the humanities was now the critical text, the text of critique."[11] The goal of work in the humanities "was an opening to culture."[12] Although the point of his piece is ultimately that the alliances out of which this brand of cultural studies was born have shattered in a post–9/11 world, and that those fragments are now recognizable as distinct from one another, he also identifies what is to him the apogee of Latin American studies—its alliance with cultural studies and transformation into a hybrid he calls Latin American cultural studies.

Moreiras believes that an alliance, albeit a transitory one, whose "real horizon" was an opening of literature to culture, allowed Latin Americanists a place at the table of the humanities, and in fact, a place at the head of that table. My book examines the ways Puig and Sarduy are able to benefit from a similar alliance, although *avant la lettre*. Their work opens literature to culture as a strategy for enfranchising the subaltern. They seem to be misfits or marvels, the latter being the positive spin of the former, according to standard and venerated literary histories. There are other sorts of literary histories—the newer ones—within which these two writers seem more at home.

A 2007 review of some recent titles of Latin American literary history for *Latin American Research Review* points to a sea change in the type of compendium that is currently being produced, such that writers like Puig and Sarduy always figure as central and canonical. In this piece, John Ochoa reevaluates the notion of the "traditional literary history"—the "holdover" from the "bad, old" days—which "reinforces the aesthetics, codes, and mores of the dominant class . . . [for] the preservation of cultural capital at the hands of the privileged few."[13] While he does point to "the dangers of cultural blindness ... always present in any sort of canon-building," Ochoa also underscores "an enormous mitigating circumstance for Latin Americanists."[14] This extenuating circumstance is that "Latin Americanists, at least in the United States, are not hegemonic."[15]

This subaltern status is one Moreiras also points to when he says, "No matter how much work we [Latin Americanists] did, our colleagues from other departments still thought our knowledge was inferior to theirs."[16] The golden age of Latin American cultural studies in the U.S., as Moreiras terms it, allowed us—for I also am a U.S. Latin Americanist—to hold our heads high for a moment; Moreiras retorts, "and there was no shame," signaling the legitimacy and pride we had attained.[17] As Ochoa puts it, "The task of many of us in the field consists of establishing not just the 'what' of Latin American literature and culture, but also the 'why,' in other words, the validity of studying it."[18] In the end, he concludes that "'old' literary history still has a place, and an ethical pedagogical function, *within Latin American studies in the United States.*"[19]

Ochoa finds the "bad, old" literary histories useful and legitimate because Latin American studies in the U.S. is, per se, subaltern and of dubious legitimacy within greater academia, within the greater family of the humanities. Although he makes no distinction in the varying fortunes of U.S. Latin American studies as Moreiras does, Ochoa does conclude that we are in an age of peripheral significance ("once more," Moreiras would add). For Ochoa, the canon—or literary history, for that matter—is "a necessary fiction," "a stable tool," "a scaffolding,"[20] that, in the case of U.S. Latin American studies, does not buttress Stephen Greenblatt's fears that the canon reflects a "potentially dangerous relationship between the idealization of aesthetic monuments and nationalism ..., [which] can create the cultural and ideological foundations for genocide."[21]

For Puig and Sarduy, writers whom I bring together in this book on the firm conceptual grounds that they are both misfits who end up fitting in—exiled intellectuals whose works and lives are in many ways responses to authoritarian regimes—the concept of the canon is a vital and necessary fiction, a "stable tool," to use Ochoa's phrase. Their canons are really alternative canons, which they attempt to archive in the greater archives of Latin American literature and culture. They primarily wield canons that are familiar, not to the hegemony, but to those disenfranchised literary subjects—women, children, gay people, political dissidents, transgendered people, the middle and lower social classes, and the like.

Although this book really focuses on the archive, the canon—an analogous, yet essentially different collection or subset—plays a role in the former's configuration, as we have already seen from my discussion of Moreiras's and Ochoa's essays. It is therefore important to consider it here briefly, if inductively, as I have already referred to the canon several times without presenting my explicit working definition of it.

THE LITERARY CANON

The literary canon is configured so as to articulate the story of a culture, a nation, a class, or an individual, by arranging its texts as though they were connected through a causal evolution. The canon allows people to see idealized versions of themselves represented within the national narrative, thus fostering a communal sense of purpose: "The canon records—in the vernacular—the history of the nation, articulating a chronological continuity of an uncertain present."[22] I would add that the canon records in a "standard" vernacular and that it could also represent a multinational grouping—the "West," for example. In other words, the present profile of a nation's people (at least of its hegemony) is what informs the process of selecting texts; a national canon's ur-text represents the genesis of the present national ascendancy, while establishing a construct of inevitability, a teleology, and a cultural homogeneity. Finally, the canon gives the impression of a more democratic collection, informed by arbiters of knowledge but not directly mediated by institutions such as the museum or library: we can each acquire canonical works, which we may fetishize and keep next to other random objects in our own collections.

The analysis of a canon must take into consideration "how texts were and are processed and to what uses they are put at specific institutional sites, such as the university, publishing house, journal, newspaper, lecture, and library."[23] Such an analysis of a text within the canonical frame must focus on that text's relative value within the hierarchy of enfranchised texts and its movement within this hierarchy, throughout history. Ultimately, a text's value derives from its interaction with other texts in the canon. Textual, and thus canonical, value is always contingent, never inherent: "All value is radically contingent, being neither a fixed attribute, an inherent quality, or an objective property of things but, rather, an effect of multiple, continuously changing, and continuously interacting variables or, to put it another way, the product of the dynamics of a system, specifically an *economic* system."[24] Canonical value exists in a context. If the context is altered, the valence of the text may also change in relationship to other texts. Ultimately, "an investigation of canon formation seeks the reasons behind the survival of certain texts and the suppression of others."[25]

The tradition preserved by literary canons is usually a diachronic one, which connects the present with its past achievements, leaving out any elements that do not conform with and/or maintain the nation's or group's identity: "The canon serves as a utopian site of continuous textuality in which a nation, a class, or an individual may find an undifferentiated identity."[26] How does one form a canon, however, if one is trying to supplement or change history and culture? What does one do with any already-existing canons and their component texts? Texts alone, as we will see, are like dismembered parts of a body. It is only when these parts come together that they form an entire corpus. If these parts are rearranged and combined with other parts, they are likely to constitute a sort of literary Frankenstein's monster: a new corpus with previously used textual parts. The life force behind this collection of texts is the collection itself; that is, the frame. This canonical assemblage can denature a text and imbue it with new significance.

According to John Guillory, an important factor in vesting a work with canonicity is whether that work holds meaning for that particular culture at that particular time; if the work reflects the ideals of a dominant group and employs the vernacular accepted and longed for as the dominant vehicle for expression at a particular historical moment. This view of the canon is similar to González Echevarría's view of the "master-stories" or "master-narratives" that influence the archive's collections at particular historical moments and the dominant discourses that the novel mimics during those same moments. Both he and Guillory believe that there are cultural forces that change with time and space—not unlike Foucault's *épistémès*—and that control a written work's value and memorialization. This is Guillory's canon and González Echevarría's archive.

I argue, to the contrary, that this notion, a version of which Curtius also relies on, does not fully explain the fact that there exist various cultures, voices, people, and discourses, at any given time and in the same place (the colonial United States, medieval Spain, present-day countries in Spanish America) that are consistently left out of the canon and the archive. As Fredric Jameson determines according to Malcolm Read, "Literary works [are] a form of ideological discourse that represses historical truth."[27] To explain away elision from the canon or from the archive as the results of historical processes, or fads, as it were, turns a blind eye to these fads as constructs of dominant social groups in the first place. These are not fads among a society's subalterns. Perhaps these subalterns have always been outside or have always been left out of history, but they need not be. These are not Zeitgeists recognized by or affecting all social groups. Instead, these subaltern groups may create their own canons, their own collections reflecting their group identities and values. These canons are not always, if ever, recognized or included in the dominant canons. Puig's and Sarduy's novels are a case in point. They bring together registers and discourses that had previously been left out.

Puig's and Sarduy's Archival Contamination

Puig and Sarduy's texts function as mini-archives, or sub-versions of their respective cultural canons—both national and alternative canons of their respective Argentina and Cuba. They formulate, as Foucault would describe the archival process, archival statements/sentences that reestablish the "law of what can be said" by means of Latin American literature's archival apparatus.[28] Their works bring together, sometimes harmoniously and other times jarringly, pieces (quotations) from and references/allusions to canonical, high literature with the pieces (quotations) from and references/allusions to the familiar and acknowledged touchstones of popular cultures, subcultures, and the mass media. Clearly this combination may create an effect of what we know of as kitsch, camp, pastiche, or even the Neobaroque. These are not my main focuses in this book, however. While enormously important subjects of inquiry, they are incidental to my thesis, and I will therefore address them incidentally as I develop my argument. I am more interested in the hybrid archives they create by melding canons of the high and the low.

As their hybrid archives enter the greater archives of Latin American literature (now that both Puig and Sarduy are canonical authors), they introduce Trojan horses of sorts within the greater archives. Their heterogeneous archives contaminate the larger archives of Latin American literature with genres and discourses that are not truth-bearing for the hegemony: popular culture, subculture, and the mass media. Their archives disassociate themselves when they come into contact with other texts in the larger archive, or by diluting the pool of canonical works within it. As Puig's and Sarduy's works enter the larger archive, they come into contact with other works and form other groupings, or the archive's user (the scholar, et al.) rearranges these groupings. I use the image of contamination here metaphorically, as a reference to the supposed generic and cultural divides between "literature" and "popular culture."

While those familiar with Latin American literary studies know that something similar is already the backbone of González Echevarría's theory of the archive, they will also remember, that he maintains that the Trojan horse in the colonial archives (and moving forward in time to the so-called Boom novels) is nonliterary discourse, which is considered legitimate, truth-bearing, and hegemonic during specific historical moments. In the case of Puig and Sarduy, on the other hand, what "contaminates" the archive is precisely the opposite—discourses that are subaltern within the greater archive. They supplement the archives of Latin American literature with discourses and voices that had been left out, precisely because they were not considered truth-bearing, at any time, to the hegemony—the creators, keepers, and users of the archive. These excluded discourses and voices were not literary, not scriptural in their origins, when the dyad of power and writing supposedly ruled Latin American literary history.

Power and writing have traditionally gone hand-in-hand throughout Latin American history and its literary tradition. This is a precept of González Echevarría's theory of the archive and of his view of Latin American literary history in general. In using the framing device of the archive, he attempts to probe how certain marginal forms become predicated upon the cult of textual erudition. One of the most influential and sweeping studies of this phenomenon, if often tendentious and poorly substantiated, is Ángel Rama's *La ciudad letrada* [*The Lettered City*]. Rama considers the reciprocal relationships among the Latin American city, power, and writing. Written discourse, he determines, deploys and reproduces institutions and laws administered through a circle of select men he identifies as *letrados*. Originally, these men were lawyers, *procuradores* [*procurators*], but as their roles in society widened, the letrados were also clergymen, fiction writers, journalists, educators, politicians, essayists, and the like; and these intellectuals would come to control the metropolis—"the lettered city"—and, by extension, the nation: "The written word conveyed to [the letrado] prestige, an enduring access to power, and an adaptability that determined the survival of the letrado even through the most apparently profound social and historical upheavals in the continent's history."[29] The prestige of the lettered city was central to Latin American and Western cultural narratives, especially from the late nineteenth to the late twentieth centuries—the peak of the nation-state.[30] The gradual downfall of the nation-state, influenced by more local rather than national affiliations as well as by globalization, led to the erosion of the epistemological authority of the lettered city. This postmodern tendency to privilege the marginal and the heterogeneous helped to displace systems of cultural practice from the nation-state.

Theoretical Underpinnings

The theoretical underpinnings of my book merit an initial unfolding and a more direct examination at this point. I have already mentioned Maria Lugones's work on the hybrid's purity or impurity as one of its influences. She examines the politics of separation as a cultural force, among others. I look at Puig's and Sarduy's hybrid works through the lens of purity and impurity as focused for us by Lugones in her piece entitled "Purity, Impurity, and Separation." Puig's and Sarduy's canons are hybrids because they purposely combine cultural and textual registers—the high and the low—that have been traditionally kept apart and seen as inherently separate. I use the metaphor of contamination above in a less innocent way as well as metaphorically.

Lugones examines the politics of hybrid identities as a strategy of resistance to dominant/hegemonic ideologies, enmeshed oppressions, and cultural homogeneity. She analyzes the concepts of those people in a given society who are made subaltern by being considered "cultural" by those who consider themselves "postcultural," or hegemonic. She ties her piece to a tradition of "resistant and liberatory possibilities," but calls "all resemblance between this tradition and postmodern literature and philosophy ... coincidental, though the conditions that underlie both may well be significantly tied."[31] Her essay itself at first strikes the reader as a hybrid confection, as it begins in the kitchen and in Spanish. The essay is actually bilingual, and plays with readers' expectations of what an academic essay should say and how it should sound. An essay, as a literary genre, is a hypermasculine space, especially within Latin American letters as far back as the nineteenth century. It is also a monological, monofocused, and monolingual space. Its purpose is to consolidate the subjective "I" of the speaker and the objective point of view on the issue about which the essay is written. Lugones's essay disarms the reader because it seems light from the outset.

The Latin American Essay and Lugones's Subversion

The essay as a literary form in Latin America is supported by the paternal authority embodied in the dictator figure—the source of the voice that bears "knowledge through the peculiarity of language."[32] González Echevarría asserts, however, that "the essay, unlike a play or a sonnet, has no given form—it is not literature simply by being itself."[33] He compares the essay to the novel because, as he sees it, the essay pretends to be something it is not, while the essay acknowledges this charade. The essay pretends to be nonliterary discourse, but an authoritative form: "a letter, a confession, a lecture, a seminar, an oration, a scientific article, or a diary."[34] The Latin American essay contains "a cluster of tropes that attempt to hold down and control Latin American texts by attaching them to a set of given meanings."[35] Lugones's essay resists this tropological cluster. She shifts the power dynamic in the voice and content of the essay. Her main strategy for rebellion is the use of a hybrid voice and persona (her literary "I") to mirror the essay's hybrid imagination—an emphasis on "mestizaje and multiplicity as tied to resistance and liberation possibilities."[36] She manages to rebel against the paternal and dictatorial voices of the traditional Latin American essay as well as against the "othering" of the postcultural gaze.

Lugones's essay begins as a bilingual, desultory meditation on the distaff. She is in the kitchen with her mother, helping to make mayonnaise. We are not in a traditionally masculine realm, yet we are reading a philosophical essay. We also hear polyphonic voices, yet we are reading an essay and, therefore, expect a monological argument from the genre. Lugones works with the techniques and strategies that have made the traditional essay successful, but she opens a space within the genre for subjects and voices previously excluded from it.

The meditation begins with a recipe for making mayonnaise, which takes us through the steps of separating an egg, followed by the steps in mixing primary ingredients that will result in mayonnaise. The first—the act of separating the egg white from the egg yolk—Lugones tells us is "an exercise in purity" because she is trying to investigate how the politics of purity bear on those of separation. She then focuses on the properties and identity of the mayonnaise itself. It is an "emulsion," that is, an unstable mixture—a hybrid—whose primary ingredients must be combined just right and in the right proportions to keep it from separating. Her exempla—the egg and mayonnaise—focus the political signification of the hybrid, which may be seen as either a "pure" entity or an "impure" entity. Her argument unfolds as she explains her terms and analyzes ideas, but it also implicitly unfolds formally, as she code-switches between English and Spanish, "male" and "female" voices, and academic and quotidian discourses. I will use Lugones's argument, and the nomenclature she distills, within the chapters that analyze particular works by Puig and Sarduy, but my point here is that she manages to work within the tradition of the (Latin American) essay while challenging and supplementing this tradition. This is precisely what Puig and Sarduy do with the tradition of the archive in Latin America.

Bourdieu's Social Fields

The work of Pierre Bourdieu on class distinction is another lens through which I look at Puig's and Sarduy's novels. I analyze the amounts of symbolic and cultural capital their characters have in novels and the degree to which they can adroitly use them within varied social and class structures. I use Guillory's reevaluation of the canon debate as a prism that refracts some of Bourdieu's ideology on cultural capital. Bourdieu's extension of Max Weber's analysis of status, the extension of the ideas of capital to categories such as cultural capital, symbolic capital, and social capital, are important to my study. He identifies the position that each individual occupies in a multidimensional social space, or *field*. For Bourdieu, the individual is not defined just by membership in a particular social class, but by the amounts of each kind of capital he or she possesses. This is an important distinction in the paradigm that is sometimes used to define social actors as class-bound or as able to move from one class to another (up or down) and sometimes back again.

Bourdieu's model ultimately explodes the notion of immutable strata to which people belong or across which they move entirely, such that these social actors are only and wholly in any given stratum at one time. Instead, Bourdieu's model posits that people may mimic the identities of those who "belong" to a given stratum, through the type of symbolic capital they possess and/or wield, and thus may indeed belong to a particular field, while still belonging to other fields as well. Therefore, people may participate fluidly in several social strata without having to declare or be identified as belonging essentially only to one. We will see later that this idea of Bourdieu's shares similarities with González Echevarría's notion of the subaltern's use of/access to discursive simulation, through the use of formulaic language, to gain access to power.

The Archive's Theorists

Lastly, but most importantly, this book is also both a critical exploration of the concept of the "archive" and a study of Puig's and Sarduy's novels as archival fiction. The archive is a central concern in this study. I will delve deeply into its configurations by Borges, Foucault, Arrom, Derrida, and Guillory in the next chapter, while examining its significance for my study. The standard archival model for Latin American studies, however, is González Echevarría's, to which I will devote considerable examination.

González Echevarría's notion about the origins of the Latin American literary tradition is that the subaltern disguise themselves as the meritorious or the literate; and that the novel (the subaltern genre, at its inception) disguises itself as the discourse of prestige at any given time in history. I hold that Puig and Sarduy had the subaltern show themselves, either through other discourses or through what, to the subaltern, were superior discourses (mass media or the middle-class lifestyle), but not through the dominant or hegemonic discourses. In other words, *el folletín* [the serial novel], in the case of Puig, for example, is seen as a valid genre by the Argentine lower classes, but is not a genre of high culture as the novel was when *Boquitas pintadas* was written. The twist in this case, however, is that Puig is really writing a novel (as evidenced by its several internal complexities, which I will go into further), which he disguises as a genre of low culture—the serial novel. Puig's novel is pretending to be a genre akin to the mass media—this is a radical departure from what González Echevarría asserts, because this genre, the serial novel, is not a truth-bearing discursive model in accordance with his paradigm.

González Echevarría's paradigm identifies three master discursive forms that have inflected colonial and postindependence Latin American narrative from its beginnings to the present day. As Carlos J. Alonso observes, "The scheme [the forensic template of the *relación* for the colonial period, the scientific travelogue for the nineteenth century, and anthropological discourse for the twentieth] is founded on the idea that the principal quality of the novel as a genre is to pretend that it is something other than literature: hence, the novel models its form after nonliterary, referential discourses that are imbued with prestige and authority at a given time in order to partake in their prominent status." (*Burden of Modernity,* 187n49) Alonso thinks that González Echevarría's three hegemonic discourses are unnecessarily limiting and artificial: "It leads him to devalue significant works that do not conform to the scheme and to focus others into harmonizing with it (e.g., the outright dismissal of *María* and *Amalia* . . .)."[37] Alonso, by contrast, sees each text as choosing from a much larger repertoire of hegemonic discourses that are invoked as models on account of their perceived prestige. Although it is often difficult to discern whether Alonso is trying to expand González Echevarría's repertoire of hegemonic discourses on which the novel might model itself or if he is trying to tear down González Echevarría's entire system, Alonso ultimately perpetuates the discursive model's being predicated upon privilege, if not writing. Puig, and Sarduy, in contrast, often show the subaltern sending up the putative superior discourses. They also privilege low cultural discourses. My book therefore examines culture as well as literature. Puig and Sarduy de-privilege writing, while González Echevarría's theory privileges it. Ultimately, Puig and Sarduy add alternatives, a different type of intertext, to the archive.

Puig's and Sarduy's Moment in Latin American Literature

The novels of Manuel Puig and Severo Sarduy have been dubbed "new Latin American novels," products of "the masters of tomorrow's novel," "revolutionary," and "post-Boom."[38] These descriptions suggest that Puig and Sarduy represent and herald a new type of Latin American narrative, which transcends the novelty of the former Boom in Latin American literature. The "marginal"—the characters and their voices—fill the works of Puig and Sarduy, often covering over or crowding the modern novel's traditional voices, genres, and inquiries. Where the writers of the Boom reckoned with the "patriarch," or the logos, as the distillation of a Latin American cultural ontology, the language of the subaltern is the evanescent and leveling protagonist of the novels of Puig and Sarduy. Language has the power to level what it describes because objects, ideas, and images are conveyed through signifiers and within discourse, both of which may be simulated. Puig and Sarduy invest their characters—traditionally marginalized and unenfranchised entities—with privileged discursive positions usually monopolized by patriarchal figures. This discursive transvestism allows the marginalized entity a position within canonical culture because this entity establishes its ability to speak with legitimacy and authority in its own social sphere like the patriarchy—the possessor of the phallus and the logos—by wielding its own discourses that, to it, are truth-bearing.[39] Sarduy and Puig suggest that canonicity is related to the degree to which one has access to rhetorical formulas that are already enfranchised and archived, or that are recognizable clichés in subaltern societies.[40] This is how the master-narratives of patriarchy have always worked. They are "inventions which nevertheless powerfully controlled interpretation."[41] The subordinate culture that these writers foreground often appears as artificially constructed as the dominant one. Therefore, patriarchal privilege is shown not to hinge on essence but on simulation instead.

It is specifically through the language of the "marginal" (for example, women, *géneros menores,* and the transvestite male, in contradistinction to the traditional hegemonic protagonist) that the epistemological musings of Puig and Sarduy are articulated. I have chosen these two writers in particular because their works seek to supplement Hispanic culture by opening up its patriarchal discourse—the medium through which authority is established and power negotiated in Latin America[42]—and adding marginalized entities to its archival repository. As Echavarren says about Puig, and I would add the analogue about Sarduy, "He was the first novelist writing in Spanish who consistently utilized popular culture and the products of the show-business industry in order to articulate his fictions."[43] Unlike texts by Luis Rafael Sánchez, Guillermo Cabrera Infante, or Reinaldo Arenas, Sarduy's and Puig's works maintain explicit references to their immediate political realities at a distance and sometimes at an ironic distance. Moreover, Sarduy's and Puig's works eschew the novel of reverent cultural knowledge, instead favoring "fictions... in which indeterminacy in all realms and the 'universalizing' force of popular culture demystify literature's claim to a deep insight into Hispanic culture."[44] For these two writers, *la cultura letrada* [literate culture], national myths, and the traditional family are no longer the teleological touchstones of Latin American identity; instead, "precarious and often perilous alliances across generations and social classes" are manifested through their language.[45] I write about specific novels by Puig and Sarduy (generally speaking, their earliest works) because it is in them that the various archival notions are already present. I skip over Sarduy's first novel *Gestos* (1963), [a combination of the objectivist technique of the *nouveau roman* and of the committed novel].[46] Sarduy abandons the *nouveau roman* with *De donde son los cantantes* (1967) and inserts himself [in the thematic and formal field of the *Tel Quel* group],[47] under the influence of post-structuralism, throughout his next four novels, which I examine here.

Latin American literature has been inflected by controversial figures and polemics concerning cultural knowledge. Within Latin American studies, a radically new frame through which to read literature has been produced: in Latin American intellectual history, although "the demand for an autochthonous cultural expression has been the dominant concern,"[48] established Latin American writers who rose to fame during the Boom subsequently abandoned the totalizing novel of cultural knowledge.[49] As part of this latter trend, "the study of Latin American literature is in a state of crisis."[50] The novels of Puig and Sarduy push the ontological envelope by undermining projects of cultural knowledge where that knowledge is defined only as that of the hegemony.[51] Their narratives avoid a totalizing nostalgia, such as the kind desired by Boom novels.[52]

By the late 1960s, when Puig and Sarduy had burst on the scene, the "new" novel was wending its way through forms such as the Neobaroque and the self-aware tome of epic scope.[53] But neither the Neobaroque before Sarduy nor the self-conscious all-encompassing novel manages to break away from treating culture admiringly and deferentially, as something sacred and apart from the (degraded) commodities of daily life. In achieving a culturally diverse space, Puig and Sarduy made an impact on leaders such as Cortázar, Vargas Llosa, and Donoso, who then produced fictions based on movie stars, melodramatic soap operas, detective novels, and erotic mysteries.[54]

This book will concern the novels of Manuel Puig and Severo Sarduy as they reproduce gestures of cultural knowledge based on the archive of noncanonical entities only to distill language, and not truth, as the novel's ultimate reality. Reality, however, has a particular inflection. In Puig's *La traición de Rita Hayworth, Boquitas pintadas, The Buenos Aires Affair,* and *El beso de la mujer araña,* and in Sarduy's *De donde son los cantantes, Cobra, Maitreya,* and *Colibrí,* the language most excluded and/or disenfranchised is that of the logos or patriarchal male—the traditional novel's center.[55] Although traditionally marginalized groups such as women, for instance, have struggled for interpretive power, they have "often had to resort to noncanonical genres that are either not within the public sphere (letters, for instance) or their writing has been reappropriated into the public sphere as a [patriarchal] male text."[56] In Puig and Sarduy's works, marginal men and women, and so-called minor genres, only pretend to be resorting to noncanonical discourses outside the public sphere. In fact, they are articulated within novels—the most canonical of genres today. Puig's and Sarduy's novels seem to offer a tantalizing new semiology, which nonetheless ultimately unravels, providing only surface signs and a leveling of culture. Puig and Sarduy neither exclusively forge nor champion noncanonical discursive spaces per se. They distill voices from reality, through empirical observation, with which they create their texts. Their creations are hybrid works, a series of vested literary and nonliterary discourses: Puig covers over the traditional patriarchy with marginal discourses, and Sarduy vests the marginal discourses in canonical narratives.

Within these hybrid texts, marginal and canonical discourses are dependent on each other for legitimacy—and none has primacy over the other all the time. Where Puig and Sarduy differ from the other mass-media texts that became much more visible in the late 1960s is that Puig and Sarduy turn these popular registers into novels—into "literature." Moreover, although their novels do not always privilege one form of discourse over another, the mere fact that they mix these discourses with *discursos cultos* [literary discourses]—in other words, the fact that they create an impure archive (as Maria Lugones might say)—already vitiates the power of those truth-bearing *discursos cultos*.

Nineteenth-century philology and romanticism in general contain the genesis of the concepts that undergirded "modern" Latin American narrative up to the Boom. At its inception, a "national" culture is really literary in nature, since literature can "mirror the nation as well as encourage the acquisition by the population of socially important values and norms."[57] In the eighteenth and nineteenth centuries, the now largely supplanted academic discipline known as medieval philology (or *romanische philologie*) "committed itself to the construction of civil and national imaginaries in western Europe."[58] By the end of the nineteenth century, "it had extended its aspirations outside the boundaries of western Europe," aiming to preserve western identity from external threats.[59]

Latin American literature was not immune to this affliction of anxiety of origins. After all, even the name—Latin America or Spanish America—signals a hybrid identity marked by Europe and America. The concern for cultural knowledge in Latin American literature (especially the novel) coincides with *modernity*. Specifically, Latin American literature is said to be *modern* "since its inception in the romantic period."[60] The acquisition and/or manufacture of cultural knowledge has a romantic source: it is a response to a crisis—a romantic anxiety of origins.[61] Positivism in Latin America influenced its characterization of having a supposed autochthonous nature as a unique essence to quell the anxiety and thus generated "a rhetorical predicament that has been the irreducible constitutive element of Latin America's relationship to modernity."[62] Although it is not my concern here to trace fully the development of this predicament, I will note that ultimately although Latin America "did not experience modernity as a historical reality . . . this *was*, nonetheless, the essence of Latin America's historical experience of modernity."[63] With writers of the Boom, however, literature no longer needed to be characteristic or representative of Latin America, yet still explored what Latin America was. Latin American literature and the archive became the fields in which to seek a totalizing self knowledge.

We will see, on the other hand, that the narratives of Puig and Sarduy deliberately plunge no deeper than the surface of official culture, reproducing popular clichés as well as official formulas. Their narratives often revel in popular culture, oral traditions, and the mass media. There is no promise of a profound understanding of identity. In fact, the authors seem to have no control over events, but often figure as another one of the characters. Most significantly, the heterogeneous elements in the works form a collage and interact with each other. This synergy gives nontraditional subjects access to the dominant status that the canonical normally enjoys. Moreover, the popular codes wielded in these works make it difficult or impossible for the traditional discourses, hegemonic characters, and voices unfamiliar with or poorly versed in those codes, to impose themselves.

THE RATIONALE FOR THIS STUDY

My work here is limited to Manuel Puig and Severo Sarduy because they are the earliest of many writers who, beginning at the end of the 1960s [parody popular culture in their Works . . . [:] Radio and soap operas, serial novels and romance novels, rhythms that are considered out of style, such as the tango and the bolero, and "B"-movie narratives end up being quoted, in several forms, in the works of this artistic aspect].[64] More importantly, I have chosen these two writers in particular [because they inscribe the use of these products in a project of rupture with the aesthetic and political ideology that was contemporary to them].[65] I share this reason for choosing Puig and Sarduy with Lidia Santos, who includes both Sarduy and Puig, among other writers, in her study of kitsch. While I am not interested in focusing on kitsch, it is noteworthy that Puig's and Sarduy's archival projects mark conscious breaks with their contemporary aesthetic and political ideologies.

Secondly, I justify my focus on only four of each of their novels—Puig's first four and Sarduy's second through fifth—because we see in these samples of their greater oeuvre the types or variants that are significant for my study. Readers might at first wonder why I did not include *Gestos* (1963), Sarduy's first novel, or *Pubis angelical* (1979), Puig's fifth novel. The answer is simple: I could, theoretically, have included every novel each of the two writers wrote, as well as more of their nonfiction work, but I am interested in using their work as practical vehicles through which I might elucidate my theories on the archive. The novels I analyze in this book allow me to display the basic paradigms of my ideas. *Pubis angelical* would have allowed me to focus on yet another subgenre—science fiction—but I would have already made my point by analyzing the serial novel (coded female) and the detective novel (coded male) in Puig's other works. *Gestos* is a novel that is perfect for an analysis of kitsch, but not a novel that sheds much more light on the theory of the archive. Every work by each of these two writers is worth reading and analyzing, and I hope that my study will inspire a desire in my readers to read these other works, too. It is my belief that these readers would be able to apply most of my ideas to many of those texts as well.

The chapters in this book are an effort to apply critical approaches that bring together theories from within Hispanism and from without. They are inspired most of all by theories of the archive, of hybrid collections, and of symbolic capital. This first chapter explains the book's thesis, grounds the reader in the critical debates, and builds the theoretical framework that will be fleshed out. Chapter 2 defines the archive and delves deeply into, and critically assesses, Borges's, Foucault's, Arrom's, Derrida's, González Echevarría's, and Guillory's notions of it, while proffering new ways to evaluate the archive. The book's last four chapters provide careful and close readings of Puig's and Sarduy's relevant works through an application of the previously discussed theoretical concepts.

Chapters 3 and 4 focus on Manuel Puig's *La traición de Rita Hayworth* (1968), *Boquitas pintadas* (1969), *The Buenos Aires Affair* (1973), and *El beso de la mujer araña* (1976), novels that have an appreciation for the marginal. In them we find mixtures of various genres, languages, and cultures. Puig focuses on and conserves the familiar but virtually forgotten art forms and idioms formerly excluded from the realm of "literature." In his narratives, Puig employs the "vulgar" *géneros menores* [minor genres] and the frame tale, thus eschewing the closure yearned for in Boom novels. Moreover, the official family patriarch (the husband, father) is not directly present in Puig's works. We learn about him through women's and children's narrations.

Through his engagement with the languages of the banal in his work, Puig reminds the reader of Latin America's heterogeneity and battles—its dialogue with various models of language. His texts reveal that these models are themselves "embattled networks of dialogues among forms of discourse that comprise [them] among the languages that make up Spanish American reality itself."[66] In Puig's writing, fictional reality emerges from the interplay of heterogeneous discourses through which a complicated and contradictory assessment is made of the languages from which that fiction is drawn. He questions certain hierarchies of literary, subliterary, and non-literary forms, themes, and languages. His work calls attention to and implicitly comments upon the hierarchies of value that inform and generate production and reception. However, within his novels, it is not clear exactly what (if any) model, language, or figure is unequivocally supported. There is "the apparent assertion of equality among diverse narrative techniques, generic forms, and languages."[67]

Chapter 3 examines how Puig works within the conventions of the archival formulas of the Latin American narrative tradition, subverting this tradition without tearing it down. In this section, I look at the use of subgenres as vehicles for altering archival configurations. In particular, I examine *Boquitas pintadas* and *The Buenos Aires Affair*. In *Boquitas pintadas,* both subgenre and frame are announced in the novel's subtitle, "*folletín.*" This supposed replication of the generic model of the serialized novel suggests a text potentially out of control, a text that might regenerate itself endlessly due to the open-ended nature of serial fiction. In fact, the entire text is an archive of various social strata. It is also a novel about collections of social discourses, as evidenced in the different compilations of letters burned at the end. The text's "plot" is further convoluted because it exists within different levels of set-in narration, or in what is commonly called Russian dolls. The most challenging portions in *Boquitas pintadas,* the ones with convoluted narration and textual inclusions, are the ones that imitate familiar registers. It is through these registers that we learn about the missing patriarchal protagonist—the town's Don Juan, who is already dead when the work opens. Puig's hybrid text negotiates the patriarchy in a fragmentary work, without a continuous first-level narrator responsible for the whole text. In the end, all of the traditional men in the novel's world are dead or dying, and women hold their memories within archives of marginal genres (letters) in their hands.

The Buenos Aires Affair as well as Puig's following novel, *El beso de la mujer araña,* convey a more palpable sense of a political background. The former, however, keeps political subjects and events at the periphery of the novelistic discourse, yet was put on the *lista de libros prohibidos* [list of banned books] by Juan Domingo Perón's government, a move that influenced Puig's decision to leave Argentina as an exile. *The Buenos Aires Affair*'s subtitle *Novela policial* [Detective novel] places us within the realm of mass-produced and mass-consumed writing—detective fiction. Although Puig frames his novel within this marginal literary genre, "the process of detection in which we are invited to participate is not criminological but psychological."[68] The novel, in fact, revels in psychoanalytic discourse and case histories as master-narratives through which to convey sociopolitical reality. This, Puig's third novel, supplements the archive of psychoanalysis—a subset of the larger Latin American archive. It is telling that the novel is primarily set in U.S. cities, creating thereby a hybrid space in which psychoanalysis can bridge the chasm that has traditionally separated it from Latin America. The hybrid title itself—the main title in English, with a subtitle in Spanish—foreshadows this bridge.

Chapter 4 analyzes the alternative discursive models Puig provides for the archive. This section applies theories about hybrid collections and Bourdieu's notion of symbolic capital. In Puig's first novel, *La traición de Rita Hayworth,* individual subjects take turns speaking and writing about themselves, the people they know, and the town's everyday world, while using discursive models from their own popular archives. As these subjects weave through the novel's monologues and dialogues that correspond to sixteen chapters, they displace each other as subjective sources of fiction. There is no one omniscient narrator upon whom the reader can rely for complete information, nor is there any privileged discourse or entity to whom we can look for an objective, final truth. The plot is secondary (the story of a boy and his mother in Argentina's interior), as is the structure of the work. What is dispositive in *La traición* is a continuum of voices—a popular archive, which both conveys the narrative and is the narrative itself.

Puig's best-known work is *El beso de la mujer araña,* a novel that was turned into a commercially successful movie and play. This novel has a more palpable political setting—a jail containing two supposed political dissidents—than any of Puig's previous novels. The novel unfolds mainly as a hybrid dialogue, mixing lofty social ideology and pedestrian personal and popular culture. This novel is therefore a rewriting of sorts of *Don Quixote,* the dialogic novel par excellence, where quixotic visions are tempered by harsh reality. Puig's novel is a twist on Cervantes's, however, for it is Molina whose confabulations are spun from the stuff of cinema and other fantasies from popular culture. The two men create an archive in their heterotopic cell, which is counter to the state's official archive. Molina's coerced complicity with the state is ultimately undermined by the relationship he forges with Valentín in the cell—in the space where dialogue levels hierarchies.

Chapters 5 and 6 focus on Severo Sarduy's *De donde son los cantantes* (1967), *Cobra* (1972), *Maitreya* (1978), and *Colibrí* (1984), novels in which the author is discredited, not only as creator, but also as an indispensable authoritative figure who controls the meaning of the texts.[69] As González Echevarría notes, [Sarduy's works parody the Boom novels' reflexiveness, which is based on the all-powerful figure of the author, that projection of romantic irony].[70] Sarduy also rejects the notion of a natural language, [of language's individual or natural property].[71] For him, language is already a translation, since he rejects the notion of a privileged central transmitter. It follows, then, that literature also is already a translation, with more than one gravitational center, not as the *grands récits* had suggested. The elision of authorial legitimacy and his view of literature and translations are two defining aspects of Sarduy's work.

Chapter 5 focuses on the alternative archives Sarduy creates within the Latin American narrative tradition through *De donde son los cantantes* and *Cobra*. He is quite aware of the different contingencies that come to bear on the value and use of texts and culture. Within his pseudocultural archive, he recreates a gesture that helps to refocus the lens of the culture machine, which processes literature to churn out literary history and literary "classics." Thus, in *De donde* we see unstable personal and gender identities, as well as a Cuban cultural amalgam composed of Spanish, African, and Chinese elements. The text is a celebration of heterogeneity and contingency. The traditional patriarch proves impotent, as he is unable to know any of the creatures he pursues. He first intends to consume them, but ends up absorbed by them. Success in this novel usually depends on having the right type of cultural capital at the right time, even if it is not a type recognized by hegemonic society.

Cobra, also a novel about identity transmutation and (re)appropriation, postulates a surgical rearrangement of identity. If signification is achieved when the signifier is rent from the signified, thus producing "violence," or a cut, then Cobra is emblematic of such signification. Or *is* s/he? Cobra is, of course, ultimately unrecognizable in a Paris Metro station, and eludes all signification, since no privileged central transmitter of meaning exists. Cobra *is* multifarious significance. She is a corporeal archive: a museum, exhibiting Cuban culture; or an archive, listing an open-ended Cuban cultural compendium. One of the text's concluding sections, *Blanco,* along with the blank-page ending of the last section, and the closing words of *Cobra,*[72] contain the same gesture of infinite meaning and language found in the frame narrative.[73] Cobra, as collection, is symbolically reconstructed through sex reassignment surgery. After the operation, Cobra has given up not only a penis, but its symbol as well—the phallus and its discursive primacy. Her body, as delimited through discourse, no longer signifies from a phallogocentric position. Cobra's corporeal collection, as arranged in discourse, is no longer framed within a phallic frame. Is Cobra divine now, after the sex change, as she has always longed to be? If so, is the divine not another dominant category? *Cobra*'s new frame, however, incorporates women, transvestites, people of color, homosexuals, and similarly marginalized figures. Sarduy has tapped into and twisted the archival tradition of Latin American narrative in which the simulation of a patriarchal frame enfranchises its marginalized content. The new frame he adopts symbolically through Cobra's "sex-change operation," that of a woman and feminine discourse, is subaltern.

Chapter 6 analyzes Sarduy's new versions of the archive within which he places the reevaluated Latin American literary traditions of the Neobaroque and Orientalism in his *Maitreya* and of *la novela de la selva* [the jungle novel] and *la novela de la tierra* [the telluric novel] in his *Colibrí*.[74] In *Maitreya*, Sarduy looks at the Western world through the perspective of the East. But this is an East that has already been shaped by the West. This novel recovers traditional Eastern minarets, an image with which *Cobra* also closes, and the modern culture influenced by Middle Eastern oil. We see Eastern images that allow the West to know itself. Sarduy exhibits the "Orient" through modern eyes while reevaluating the archival tradition. By locating the archive in its dispersed adumbrations and Imperial body cavities—"annals"—Sarduy sends up the archive as the locus for the origins of the Latin American literary tradition, especially that of Boom novels such as *Cien años de soledad*.

In *Colibrí*, Sarduy raids the archives of Latin American literature, burns their stories, and infuses their remnants with new stories and characters. He is able to tap into the hidden and unrealized tensions within *la novela de la tierra* and *la novela de la selva* to tease out and display the sexual, gender, and racial anxieties that have been covered over within the bona fides of the traditional archive. He uses the East as a foil for Western desire whose initial misdirection in the fifteenth century was never fully resolved. This novel is set in and near the jungle, often the boundary where native and European cultures met and created a hybrid world at the beginning of the Spanish-American encounter. *Colibrí*'s world is a hybrid of East and West. Ultimately, this novel creates an archive where misfits can belong.

In this book, I will rely on postulates, which I have presented in this introductory chapter, about the configuration of the novel as archival fiction. González Echevarría hypothesizes that "the novel, having no fixed form of its own, often assumes that of a given kind of document endowed with *truth-bearing power* by society at specific moments in time."[75] Furthermore, he maintains that "the only common denominator [to all of prose fiction] is the novel's mimetic quality, not of a given reality, but of a given discourse that has already 'mirrored' reality."[76] In contrast, the nub of my thesis is the following: Puig's and Sarduy's novels' mimetic qualities are of given discourses—generally speaking, of discourses that lack prestige, such as those of popular culture and the mass media—that also have already mirrored reality, but the reality they have mirrored is that of groups that are often illiterate or functionally literate, or whose cultural variants had not previously been included in the archive as legitimate models—gay people, children, the poor, ethnic and racial minorities—for contemporary writers. It is my view that Puig's and Sarduy's novels, having no fixed forms of their own as hard-boiled novels, often assume that of alternative cultural idioms endowed with truth-bearing power by segments of society whose cultural and political agencies have previously been elided from or ignored in the Latin American prose-fiction tradition.

The fact that Puig and Sarduy both ultimately do write novels (canonical prose fiction) brings over these marginal discourses and entities into the greater archive of Latin American literature. These formerly marginal entities then become established tropes, once ensconced within the archive, and may later serve as legitimate discourses on which subsequent fiction might be modeled. Puig and Sarduy set up antecedents of credibility (or credibility because there are antecedents) so that the authority and veracity of future narrators who tap into these alternative archival sources will not be vulnerable. Gayatri Spivak observes that "the status of a language in the world is what one must consider when teasing out the politics of translation."[77] Analogously, the status of a discourse in the archive is what one must consider when teasing out the politics of Latin American literature. This is how Puig and Sarduy provide alternative archival models. Their work, and my own, does not tear down the theory of the archive as a source for and origins of Latin American literature. Rather, their work and my own, supplements that archive.

2
Raiding the Archive: An Analysis of an Archival Tradition and Its New Configurations

WHAT IS "THE ARCHIVE" AND WHAT ARE ITS HISTORICAL RESOnances? The archive is both a "paradigmatic entity" and a "concrete institution."[1] There has been perennial interest in the archive in general as well as in a mythical, all-encompassing type throughout history and in different cultures. Humanity created storage vessels for its most sacred writings from the beginning of scriptural culture and even dreamt of a universal library: the Hebrew Ark of the Covenant (also appearing later in the Qur'an) held the stone tablets containing the "Ten Commandments" and other sacred objects; the Royal Library of Alexandria (ca. 300 B.C.E.) attempted to collect all of the papyrus scrolls in the world and, for the first time, shelved them alphabetically; and the Archivo General del Reino (The National Archives of Spain)—ordered to be moved to Simancas, in Valladolid, Spain, in 1540—became the first permanent repository for the narratives and chronicles of the encounter and colonization in the Americas.[2]

Within the last forty years, especially, several remarkable raiders of the archive have attempted to plumb its depths, unlock its mysteries, and synthesize theories based on its seemingly unfathomable contents. Scholars and writers such as Jorge Luis Borges, Michel Foucault, Jacques Derrida, Roberto González Echevarría, and John Guillory wrestle with the idea of the archive and provide critical frameworks for understanding its interactions with society, history, literature, language, and culture.[3] Moreover, evolving technology allows other types of archives to be created. In 1990, the U.S. Human Genome Project officially began; it was completed in 2003. It archives maps and formulas of all the DNA in an organism, including its genes. In our increasingly digitized world, some of the most powerful Internet search engines today have already created virtual archives.

Archive fever was rekindled in 2004 when Google announced that it would create the universal library.

This book engages Hispanic literature and specifically Spanish-American cultures. I will unfold the major considerations of the archive, most of which do not focus on Cuban and Argentine works in particular, while inserting myself within the existing debates and theoretical positions, and rereading and challenging canonical texts by Borges, Foucault, Arrom, Derrida, González Echevarría, Guillory, and Bourdieu. One of my main goals is to revisit these traditional definitions of the archive and to uncover how Manuel Puig and Severo Sarduy insert themselves into this tradition by staking new ground through their most important and best known works. Puig's and Sarduy's novels implicitly reevaluate the theories of the archive, without destroying or abandoning the notion. Instead, their works offer cultural variants and voices that were previously excluded from the traditional archive. The main goal of this chapter is to distill the essential aspects of the archive, which I will apply in subsequent chapters to study Puig's and Sarduy's work.

The archive has been the object of much consideration and study, particularly since the latter half of the twentieth century. Jorge Luis Borges considers archival issues most remarkably in three works: his essay "The Total Library" (1939), his short story "The Library of Babel," first published in 1941, and "The Analytical Language of John Wilkins," first published in 1952. This second essay is later inscribed within Michel Foucault's own study of the archive in *The Order of Things* (1966). Foucault expands his study of the archive into an all-encompassing system in *The Archaeology of Knowledge* (1969) and teases out significant theoretical and real-world aspects of it in "Of Other Spaces" (1986). Roberto González Echevarría's *Myth and Archive* (1990) propounds a theory of the origins of the novel. John Guillory's *Cultural Capital: The Problem of Literary Canon Formation* (1993) is a major study that uses the figure of the archive, albeit with a different focus than my own.[4] Jacques Derrida's *Memoirs of the Blind* is first published in French in 1990 and then in an English translation in 1993, and his *Archive Fever: A Freudian Impression* is first delivered as a lecture in 1994 and published in 1995. Because these major writers and critical theorists have nuanced or different views of the archive, I will present my use of the term as well as theirs. The word "archive" carries much freight, so I will tease out the aspects of this term that have bearing on my book.[5] The most apposite configuration of the archive is González Echevarría's, which itself derives partly from the anthropological and anthological considerations of José Juan Arrom, while springing from Foucault's epistemic molds.

Borges's Archive

Borges is certainly the most appropriate lens through which to start looking at the concept of the archive as it developed in the twentieth century. "The Total Library," also translated as "The Complete Library," ("La biblioteca total") (1939) is one of the earliest works in which he focuses on the concept. This essay is, in many ways, extraordinarily modern, given that it prefigures the totalizing archives provided by the Internet and digital media. Borges traces therein "the fancy or the imagination or the utopia of the Total Library."[6] His ultimate message is that human beings' quest for the complete library is, worse than a fool's errand, "the invention of horrible imaginings,"[7] for the complete library's characteristics "are easily confused with virtues."[8]

The Total Library consists of "twenty-five symbols (twenty-two letters, the space, the period, the comma), whose recombinations and repetitions encompass everything possible to express in all languages. The totality of such variations would form a Total Library of astronomical size."[9] Borges sees the first "glimpse" of the total library in Democritus and the atomist cosmogony of Leucippus in Aristotle's *Metaphysics*. He subsequently traces this archive's history in Cicero's *De natura deorum*, Blaise Pascal's academic discourse, and Jonathan Swift's "museum of commonplaces," until he reaches his own time. He ascribes the belated invention of the Total Library to Gustav Theodor Fechner, and describes its first exponent as Kurd Lasswitz. At this point, Borges indicates that there is an idiomatic and conceptual change, in which the so-called infinite monkey theorem is employed.[10] This allows Borges to conduct a thought experiment in which he imagines the contents of the Total Library, which this endeavor would produce if carried to its extreme.

Because the library would be total, complete, it would contain "Everything: . . . the complete catalog of the Library, the proof of the inaccuracy of that catalog. Everything: but for every sensible line or accurate fact there would be millions of meaningless cacophonies, verbal farragoes, and babblings. Everything: but all the generations of mankind could pass before the dizzying shelves—shelves that obliterate the day and on which chaos lies—ever reward them with a tolerable page."[11]

Borges ultimately warns against this desire for a Total Library. He realizes that such an archive would contain self-destructive elements, which Derrida will go on to define in his *Archive Fever* as analogues of Freud's death drive. Borges tells us that this archive will be a "horror: the vast, contradictory Library, whose vertical wilderness of books run the incessant risk of changing into others that affirm, deny, and confuse everything like a delirious god."[12]

The archive, according to Borges in "The Total Library," results from, in the end, a misguided and futile enterprise. Instead of summing up all knowledge, creating a metacatalog, and allowing for a godlike knowledge of the universe, the archive—the Total Library—belies itself, erases itself, obscures itself. The library's totality means that it contains all books: books of lies and falsehoods as well as books of truths and facts. Enlightening knowledge is buried in deception. Carried to its fullest extreme, this totalizing archive would, in sum, hold a Babel of voices that would, ironically, contain zero or very little useful information.

Borges's best-known work on the concept of the archive is his "La biblioteca de Babel" ["The Library of Babel"] (1941). He develops the significant concept of an inscrutable, unintelligible, and untrustworthy archive *sous rature*, however, in "The Total Library." The interpolation of "Babel" in his short story from 1941 will become clearer now that I have examined his 1939 work. Borges fleshes out his notion of the totalizing archive as he creates the universe of the ultimate library for us.

"La biblioteca de Babel" is a library cum universe. This is the totalizing archive, which consumes even the archivists themselves. Borges's story highlights two points that are significant for my study: the inside-outside binary and the archive's counterintuitive impulse to erase and confuse rather than to accumulate and illuminate.

Borges's library contains not just books and records, but people as well. The library has "inquisidores," librarians or pages, who spend their entire lives in the library. It is built with facilities that accommodate its denizens' most basic needs—sleeping quarters and bathrooms. In fact, Borges's story is told from the point of view of one of these residents, [the men of the Library] who are born there.[13] Although we are told that the library is the universe, we are told this "fact" by someone who has never left the library. How does this "man of the library" know that his home is infinite and contains all possible books if he has never left it?

This uncanny relationship between man and the library reveals the quandary of defining what is within the archive and what is without. This is an issue that I will explore further when I get to Foucault's and Derrida's work. Although Borges tells us that the library is preexisting and immutable, [the Library exists *ab aeterno*],[14] he implies that the archive does not have an internal logic or transcendental order. Instead, he tells us that pages or librarians rummage through the books, trying to make sense of them in their quest for one book: [the catalog of catalogs].[15] Borges speculates on the existence of the [Crimson Hexagon][16] that contains the log of all the other books, giving its reader omniscience. We are told that the quest for this holy grail drives many librarians mad and to the point of suicide.

If we thought about Borges's proposition—that there could actually be a book that contained the catalog of all other books—we would realize that this is an impossibility in real time, a tautological hell. Borges is here suggesting that the archive always opens toward the future, an idea that I will discuss further when I explore Derrida's work. Closure—the totalizing catalog—is impossible because such a thing could never include itself without generating another variant. As soon as there were a catalog that included the universal catalog, it itself would be incomplete because it would not catalog itself, and so on, and so on, in an infinite progression of master or metacatalogs that can never include themselves.

As a result of this open-ended nature of the archive, the total library or archive is a futile enterprise. Borges tells us that censors and book purgers in his library attempt to destroy all false or imperfect texts and copies of texts. Because the library is complete, it contains all of these inchoate texts: [since the Library is total there are always several hundred thousand imperfect facsimiles: Works that differ in only a letter or a comma].[17] The act of purging books is counter to the purpose of the archive—to collect books—yet, as we will see Derrida argue, purging is also a natural part of the economy of the archive—of its inherent destructive drive. The act of purging presupposes a value judgment, a critical judgment, in the guise of epistemological purity.[18] Borges includes an intruding "Editor" figure—a metalibrarian of sorts—through his intercalation of footnotes, as is his custom. This would seem to be an exogenous force acting upon the "men of the Library" and correcting or ratifying their assertions. Once more, Borges manages ironically to vitiate the authority and to taint the purity of the archive's interior through this intruder's putative bona fides.

Borges shows us that we implicitly associate totality and universality with truth and purity. To the contrary, however, a collection of everything, naturally and logically, would contain *everything*, including the ersatz, the contradictory, the false, and the similar. Archival purity is the desire, but heterogeneity and incoherence is the reality, as anyone who has spent time in any of the world's major libraries or archives can tell you. Records are not always easy to find, if retrievable at all.[19] Oftentimes, the document or book that one finds interesting, helpful, or relevant is not the one looked for, but, serendipitously, the one next to it, or the one lying on a table. The collection in the archive, therefore, always presupposes a mark (a judgment) imposed on it by an outside force—a critic or scholar, without whose choice and ratification of texts the archive would simply be chaos or Babel.

Borges and Foucault come together in the consideration of a general system for the classification of archival entities. Foucault inscribes Borges's essay "El idioma analítico de John Wilkins" ["The Analytical Language of John Wilkins"], first published in a collection called *Otras inquisiciones* (1952) [*Other Inquiries*], in *Les mots et les choses: Une archéologie des sciences humaines* (1966) [*The Order of Things: An Archaeology of the Human Sciences*] (1970). Foucault's preface begins, "This book first arose out of a passage in Borges, out of the laughter that shattered, as I read the passage, all the familiar landmarks of my thought—*our* thought, the thought that bears the stamp of our age and our geography—breaking up all the ordered surfaces and all the planes with which we are accustomed to tame the wild profusion of existing things, and continuing long afterwards to disturb and threaten with collapse our age-old distinctions between the Same and Other."[20] Borges makes reference to [a certain Chinese encyclopedia],[21] in which animals are categorized or cataloged in ways that are surprising, disorienting, and, as Foucault's own laughter indicates, comical to the Western mind.

Borges's Chinese encyclopedia challenges not only the meta-tags, to use a contemporary term from our cyber-age, that dominate Western thinking and cataloging, but also the West's concept of purity and homogeneity. This encyclopedia, by all accounts apocryphal, categorizes objects in a way similar to that found in non-Western cultures: "It comes close to the impression a Western reader gets when reading descriptions of nonwestern languages and cultures. The fact is that people around the world categorize things in ways that both boggle the Western mind and stump Western linguists and anthropologists."[22]

Beyond mere taxonomic dissonance, Borges's Chinese encyclopedia contaminates the category of the pure and threatens the distinction between the Self and the Other, as Foucault himself tells us. The encyclopedia's list contains both the real (stray dogs) and the fanciful (mermaids), the obviously recognizable (pigs) and the metaphoric (from a distance look like flies), the integral (embalmed) and the oblique (belonging to the Emperor). We are invited, or perhaps challenged, by Borges to figure out what it is among these categories that binds them together as a list. What makes them all similar in kind, or pure? The apparent heterogeneity of these categories—their impurity—is normalized by the list itself. The mere fact that they appear together unifies these seemingly disparate and impure categories. Borges thus makes us aware of the arbitrariness in list-making and the arbitrariness resulting from archiving.

The economy of the archive works this way as well. The archive is open to everything and therefore may contain everything. They who mark it, who shape it, are both they who organize and oversee it—archivists and librarians—and they who use it—scholars and critics. Dipping into the archive and creating lists are reflections of the constitution of the Self. The Self is defined by that which is similar and pure. The Other is what is different from the Self. Both the unordered archive and Borges's Chinese encyclopedia collapse this Self-Other binary and create a state of impurity, a state in which the heterogeneous, and the Self and the Other, are grouped together.

Foucault's Archive

Foucault's ultimate claim in *Les mots et les choses* is that all periods of history possess a particular overarching *épistémè* that grounds knowledge and its discourses, and therefore represents the conditions of truth and of their possibilities. Foucault argues that these conditions of discourse have altered throughout the ages, producing epistemic shifts. Just as Borges's Chinese encyclopedia causes us to scrutinize the bases for knowledge, the consciousness shifts (*épistémès*) that Foucault identifies make us question the projection of our categories of knowledge and the bases for knowledge in our own time. In subsequent writings, Foucault goes on to say that different historical periods may have more than one *épistémè* at a time. His original claims in *Les mots et les choses* will be central to understanding González Echevarría's concepts of master-narratives that inform his theory of the archive, as we will examine later on.

As we see above in *The Order of Things,* Foucault discusses the historical conditions resulting from the classification of information. In *The Archaeology of Knowledge* (1969), he posits his "archive" as a "unified field theory" of sorts. This latter work, translated into English in 1972, is his concerted effort to sum up his own methodological assumptions, to describe a system that would encompass the different types of knowledge he previously identified in cultural formations—illness and medicine, madness and psychology, science, philology, and so forth. These discursive formations,[23] as Foucault considers them, are the very accumulation of statements, which are systematically recognized through their own internal and particular rules. The archive is his nexus for bringing together seemingly distant cultural formations, but not through a structuralist method.[24] It is, as he says, "the system that governs the appearance of statements and unique events."[25] The archive is not a culture's collection of texts, but instead "the law of what can be said, the system that governs the appearance of statements as singular events."[26]

In the end, Foucault's archive unifies a culture's discursive statements. It is an attempt to find a single way to analyze and talk about that cultural knowledge. He traces the history of the formation of discourse within culture by focusing on the historical conditions that result through the classification of information. He argues that when real, concrete archives are created, they become authoritative institutions, which later become symbols of or metaphors for the heterogeneous groupings of a culture's discursive formations. Foucault specifically studies French archives that first came into being in the eighteenth century (the National Archives in France, 1790), that grew very powerful in the nineteenth century as they became allied with the nascent modern nation-state. These archives "housed the proliferation of files and case studies as populations were subjected to disciplinary power and surveillance."[27] Archives define what is possible and what is not in terms of what can be spoken. The accumulation of statements recognized as "madness," for example, by a given culture and at a specific moment in time, is predicated upon the "associated field,"[28] a field of possibilities that can produce or contain other statements on madness as components of sameness. Discursive breaks and discontinuity are not to be ignored, however, according to Foucault. He suggests that we have preexisting assumptions of continuity and sameness and that these must be set aside in order to analyze discursive statements properly. His associated field of statements that may make up the discourse on madness, for example, is ultimately heterogeneous. It contains aporias—a link to Derrida, which I will explore later—and contradictions when amassed as a historical continuity viewed outside of a specific context. Foucault's theoretical archive is a shifting and contextually contingent set of relations and institutions, which allow discourse to exist. His archive is not just a static collection of real texts and is certainly not universal.

Foucault's notion of the archive, "a sustained polemic against dialectical thinking in the philosophy of language," rests on the identification of discourse's constitutive elements.[29] He differentiates among a sentence's grammatical identity, its enunciative level, and the logical level of its proposition. Moreover, he defines a discourse as a grouping of utterances for which conditions of existence can be defined. Discourse is consequently a historical event or, as he would put it, an archive of historical statements: "Discourse [is] a group of statements in so far as they belong to the same discursive formation;

it does not form a rhetorical or formal unity, endlessly repeatable, whose appearance or use in history might be indicated (and, if necessary, explained); it is made up of a limited number of statements for which a group of conditions of existence can be defined."[30] An archive, therefore, is a system that controls the manifestation of utterances as historical events: "the general system of the formation and transformation of statements," the "law of what can be said, the system that governs the appearance of statements as unique events."[31] Each society, culture, civilization, or social system has its own archive in which statements are created and changed, but may no longer be said. This is what Foucault calls an archaeology—the description of any discursive formation, with the essential quality of discontinuity.

Foucault uses the term archaeology as a rubric of study through which he might discover the set of laws that defines a discursive formation's essence. The term is not intended to construe the meaning or history of the discursive statement: "it is rather an inquiry whose aim is to rediscover on what basis knowledge and theory became possible; within what space of order knowledge is constituted. . . . Such an enterprise is not so much a history, in the traditional meaning of the word, as an 'archaeology.'"[32] Nor is it an attempt to understand how entities put together ideas. Instead, the archaeological conception seeks the set of laws and codes specific to the very discourse for a given culture and at a given time: "Foucault . . . reformulates the archive as archaeology and shifts the meaning of the archive away from the unifying structure we find in traditional humanist accounts to a system in which a multiplicity of discourses are created from a given set of data. . . . The archive cannot provide a direct access to the past, but only a textual refiguring of it."[33] Through this method of discourse analysis, Foucault is able to uncover "a process of the formation and transformation of bodies of *statements* according to isolable rules,"[34] and therefore is also able to uncover epistemic spaces, or discontinuities, in the conditions of human knowledge.

This archaeology, or study of a given discursive formation, describes how such a collection of statements comes to be possible and to constitute a discipline or knowledge. What is actually uttered, as statements about madness for example, is addressed against specific if relational contexts: the statement's value, how the statement's utterance affects the position of the subject who enunciated it, the culturotemporal conditions that allowed the statements to be uttered, and, among other things, but perhaps most importantly, the power struggle implied in the appearance and transformation of the statements. The archive itself, according to Foucault, is therefore not a collection of a culture's documents or the site of their preservation. It is instead "that which differentiates discourses in their multiple existence [sic] and specifies them in their own duration."³⁵

Another way to understand the archive according to Foucault, and a way to see the archive as a space, is through his notion of heterotopia, which he expounds in "Of Other Spaces," a lecture he gave in 1967 and published in the 1980s. This idea of the archive as a heterotopia does not contradict his scheme of the archive as neither a collection of a culture's documents nor the site of their preservation, as described in *The Archaeology of Knowledge*. A heterotopia, according to Foucault, is a space parallel to the real world. It is not itself the real world. An archive is therefore not a space or a collection that functions as would other parts of a society. An archive is ultimately linked early on "with the consolidation of Empire, with national definition, and with the acts of incorporation and exclusion that canon formation . . . inevitably mobilizes."³⁶ An empire's archive is usually physically located in the "mother" country, of course, and not in the colonies. The archive is only ever parallel, in this sense, to the empire, which is defined as both the motherland *and* its colonies. The archive is never really in "the empire"—in the entire thing—because it is apart from the colonies. I will examine this notion of archives further, as a pretext for my reading of Puig's *El beso de la mujer araña* at the end of chapter 4. Ultimately, for Foucault, the archive itself is therefore not just a collection of a culture's documents or the site of their preservation.

Derrida's Archive

Derrida, on the other hand, sees those very collections as the basis for his archive—a term he also uses for the reification of memory. His more significant, if indirect, elaboration of a notion of the modern archive is born of his study of Freud's work, specifically *Civilization and its Discontents, Beyond the Pleasure Principle, Moses and Monotheism,* and Freud's writings on the death drive. As such, this text is concerned "not only with what a knowledge of psychoanalysis (as a body of content or discipline) can contribute to an understanding of the archive, but also with the archive of psychoanalysis itself."³⁷ Derrida's *Archive Fever: A Freudian Impression* seeks to naturalize the human being's impulse to collect within the archive. This text, which uses psychoanalysis as a vehicle for understanding the archive, is ultimately really concerned with the "post-Freudian" depths of the archive's subject—with the archivist himself.³⁸ *Archive Fever* was first delivered on June 5, 1994, in London as a lecture during an international colloquium entitled "Memory: The Question of Archives," which was organized by the people in charge of Freud's archive and close to Freud's house in London. The work sees psychoanalysis—the pretext for the lecture on Freud—as aspiring "to be a general science of the archive."[39] Derrida explains that archivization is a universal human impulse that cuts across historical epochs and that lies between two opposing forces—memory and forgetting.

Derrida begins his text with an etymological investigation of the Greek roots of the word "archive," isolating its two variants, *arkhē* and *arkheion*. These etyma reveal the principles derived from his study of the archive: a locus where things are instituted ("commencement") and where social order and law are exercised ("commandment"): "[*Arkhē*] apparently coordinates two principles in one: the principle according to nature or history, there where things commence—physical, historical, or ontological principle—but also the principle according to the law, there where men and gods command, there where authority, social order are exercised, in the place from which order is given—nomological principle."[40] In addition, there is a house or residence of the *archons*, or chief magistrates, respectively. These *archons* enforce control over both the documents and their interpretations. Thus, the archive is housed by those with the power to interpret it and to impose it as law.

He goes on to consider the Latin etyma of "archive"; unfortunately, Derrida relies too heavily on etymological origins for grounding his ideas about the archive. His attempt is to return to the source of the modern concept of the archive. Thousands of years have passed since these terms were first coined, however, and many acceptations of the terms have since developed. He leaves out the fact, for example, that the archive and archivization have developed their own lexicon—a meta-language of sorts. Derrida's superficial, if evocative, lexicon dilutes the strength and universality of his argument and seems to promote a strained teleological connection.

Derrida's next consideration is the topological significance of the word *arkheion*—the site where the archive rests as well as the "archic, in truth, patriarchic, function" of keeping.[41] This aspect of the archive calls attention to the privileged site where a collection of knowledge is kept, by a privileged archivist. The archivist's privilege, his legally sanctioned "right" (*droit*, in French, and *derecho*, in Spanish) of keeping the archive, and his concomitant hermeneutic authority, metonymically transfer that authority to the archival content so that these documents become the "law" (also, *droit* in French and *derecho* in Spanish, in certain contexts); they speak or recall the law:

> the meaning of "archive"... comes to it from the Greek *arkheion:* initially a house, a domicile, an address, the residence of the superior magistrates, the *archons,* those who commanded.... On account of their publicly recognized authority, it is their home, in that *place* which is their house ... that official documents are filed. The archons are first of all the documents' guardians. They do not only ensure the physical security of what is deposited and of the substrate. They are also accorded the hermeneutic right and competence. They have the power to interpret the archives. Entrusted to such archons, these documents in effect speak the law: they recall the law and call on or impose the law. (Derrida, *Archive Fever,* 3)

Location is therefore an essential aspect of the archive, as the archive is not a living memory, but a "location" instead. This explains the significance and the political power of the *archons.* Location implies exteriority. The archive is predicated on the binary "inside-outside." Exteriority, ironically, makes that which is archived (that which is supposed to be safe) threatened by the possibility of destruction. According to Derrida, Freud says something similar about the psyche, "that within it, there is an interior and an exterior, containing many areas where traces are stored."

Derrida moves on to discussing the relationship of the archive to power by defining the "*achrontic*" as related to place and law, what he terms "topo-nomology," and to the gathering together of signs, which he calls "consigning"—the marking on a substrate (through impression on paper, through circumcision on the human body), which implies both process (the power of consignation) and place (the place of consignation). Consignation, he says, is the wish to "coordinate a single corpus, in a system or a synchrony in which all the elements articulate the unity of an ideal configuration."[42] Political power is ultimately dependent on controlling the archive, if not memory itself. The archive, he goes on to say, "takes place at the place of originary and structural breakdown of the said memory."[43] The archive, he predicts, will never take the place of spontaneous, alive, and internal experience.

In explaining the full title of his work, *Archive Fever: A Freudian Impression,* Derrida gives three meanings of the word "impression." First, he ponders what constitutes the "archive proper" by inquiring into the point at which the archive occurs. For him, it is literally at his word processor—so that the first meaning of the archive is typographic, "that of an inscription."[44] The second meaning of "impression" has to do with our sense, our impression, of what an archive is. According to Derrida, we can never fully know the archive; we can only ever have a series of impressions of it. Lastly, "impression" points to the influence of Sigmund Freud.

Derrida goes on to perform a close reading of Yosef Hayim Yerushalmi in turn performing a close reading of Freud through an interrogation of his ghost. The result of this thought experiment is to posit that there can be no archive without taxonomy and titles, without classification and hierarchization.[45] Derrida sees the archive, therefore, as a form of repression. He claims that it is ultimately achieved by the death, aggression, and destruction drives. Archive fever, then, is "the attempt to return to the lived origin, to the everyday experience [*sic*] which are the source of our distorted and refracted memories whose transience and forgetting makes us uneasy."[46]

Such distortion and discontinuity preoccupy Derrida in *Archive Fever*. One of his goals is to ponder the archive's stability, its contradictions. In this and in other writings, he questions the human's fascination with creating archives in the first place, given that they appear to be cohesive, but are, in reality, fragmentary:

> This deconstruction [of the history of the right that authorizes the archive] . . . concerns . . . the institution of limits *declared* to be insurmountable, whether they involve property or access rights, publication or reproduction rights, whether they involve classification and *putting into order:* What comes under theory or under private correspondence, for example? What comes under system? under biography or autobiography? under personal or intellectual anamnesis? In works said to be *theoretical,* what is worthy of this name and what is not? . . . In each of these cases the limits, the borders, the distinctions have been shaken by an earthquake from which no classificational concept and no implementation of the archive can be sheltered. Order is no longer assured. (Derrida, "Archive Fever," 40, 42; emphasis in the original)

As we saw earlier with the metonymic transfer of authority from the archivist to the archived, Derrida is questioning the inherent and transcendental affinities between and among the various discrete objects in an archive. In fact, he concludes that it is the erosion of the categorical distance between archivist and archived (subject and object)—a natural impulse, which is activated by the close contact of the former with the latter—that actually contaminates the archive; its contents become ordered by the archivist and therefore adulterated by the archivist, if we are to believe that there was some sense of ideal, Platonic form of the collection in the first instance that is more legitimate than a derivative one. Nonetheless, the mere act of collecting creates a dispersal of meaning, a rupture with the dynamic of recording. Almost like the observer effect in the natural and physical sciences, "the archiving trace, the archive, is not simply a recording, a reflection, an image of the event. It shapes the event. 'The archivization produces as much as it records the event.'"[47] Therefore, "the archive doesn't simply record the past. It also, of course, constitutes the past, and in the view of a future which retrospectively, or retroactively, gives it its so-called final truth."[48]

Whether an archivist or a scholar, the user of the archive is never outside the archive; he or she is never just an exogenous force acting upon the edge or frontier of the archive. Instead, scholars are "marked before they interrogate the markings [of their objects], and this pre-impression shapes their interrogation."[49] As we might have already surmised, the scholar's interrogation of the archive does not yield answers directly from the archive, but from the scholar himself or herself. Much as a historian would interpret artifacts and other data, the scholar interprets the collection of objects within the archive: "The object does not speak for itself. In interrogating and interpreting the object, the archive, scholars inscribe their own interpretation into it. The interpretation has no meta-textual authority. There is no meta-archive. There is no closing of the archive. 'It opens out of the future.'"[50]

Derrida's discussion of consignation might seem to contradict his notion of the archive's inherent inconsistency, which is due to the archivist's disordering access to it. The desire to coordinate the archive in a single corpus—the impulse to consign—gives it an interior and an exterior. The archive does not consist simply of remembering, of living memory, "in anamnesis," but of consigning, of inscribing a trace in some external location—there is no archive without some location, that is, some space outside. Exterior space is predicated upon interior space, which allows for repression: "To repress is to archive, to form a kind of inner exterior (unconscious) writing."[51] Derrida's notion of consignation does lend cohesion and fixity to the archive. As he puts it, the archive does not exist "without consignation in an *external place* which assures the possibility of memorization, of repetition, of reproduction, or of reimpression."[52] Derrida attempts, to a degree, to define this order as that of memory. He uses the term "hypomnesic" to describe the archive as a stand-in for the propinquity of earlier experience.[53]

At the end of the day, however, Derrida's archive does generate uneasiness—a tension between order and disorder. The archive, "as concept, is cleft, contradictory and always dislocating itself, because it is never one with itself."[54] He addresses this through the term "archive fever," which results from this critical tension. His original

French term, *mal d'archive,* may seem more apt because it connotes illness—"the feverish hunt for something in an archive that has presumably been lost or that has been kept secret,"[55] malfunction, or even evil: "It is a holocaust we could and probably should associate with the burning down of archives, and not just of Jewish books in Nazi demonstrations of the 1930s, but of archives like the Library of Alexandria, that, for Western civilization, is perhaps paradigmatic of archive trauma. . . . What is worse than the destruction of the archive by those who want to liquidate culture is their desire to archive their evil, to painstakingly record the physical destruction of the very people they execrate in order that future generations may inherit the legacy of their evil *as* evil" (Derrida, *Archive Fever,* 12). This destructive potential of the archive may be aimed at the archive itself as well as at the other (as a tool of genocide, for example, as we see above). In relating the archive to Freud, the original motivation for his talk, Derrida focuses on the death drive as a metaphor for the archive's self destruction. At work, this drive functions silently and without leaving traces of it's own archives. Derrida says,

> It destroys in advance its own archive, as if that were in truth the very motivation of its most proper movements. It works *to destroy the archive: on the condition of effacing but also with a view to effacing* its own "proper" traces – which consequently cannot properly be called "proper." It devours it even before producing it on the outside. This drive, from then on, seems not only to be anarchic, anachrontic (we must not forget that the death drive, originary though it may be, is not a principle, as are the pleasure and reality principles): the death drive is above all *anarchivic,* one could say, or *archiviolithic.* It will always have been archive-destroying, by silent vocation. (Derrida, *Archive Fever,* 68)
>
> Right on that which permits and conditions archivization, we will never find anything other than that which exposes to destruction, and in truth menaces with destruction, introducing, *a priori,* forgetfulness and the archiviolithic into the heart of the monument. . . . The archive always works, and *a priori,* against itself. (Derrida, "Archive Fever," 44; emphasis in the original)

In this way, a social and political institution, a construct really, is created to warehouse, organize, and make accessible cultural touchstones, which paradoxically dissociate as cultural metonyms when they are collected. In the archive, the individual records (texts) develop new affinities and meanings based on the archivist's organization, the scholar's use, and the overall resonance of the palimpsestic economy of interpolation and intercalation. As Derrida puts it, "One will never be able to objectivize [the archive] with no remainder. The archivist produces more archive, and that is why the archive is never closed."[56] That is why the archive always opens out of the future and why a Total Library is always a fool's errand.

The destruction of the archive is not just due to the danger posed by the exteriority of its location, but also to what Freud called the death drive—a drive to destroy the memory or trauma without any remainder or trace. What is repressed is kept safe (archived) in some other part of the psychic apparatus. In some situations, the repressed can come back. There is a destruction even more radical than repression: "the archiviolithic power." This is when something in the psychic apparatus is driven to destroy the trace without any remainder. The desire for archiving is a burning one (archive fever) because the death drive (drive for destruction) is always at work. Derrida says there is a passion "because we know that not only the traces can be lost by accident or because the space is finite or the time is finite, but because we know that something in us . . . , something in the psychic apparatus, is driven to destroy the trace without any remainder."[57] The desire to archive, therefore, is equivalent to Freud's death drive or compulsion to return to a pre-organic, inanimate state—toward destruction, or also toward forgetfulness. We want to forget, traumatic events, for example. Archives, says Derrida, "take place at the place of originary and structural breakdown of . . . memory."[58]

The original can never be retrieved, according to Derrida, because the mere act of archiving it or of recalling it once it has been archived changes it, adds to it. As with the observer effect in the physical sciences, "the archivization produces as much as it shapes the event."[59] In dipping into or consigning texts to the archive, scholars change both the texts and the archive. Scholars inscribe their own interpretations of the texts and the archive. Because there is "no meta-textual authority . . . , there is no meta-archive, There is no closing of the archive"[60] and the archive "opens out of the future."[61] The original, the event or origin, the *arkhé* is unique—irrecoverable: "The faithful memory of such a singularity can only be given over to the specter,"[62] and "It remains unfindable."[63] Again, as we saw in an earlier part of this chapter, Borges also suggests that the archive always opens toward the future, as there can never really be a book that contains the catalog of all other books in real time.

Derrida reveals through his spectral resonances among himself, Yerushalmi, and Freud that, at best, contextualizing texts reveals only the multiple layers of construction in texts (and by doing so adds another layer—as in a palimpsest of infinite progression). This is a rebuttal of the long-cherished notion of archivists that in contextualizing text they are revealing meaning, resolving mystery, and closing the archive. Derrida says that archival endeavors actually open the archive, always toward the future. This is the tension within the archive—depositing, protecting, and hiding versus disclosing, demystifying, and opening. Derrida reveals the analogical tension in Freud's memory, versus the death drive. Derrida shows that there is no remembering without forgetting, that there can be no remembering that does not become forgetting. "The archive, then, is a trilectic, an open-ended process of remembering, forgetting, and imagining."[64]

Derrida further explores the archive's ontological groundings in his *Memoirs of the Blind: The Self-Portrait and Other Ruins*—a selection of drawings from the Louvre's collections with an accompanying text. This work is more than simply a catalogue of an exhibition, however. Like the archive itself, *Memoirs of the Blind* is polymorphous and protean. The text presented along with the drawings and paintings at the exhibition is not the same as that found in the published version. Furthermore, a number of works that could not be exhibited are included in the 1993 publication, and they are not presented in the same order in the book as in the exhibition.

In this work, Derrida relates a parable about the Christian god Jesus, who applies a mixture of mud and saliva to the eyes of a man who is blind from birth and thereby gives him sight: "This man had not sinned, nor had his parents, but it was necessary that he bear witness to God's works through his restored sight. By a singular vocation, the blind man becomes a witness; he must attest to the truth or the divine light. He is an archivist of visibility."[65] Derrida interprets the parable ironically, for the blind man has in-sight and vision when he is sightless. He is given sight so that he might bear witness to the "truth or the divine light." However, seeing or bearing witness to the light is a function of blindness or the removal/lack of sight. The act of seeing is always a deferred action. Our minds must process images so that we might understand—see—them. When we draw these images or try to remember them, we are not actually looking at the images—we are metaphorically blind. We are instead remembering what we have just seen.

What the "West" archives, according to Derrida, is memory—that which exists in memory, that which can be remembered, and not that which actually exists—despite Western thinking's insistence on preserving the binary opposition between sight and blindness, the former being associated with knowledge and the latter with ignorance. In other words, that which is archived is that which was once seen, but which subsequently can only exist as an aura in memory, can only be preserved as memory. So, it seems as though the West's binary leads paradoxically to the conclusion that what is archived is ignorance, or that which is ignored, not known—*in* (not) + **gnōr-āre*, f. stem *gnō-* (to know).⁶⁶

Derrida's and Foucault's archives seem to have a number of things in common, but they do seem to be more different than similar. Although Derrida is really interested in the ontological status of the archive while Foucault stresses its epistemology, they both in the end are concerned with the ways in which culture and knowledge can be performances of power.

González Echevarría's Archive

The archive as defined by Roberto González Echevarría in *Myth and Archive: A Theory of Latin American Narrative* (1990) is the most apposite to my study. His work assembles a new theoretical model for the study of Latin American narrative: the archive (a physical, historical, and imaginary concept) is at the heart of the development of both the modern Western novel and Latin American narrative. This model affected scholars' approaches to both the historiography and the theory of Latin American literature and culture. It is a theory with which many scholars have had to contend, despite the fact that some have not found it capacious enough. This is a theory that focuses on lettered culture—the culture that is marked by reading and writing, primarily—to the exclusion of other segments of society and culture.

Let us see a view of the model and its key ideas:

> The first is that both the Western novel and Latin American narrative emerge less from inherited literary traditions than from writers' interaction with dominant non-literary discourses specific to given historical epochs. Thus, writers construct a position from which to legitimate their own stories by mimicking the rhetorical strategies of these hegemonic discourses. This process of constraint and imitation creates a "simulacrum of legitimacy" ([*Myth and Archive*] 8), and constitutes an escape from authority by revealing the conventionality of writing and its complicity with power and by providing ways for new stories to be told. (Unruh, "Review of *Myth and Archive*," 76)

These writers borrow nonliterary discursive models from those contained in the archive, the exact concept of which we will see in great detail in a moment. In the case of Latin American narrative and history, the archive was a true, physical, and political institution: "As figures of 'cultural retentions' ([*Myth and Archive*] 29) and novelistic hoarding, archival fictions incorporate and critique all prior historical engagements with official discourse and all narrative possibilities for telling Latin American stories."[67]

González Echevarría defines the archive as the repository containing the legal origins of Latin American narrative and, ultimately, of Latin America itself. The origins of Latin America, after all, were prefigured in a contract between Columbus and the Spanish Crown prior to October 1492, and then in legal and notarial documents between Habsburg Spain and its subjects in the Americas. The vast Spanish bureaucratic machine of the Habsburgs provided a discursive formula for addressing the Crown. Rhetorical privilege was afforded all those who took part in the archive's scriptural economy, because this economy recognized those who were able to simulate its discourse. Even the illiterate were able to have letters written on their behalf, using the recognized conventions. The archive was, indeed, a real building, then two major buildings, and then others, where the overwhelming number of written documents that grew out of the American encounter were, and many still are, housed in Spain.[68]

González Echevarría sheds some light on his use of the concept of the "archive," "*archivo*" in Spanish, by tracing the etymology of the word as according to Corominas: "*Archivo,* 1490, Tomado del latín tardío *archivum,* y éste del griego *archeion* 'residencia de los magistrados,' 'archivo,' derivado de *arkhē* 'mando,' 'magistratura.'" ["Archive, 1490, Taken from late Latin *archivum,* and this from the Greek *archeion,* 'residence of the magistrates,' 'archive,' derived from *arkhē* 'command,' 'magistracy.'"] (González Echevarría, *Myth and Archive,* 31). González Echevarría highlights the fact that the 1490 date given for *archivo* coincides with the reign of the Catholic Monarchs, Ferdinand and Isabella,[69] and, more significantly, with the beginning of modern archival practices, ushered in by the "discovery of America" in 1492, the beginning of Spanish imperial expansion, and the Habsburg rush to historicize the discoveries.[70]

A tremendous number of contracts and letters crisscrossed the Atlantic in the sixteenth century, many of which were tendentious and full of embellishment in efforts by explorers and colonists to gain the Crown's favor. Therefore, these writings may be read as fiction, after all. As a result, the Latin American narrative tradition was born out of this intercourse. Writing in Habsburg Spain and in its colonies was an act of submitting to a prescribed formula of address to authority, the specifics of which are perhaps beyond the scope of this study.[71] Those who could write, or who could get someone, such as a scribe, to write for them, could simulate the discourse of power and could address power itself—the king of Spain directly or his representatives. The Latin American narrative tradition was therefore born out of the derivative relationship between power and writing issuing from this epistolary intercourse.

The Spanish Habsburgs—Charles I of Spain (also known as Charles V of the Holy Roman Empire) and his son, Philip II—as well as Ferdinand and Isabella themselves, are known as the "papermonger kings" for their insatiable need to collect—accumulate, preserve, and manipulate—information.[72] Their penchant for archiving achieved its apotheosis in the institution of the archive—the actual space in which all of this paper was kept. The empire they came to build has been called by J. H. Elliott, a historian of Spain, an empire of paper, a government by paper.[73] This was never truer than during the reign of Philip II, who was almost literally cloistered away at his palace of El Escorial, ruling his vast empire on paper, on the basis of *consultas*—advice presented to him by his ministers via reports and memoranda. The physical legacy of this rule by paper is the Spanish Archives.

The Spanish Crown's first modern archive was organized by Ferdinand the Catholic in 1509, but, just like the Spanish court itself, it was itinerant, moving from one royal residence to the next, depending on the time of year.[74] Although Cardinal Ximenes de Cisneros suggested to Charles V that the national archives be transferred to a permanent repository—namely to a ninth-century citadel (dating from the period shortly after the Muslim conquest of the Peninsula) in Simancas, Valladolid—it was Philip II who actually effectuated the transfer fully. Charles V did indeed order in 1540 that an important collection of documents be kept in one of the citadel's towers, which was specifically refurbished for that purpose. It was Philip II, however, who truly looked upon the citadel as a living, national archive, where a rapidly expanding empire's new discoveries could be documented and stored in writing, and from where that same empire's precarious order could be controlled through the promulgation of regulations that would be codified within the citadel's walls. Phillip, a bureaucrat's bureaucrat, also had El Escorial built and the capital of Spain transferred to the very center of the Peninsula—Madrid. It was he who ordered the national archives removed to Simancas in 1563. The old citadel was also extensively altered in the middle of the sixteenth century by, among others, Juan de Herrera—the architect of the Escorial. This then became the first building built expressly as an archive in modern times—"possibly the most voluminous of such storehouses in Europe"[75]—and "the first fire-proof Archive known to Europe."[76] In 1588, Philip signed a statute widely held to constitute the world's first archival bylaws. The archive continued to function as the Spanish Crown's primary repository until 1844, when the political regime changed, at which point Simancas was opened for historical research. Earlier, in 1784–85, the archive of the Indies was transferred to the Lonja of Seville.

La casa Lonja de Mercaderes de Sevilla (the merchants' exchange) became the building in which the Archivo General de Indias, General Archive of the Indies, organized by the Bourbon Spanish king Charles III, was housed. The building, designed by Juan de Herrera in an Italianate Spanish Renaissance style in 1572, was first built in 1584 as La Casa de Contratación (The House of Trade), and officially known as La Casa y Audiencia de Indias (The House and Audience of the Indies). Because of a lack of space in the archive at Simancas, in "1785, 253 trunks full of documents arrived at Seville in two expeditions consisting of thirteen and eleven carts respectively."[77] This archive was created to house documents related to Spain's possessions in the New World and ultimately housed only documents that were created prior to 1760.

The third great Spanish archive is the Escorial (also known as Monasterio de San Lorenzo de El Escorial and Monasterio de San Lorenzo El Real), and it was built for Philip II beginning in 1563, just outside of Madrid, by Juan Bautista de Toledo and Juan de Herrera. This building became a palace for Philip II, for the Habsburgs, and for the Bourbons; the Royal Crypt or Pantheon, a necropolis where most of the Spanish kings of the last five centuries are buried (both Habsburgs and Bourbons) as well as other Spanish nobility; a basilica; a convent; a museum; a royal library; a school; a seminary; a hospital; and a chemist's laboratory, among other things. The Escorial became an archive of bodies—in reliquaries and tombs—as well as of documents.

González Echevarría argues that the novel and the archive are roughly coeval as part of the same discourse of the modern state and are, therefore, causally connected. The modern novel, dependent on the printing press, was created from and in the archive, just as knowledge and the idea of Latin America were also created in the archive. He claims that Columbus's "discovery" was nominal because it was not as widely disseminated at the time as it would later be in history and literature. History and literature really discovered Latin America in the archive—in all of the narrations and chronicles contained therein, which subsequent historians and fiction writers tapped into for sources and material for their works. As a repository of the narratives and chronicles of the conquest of the New World, the archive purportedly always already contains all of the narrative possibilities for telling the story of the origins of Latin America.

Arrom's Influence

The relationship between the twentieth-century Latin American novel (the Boom novel) and the early chronicles and letters of the Spanish Empire in the Americas had previously been championed by José Juan Arrom. The critic and professor was an early scholar of the epistolary and chronicle origins of Latin American fiction. Regarding the generic identity of that early writing, he says, [There are parts of those chronicles that turn out to be more novel-like than historical, and authors who end up making of themselves characters that are more made up than real].[78] Arrom identifies the Boom novel's penchant for mining and appropriating these early texts: [They reach back to even the very origins of our narrative, and with the utmost skill they examine the old chronicles of the Indies. . . . That is why, in some of this group's works, . . . intertextual dialogues with Columbus's *Diary*, Oviedo's histories, and Las Casas can be found].[79]

The twentieth-century Latin American novel is linked to these early American chronicles through its own penchant for discursive simulation. In particular, this simulation manifests itself, as González Echevarría puts it, in "the novel's persistent disclaimer of literary origins and its imitation of other kinds of [nonliterary] discourse."[80] This nonliterary discourse that the novel imitates, however, is always one that happens to be invested with truth-value, power, or privilege at that moment in time and by that society.

Myth and Archive identifies three historical moments and nonliterary discourses that shape Latin American narrative. The first period begins around the moment when "Latin America" comes into existence—the binomial nomenclature (the composite name) highlights the encounter between Europe and the "New World." This is the epoch of the coeval emergence of both the novel and Latin America.[81] In this stage of the consolidation of the Spanish state, the Habsburgs continued and stepped up the bureaucratic management of power that the Catholic Monarchs had begun—they predicated power on writing. The Crown recognized authority and power only in written form. Therefore, in sixteenth-century Spain, the discourse of legitimacy was a legal one.

This is a discourse that might be mimicked by the disenfranchised and, in general, by the illiterate. Those seeking power or recognition from authority needed only have a scribe relate their tale to men of influence if they themselves could not write. This is the discourse that frames the picaresque novel, which González Echevarría traces to a legal deposition of sorts. *La relación*, as he identifies the legal confession, provided formulaic language that bestowed legitimacy on him who could use it.

In a similar vein, other discourses, or, as González Echevarría calls them, "masterstories," provide legitimacy and enfranchisement to their users in the two other epochs that he identifies—the discourse of modern science in the nineteenth century and the discourse of anthropology in the early twentieth. Each epoch seems to promote the dominance of one of these discourses as scriptural vehicles of legitimacy. European travel literature (think of that of von Humboldt and Darwin) provided nascent scientific language, or quasiscientific language if you will, that dominated Latin American writing in the nineteenth century. Anthropological discourse frames the search for the myths of Latin American cultural origins in the twentieth century. González Echevarría sets up master "myths" in analogy to the topics Ernst Robert Curtius had already "discovered" as constituting late classical and medieval literature. Curtius's themes and the tradition in which he finds them are not the same as González Echevarría's. This is clear to anyone who has given both even the most cursory of readings. But they are similar in that they both hew to the structuralist belief that one can find a hidden unity in, in this case, literature. González Echevarría's three major types of discourse come out of more direct and particular traditions and phenomena in Latin America. What is particularly significant about his three major types of discourse is that none is literary.

Despite such a disavowal of the literary, both the twentieth-century novel and the early chronicles of the "New World" presume a literate subject who may access dominant forms of writing, or high culture. After all, the archive is a repository for the idiom of power or its simulation. The novel, for its part—according to Bakhtin as well as González Echevarría—is omnivorous, as it were, embracing, ingesting, and devouring other genres while still maintaining its non-canonical generic status as a novel. For Bakhtin, in "Discourse in the Novel," this is equivalent to the novel's welcoming of the heteroglossic into its realm of literary language. According to González Echevarría, the essential characteristic of the modern novel is that it simulates the nonliterary discourse, or metadiscourse, that dominates a particular epoch. When the twentieth-century novel sought literary models to emulate, it turned to the archive. What it found were models that had already been modeled on nonliterary, yet enfranchising, discourse. In other words, colonial narrative fiction simulates nonliterary discourse.

This is the key for which González Echevarría is searching—a "unified field theory" of sorts, within a structuralist vein. As he puts it in another one of his influential works, *The Voice of the Masters*, "My intention is to find a hidden unity in Latin American literature, a key to its various articulations."[82] The search for the unified theory of everything reminds us of the search in Borges's "Library of Babel" for the "Hexágono Carmesí" [Crimson Hexagon] that contains the log of all the other books, giving its reader omniscience.[83] To evaluate just what is contained in the archive, however, is to restrict the empirical evidence one analyzes for one's theory. Puig and Sarduy supplement the archive with those other voices and characters that it was missing. González Echevarría's conclusion, in any case, is that the origins of the Latin American literary tradition, and of Latin America itself, are in the archives of Habsburg Spain.

The fact that González Echevarría has identified three major epochs whose Zeitgeists have provided nonliterary discursive models (masterstories) for the development of Latin American fiction and the novel leads one to the natural conclusion that there may very well be other epochs to come with similar influences on Latin American narrative. He himself poses the question of what kind of hegemonic discourse will follow anthropology and, ultimately, archival fictions. He wonders what kind of new stories will be generated: "Is there narrative beyond the Archive? Do archival fictions give way to new kinds of narrative that announce a new masterstory?"[84] Ultimately, he asks what is perhaps a more interesting and powerful question: "Can narrative ever really break the mimetic bond sealed by the law in the sixteenth century?"[85] What he is really also asking is whether the archive can ever be subverted. One of the aims of my book is to answer those very questions. Or—to put it more accurately—as I write this book, those questions seem to come up naturally and to become one of the motivating forces for my study.

One of the ways González Echevarría's thesis diverges with Foucault's, and with my own, is his construction of a Latin American literary evolution that culminates with the Boom novels, but that is also, thereby, limited in critical scope. Antony Higgins has described his own "conviction that in seeking to produce a teleological narrative of the emergence of Spanish American intellectual subjectivity that culminates in the twentieth-century novel, González Echevarría tends to restrict the concept of the archive to the level of a timeless discursivity."[86] Both Higgins and I are interested in expanding the semantic range of the term "archive," beyond a term to designate the authority of writing and law, much as Foucault's concept of the modern *épistémè* sets a place at the table for eighteenth-century "man": "Before the end of the eighteenth century, *man* did not exist. . . . The

Classical *episteme* is articulated along lines that do not isolate, in any way, a specific domain proper to man . . . and man, as a primary reality with his own density, as the difficult object and sovereign subject of all possible knowledge, has no place in it."[87] Puig's and Sarduy's novels' expansion of the theory of the archive does the same for marginal, unlettered people, setting a place at the Latin American cultural banquet for them. These two writers bring marginal figures into the fold through language and linguistics, however, and this is what Foucault ultimately predicts. "Foucault cryptically asserted [in the 1960s that this figure of man was] poised to disappear. The signs of the appearance of a new *épistémè*, one that replaced and upended the modern, were unmistakable. Foucault found them in the growing importance of *language*. In theoretical discourse, linguistics was emerging as a model for the analysis of formal relationships in other areas; . . . with literature itself as an authorless event, as an effect of language."[88] Puig and Sarduy are ultimately able to reduce all cultural variants to their linguistic components. At that level, they may be inserted into the archive and exist side-by-side with other texts. Puig and Sarduy's archives are not the official repositories of a hegemonic state (such as the Spanish archives), however, but collections of mass media or popular culture, and like these subgenres—these popular genres—their archives are also unofficial and "popular"; they are archives without a state, at a moment in history when the mass media were creating a globalized culture. The difference is that, where archives are official state apparatuses that enfranchise and bestow legitimacy on their collections, Puig and Sarduy's archives—their novels—are literature. For them, literature performs the functions of the state for strata of cultures that have traditionally been unrecognized or unacknowledged. Ultimately, Puig and Sarduy expand the possible repertoires of the archive by adding Trojan horses—works of popular culture and the mass media cloaked as novels—to its collections. Now that their novels are canonical, the archive contains their work, within which they have archived popular culture and the mass media. One of the questions I will ask when I analyze their novels directly will relate to the amount of their symbolic and cultural capital and the degree to which they can be deftly wielded by Puig's and Sarduy's characters within varied social-class structures.

Guillory's Archive

John Guillory's work, while somewhat far afield of my own work here, is useful for his considerations of Bourdieu's concept of cultural/

symbolic capital. The purpose of importing Guillory's ideas about the canon into a discussion of the archive is to use his view of Bourdieu. The latter is important in my work because I will be focusing on novels whose characters have little access to symbolic capital and which, when they do have that access, do not know how to wield that cultural currency for profit. The reason I need Guillory at all as a mediating source, as opposed to going directly to Bourdieu in this chapter, as I will do when I look at particular novels further on, is to display a multifaceted point of view, as Guillory dissents on occasion from particular conclusions of Bourdieu's.

Guillory's main divergence from Bourdieu's view of symbolic capital relates to the latter's reliance on the concept of class as the underpinning of his theory. Bourdieu's revisionary sociology is predicated on the division of a society into classes, but such divisions are not universal; they may not be mapped onto other societies. Instead, Guillory focuses on race and gender as two markers that exclude from the canon. Guillory's work is significant because it argues for the disentanglement of the categories of race and gender from that of class—the traditional triad in cultural studies. He does not relegate the third category to insignificance, but instead identifies it as the hurdle or "mechanism of social exclusion" that determines "whether and how individuals gain access to the means of literary production."[89]

In unbundling these three concepts, Guillory—to my mind—is not trying to assign a lesser importance to one than to the other two in what might be called layered, or even enmeshed, oppressions—to invoke cultural studies again. As he puts it, "What *should* go without saying is that the emphasis on class in the following argument does not imply the theoretical privileging of class over race and gender."[90] Guillory ultimately situates the problem of canon formation in the crosshairs of "the constitution and distribution of cultural capital" and "the problem of access to the means of literary production and consumption."[91]

I am really studying the archive here, however, and not the canon. Although Guillory makes scant reference to the former, he is not merely making a desultory observation when he does. For him, the archive represents the heteroglossic repository of texts, which contains, or may contain, canons. Ultimately, Guillory's views of the archive are the reason for including him here at all. The archive is for him a "complex continuum of major works, minor works, works read primarily in research contexts, works as yet simply shelved," containing "an indefinite number of works of manifest cultural interest and accomplishment."[92] The archive denatures the value system, the contingencies, of the canonical worth. It is heterogeneous and polyphonic. As such, the archive is the anti-canon because it does not organize or order solely and always through value judgments. The archive's collections are in a latent state that, when activated—used by a scholar, or ordered by an archivist—do become organized and ordered through value judgment. The archive resists and erodes this organization and judgment, however, because of its vastness and heterogeneity.

The Universal Archive

The digitized age of the late twentieth century and early twenty-first century has not only made a universal archive—the ultimate collection—seem possible, but it has also made it seem more democratic. Readers write much of the content that does not already exist in cyberspace, and in that way consumers become producers. Practically, it often appears as though we already have access through our computers to universal content from Google and Yahoo, for example. Despite this, archive fever was rekindled in 2004 when Google announced that it would scan books from five key research libraries into one digitized database, which might eventually contain all books and be searchable in many different and intersecting ways—the Google Library Project. Its origins date back to the 2002 Google Book Search project, which aimed to "build a comprehensive index of all the books in the world."[93] Now, at the time this book was written, Google Book Search aims to be the service through which users will have access to the Google Library Project's collections.

The dream of the universal library has now been reborn and made to seem attainable. Many of us walk around with our own audio and video archives in our pockets; our iPods and Kindles are archives and one day may contain the "universal archive" as well. Ultimately, however, this truly is a mythical, theoretical concept. There can never be one "universal archive," for several reasons—the constant expansion of information overwhelms our capacity to contain it; the archive, a secondary entity, will always be one step behind its latest content, or so science's observer effect would have us believe. As soon as the content of the archive is observed, that is, as soon as this content is deemed a collection, it becomes fixed. At this point, the archive ceases to collect, to amass. All the while, however, archiveable material continues to be produced. There will always be something produced outside the archive before it is contained within it, *ad infinitum*. There will be no universal archive "in real time"; furthermore, the archive will not truly contain every piece that is written, recorded, published, and so forth, and so forth. It has always been and will continue to be somewhat of an exclusive club. An item may only belong if it conforms to the archive's rules, or if it is able to simulate conformation to the archive's rules: items must be able to be digitized, and the like. Finally, the archive must be accessible in order to be effective.

Let us not forget, as well, that an archive—and especially an archive of this magnitude and variety—is only as good as the technology that allows users to search accurately and practically. If search software pulls up a web of hundreds or even thousands of cross-referenced entries, users might choke on the data, unable to digest this information in a meaningful way. Classifications by archivists or librarians as well as user-friendly technology will be crucial if we are to continue to have online those fortuitous yet felicitous encounters we used to have in the stacks while searching for our scribbled leads. It is also obviously important to have readable scanned versions of pages. The de facto archive that is the World Wide Web often allows viewers to add tags of their own categorization to a file. A tag is "a public annotation, like a keyword or category name, that is hung on a file, page, or song, enabling anyone to search for that file. . . . Because tags are user-generated, when they move to the realm of books, they will be assigned faster, range wider, and serve better than out-of-date schemes like the Dewey Decimal System."[94] This aspect of the Web conforms to Derrida's notion of the diverse categorizations that might be given to the archive, depending on the archivist.

And then there is the issue of copies. The digitized archive will not contain every variant of every item. Practically, it would contain one copy of each. It will be a Noah's ark of data, containing only variants that can reproduce essential differences. But, as we know, multiplicity or uniqueness can be as much a part of the identity of a written work, for example, as is its content. Even if variants are archived, one cannot digitally archive the aura or essence of a first edition of a text, signed by its author, whose primordial condition is not derivative; or an original manuscript on vellum, whose palimpsestic nature makes it as unique as what it says. Time and space are two dimensions that are crucial to the identity of an archived item, and a digital archive stores only deracinated facsimiles.

Walter Benjamin already made clear in his essay "The Work of Art in the Age of Mechanical Reproduction" that a work of art exists as a unique entity in time and space. It becomes an "original" only when a copy of it is made. Only when a variant exists does the work take on a dialogical relationship to its copy or multiples. Copies do not bear the same physical marks or inscriptions—such as brushstrokes on a canvas, for example—that their predecessor does. Anthony Grafton gives us another similarly interesting example when he recounts Paul Duguid's observation of a fellow historian who "systematically sniff[s] two-hundred-and-fifty-year old letters in an archive. By detecting the smell of vinegar—which had been sprinkled, in the eighteenth century, on letters from towns struck by cholera, in the hope of disinfecting them—he could trace the history of disease outbreaks."[95] Grafton's eccentric and quaint object lesson hits home: "Original documents reward us for taking the trouble to find them by telling us things that no image can."[96] The digitized copy of an item denatures and decontextualizes the item.

When a work of art is created, it appears in a particular place and time, and therefore belongs to a particular age and culture. Copies, by definition, belong to a different time and place, and are therefore never the same as the "original." We also know that copies exhibit an anxiety of influence, to use Harold Bloom's term. They are created in a world where there is already an ur-text, for example. Copies always strive to be faithful to or to distinguish themselves from another, whereas "originals" do not seek exact symmetry with anything, excepting, of course, with nature if the original aspires to a high degree of mimetic fidelity; but in this case the original creation would not supplant the natural object's sole position in a collection—in an archive—as a digital copy might do.

Even in the age when mechanical reproduction allows one to go beyond the simulacrum to the exact facsimile, the copy is still deficient. It lacks presence, gravitas, a "soul." The copy lacks what Benjamin calls an "aura." Perhaps there is another way to look at the copy, however, which shifts the paradigm of primacy. I would argue that in a digital environment, items acquire a new aura. They become "the" item, the essence that represents the item in the archive. The archive functions with the currency of synecdoche. As a collection, the digital archive gives importance to representation. One copy of a text, for example, can stand in for all of the existing copies of that text because it will have met the criterion of representation. Older books have typographical errors, and this is part of their significance. Much can be learned from the errors and/or their correction, but nonstandard letters or characters may throw off keyword searches.

Politics will also play a role in determining the content of a universal archive. Does such an archive imply that every piece of material culture will be represented as a digitized copy? Will the disenfranchised and poorest segments of a society or of the world have their cultural variants represented (or equally represented) in the universal digital archive, or will the non-Western world, for example, be provided with access to Western culture? Will the digital archive lead to greater homogenization of world cultures, such that Western culture continues on its hegemonic assent? And who will choose what material gets digitized? Will ephemera in general and that from marginal groups in marginal parts of the world be recognized as valid or as equal to other content? Will marginal cultures be represented as "types," such that individuality is lost? Will obscure and less serious scholarship, for example, be given the same weight and gravitas as the hard-boiled analytical work? Certainly not if the item does not conform to the physical limitations and expectations of the archival system: "If the archive cannot or does not accommodate a particular kind of information or mode of scholarship, then it is effectively excluded from the historical record."[97] Even if items of diverse quality are included, how will a serious scholar be able to distinguish at first blush between those truly important and relevant works and the text of dubious importance without having first wasted hours on a fishing expedition? One of the quandaries of the Internet as archive is its seeming contradiction "between the secrecy or unavailability of the Archive and the open access of the Internet."[98] The Internet as archive is a vast, virtual domain, that holds out the possibilities of both infinite knowledge because of its bountiful content and oblivion because of its babble of voices.

Similarly, the Human Genome Project, which proposes to map and, therefore, to archive all of the genes in human DNA, is based on synecdochic representation because of the negotiation between, as Derrida would say, Eros and Thanatos. The project is not mapping the genes of any one individual, but rather the genes that every person might have. In this way, an archaeology of DNA, to invoke Foucault's term, is created. This archive will be complete—barring any mutations, of course. It can be studied and reconfigured. It can inspire scientists to create cures for human disease. Moreover, archives of mitochondrial DNA and world populations are indeed being created, such as through the DNA Ancestry Project. People may now search these databases or have their ancestry traced for a fee. Open access to these human archives is, however, also fraught with dangers. In the hands of the wrong person or entity, one's most intimate genetic information could be used for exclusionary or punitive purposes in social, legal, economic, or bureaucratic settings.

The Archive as Pre-text

I have considered several relevant examples of archives and have explored various notions and theories of the origins and functions of archives. The archive is a pre-text in this book for reexamining the major novels of Manuel Puig and Severo Sarduy. It is a lens through which we might understand better these two iconoclastic authors' relationships to Latin American literature and literary criticism. It has always been difficult to situate Puig and Sarduy within traditional literary history. Do they belong to the writers of the Boom? Are they post-Boom, postmodern? When seen through González Echevarría's established theoretical trope of the archive, Puig's and Sarduy's novels do seem "traditional." They do seem to fit within conventional literary histories. The twist, however, is that their novels, while engaging the archive, do not venerate it—as we shall see later. Puig and Sarduy want to elude hegemonic, canonical, and teleological narrations. The archive for Puig and Sarduy is a tradition to be invaded, raided, and expanded.

We in academia today find ourselves in the crosshairs of our profession and of our craft. We must often define for ourselves our roles, without the benefit of being ensconced in a hard-boiled movement or philosophy. We have decided that the New Critics are old, that theory is dead, and that cultural studies is effete—as movements, that is. Many of us are waiting for or trying to create the next big thing, while still others are practicing, as they always have, some or all of these methodologies and approaches, without defining themselves as being of one stripe or another.

Beyond an epistemological quandary, what we are experiencing is the questioning of what counts as knowledge, especially as our work becomes more and more interdisciplinary:

> Scholars are raising questions about what counts as knowledge and what are appropriate objects of study in specific disciplines. One way these issues are framed is as a question about what legitimately belongs in the archive. Growth in the academic study of popular culture, for example, has led to the expansion of materials deemed appropriate for research library collections. These now include comic books, romance novels, and even video games. What is considered a legitimate contribution to the archive changes over time and is a function of the transformations of the disciplines and the shifting boundaries among them. (Manoff, "Theories of the Archive," 13–14)

Puig and Sarduy were among the very first Latin American novelists who consciously sought to expand "materials deemed appropriate for . . . collections." Thanks to them, in great measure, what is now considered legitimate to archive and for which to mine the archive has been expanded to include popular and marginalized cultures. Their works redress "the limits of the official record . . . , write [subalterns] back into the historical record . . . , [and] fill the gaps and correct the omissions in the archive."[99] By doing these things—by providing sub-versions of the archive—they also subvert the archive. As we saw earlier in this chapter when we studied Derrida's notions of the archive, the economy of the archive is a negotiation between collecting and destroying, between remembering and oblivion, and between Eros and Thanatos.

I have established that the major influence on the concept of the archive in this book has been Roberto González Echevarría. My book, however, seeks to stand as a supplement to his theory. That theory is predicated upon the simulation of truth-bearing discourses by the disenfranchised (be they genres or people). Essentially, that theory relies heavily on the cultural binary "high-low." Puig's and Sarduy's novels engage various levels of cultural influence and power, which are often intermingled, as in Sarduy's famous metaphor of the Möbius strip.[100] In the end, culture in these two writers' novels is as nonorientable as the Möbius strip itself. Cultural superiority and power, in their novels, are not absolute and are neither derived from nor based on a universal archive. Instead, cultural legitimacy in Puig's and Sarduy's novels is ultimately based on relational oppositions and contextual hierarchies.

3
Manuel Puig:
El "doble irrisorio" de un subgénero: Entering the Archive through *Boquitas pintadas* and *The Buenos Aires Affair*

MANUEL PUIG'S NOVELS ARCHIVE BOTH MARGINAL IDIOMS AND MARginal characters. His second and third works, *Boquitas pintadas* and *The Buenos Aires Affair,* announce themselves as nonliterary genres—the serial and the detective novel, respectively—as they collect and display the "law of what can be said" within marginal cultures.

We will remember that Foucault defines his archive not just as "that whole mass of texts that belong to a single discursive formation," but also as the "law of what can be said, the system that governs the appearance of statements as unique events."[1] In a Foucauldian context, Puig's use of registers from the mass media and popular culture within a high-literary genre (the novel) that pretends to be a subliterary genre (the serial or detective novel) establishes these registers as archival "statements/sentences" that rewrite the "law of what can be said" in literature. González Echevarría's archive only recognizes the literary, or that which can simulate the literary. The "subaltern" cannot speak per se in his archive, to borrow Gayatri Spivak's term. González Echevarría's subaltern may only enter the archive through a redemptive translation into hegemonic discourse—master-narratives. Puig's subalterns not only speak, but they speak to the exclusion of patriarchal and other hegemonic figures.

González Echevarría's archive recognizes the authority of writing and the law. His work privileges "the regime of textual authority."[2] He clearly illustrates this through his study of the Inca Garcilaso de la Vega's writing. Writing in the Renaissance took place "within a grid of strict rules and formulae which comprised what could loosely be called rhetoric. Therefore, writing the story of America [as the Inca Garcilaso did] had to take place through such a network, which had connections to broader systems that regulated social activity."[3] Puig and Sarduy must write through a network of mass media and popular culture: subliterary, paraliterary, and nonliterary genres.[4] This is the archive in which they must insert their own works—an archive of ephemera.

The "grid of rules and formulae" within which Puig and Sarduy work is made up of the rhetorical models of the marginal in their societies. Puig's use of the serial novel and the detective novel conforms to the "law of what can be said" within the rhetorical standards of those subaltern groups. Sarduy creates his own archive to compete with the official Cuban one. Puig also creates his own archive to compete with the canonical one. In Puig and Sarduy's time, just as in the eighteenth-century moment studied by Higgins in his *Constructing the Criollo Archive,* the regime of textual authority on which González Echevarría relies "is being reformulated in the face of interrelated factors of economic, social, and intellectual change," and "the discursive is seen to be inextricably bound up with material factors, particularly institutional matrixes, class, and race."[5]

Marginal figures in Puig's and Sarduy's novels are not beholden to the regime of textual authority; instead, they are influenced by the mass media. Much of the popular culture these marginal figures wield hews closely to that which is represented in the mass media. Verging on a chicken-and-egg conundrum, the relationship that socially marginal people have to the media in Puig's and Sarduy's novels threatens the popular tradition, as García Canclini claims. After all, the media are not controlled by marginal people, but by those in the hegemony. Radio—the radio serial *El capitán herido* in *Boquitas,* for example—and film—incorporates or "stages the language and myths of the people that the dominant painting, narrative, and music almost never collected. But at the same time it induces another articulation of the popular with the traditional, with the modern, with history, and with politics.[6] The media are, of course, influenced by popular culture, as they mine it in order to be able to create programming reflecting some simulacrum of reality for its consumers. The mass media collect and feed back culture rejected by dominant society by putting themselves in charge "of adventure, serial fiction, mystery, fiestas, humor, a whole zone that is looked down upon by high culture."[7] This is not necessarily a cynical act, as "it was decisive that radio take up, in a solidary way, the oral cultures of diverse regions and reclaim the proliferating 'vulgarities' in urban centers. . . . [Radio] translated 'the idea of the nation into sentiment and the commonplace.' "[8]

To the degree that marginal figures in Puig's and Sarduy's novels control their environments and make the rules for their literary discourse, they do so by following models from the mass media. Understanding Puig's and Sarduy's novels hinges on understanding the rules of the disenfranchised world and on recognizing its touchstones. If the mass media are a threat to popular culture because they are a part of "the process of homogenization,"[9] then Puig's and Sarduy's archive-novels lay bare and vitiate that homogenization by showing us both the media's version of popular culture—a version predicated on an economic exchange for commodities such as toothpaste and soap via commercials—and the subaltern characters' own versions of popular culture. [The showing of the mercantile process in which literature is the goods exchanged is another instance that disappoints the credible serial novel's conventions].[10]

Regardless of the source of the popular culture exhibited and performed in Puig's and Sarduy's novels, we, the cultured readers, are meant to be alienated and to look for enfranchising codes in popular culture. Their novels seek enfranchisement and legitimacy from popular culture, the mass media, and the oral tradition. Their novels do not pretend to be literary creations, but instead actually pretend to be subliterary or nonliterary. In Margarita Zamora's article, "Language and Authority in the *Comentarios reales*," another study of the Inca Garcilaso's work, the author discusses the different types of truth-bearing discourses throughout history, on which Garcilaso would have modeled the *Comentarios*. Analogously, in Puig and Sarduy's time, Latin American popular culture was "a discourse without antecedents," so "its credibility was very vulnerable and the authority of its narrator was constantly in question."[11] Puig's and Sarduy's novels mark a change "in the concept of historical truth and its representation."[12]

Puig represents vernacular dialogue and commoditized cultural references in his novels. Both he and Sarduy subvert the dominant (logocentric) ideology of contemporary Western culture, as they move away from literary language. We see "the erasure of the impossibly knowledgeable author figure and the provisional empowerment of normatively marginalized voices" in Puig's novels.[13] Puig reconstructs the identity of the marginal through his archive-novels. His archive is a "prosthetic memory device . . . to invent a place to be at home" for the marginal.[14]

This idea of the archive as "home" takes us to a consideration of Derrida's notion of the archive, as it relates to Puig's novels. In Derrida's *Archive Fever*, "the concept of the archive shelters in itself the memory of the name *arkhē*, but it also shelters itself from this memory which it *shelters;* which is the same as saying it forgets it."[15] The archive occurs, for Derrida, at the breakdown of memory. As he points out, it is at the moment of forgetting that we archive. As scholars of modern computer nomenclature have noted, to archive means to "transfer to a store of infrequently used files."[16] Puig's alternative archive is not just a haven for or a place in which to memorialize cultural variants of the middle class. It is also a sendup of that group's duplicity and prejudice. Puig's archive, seen this way, is also configured then to encapsulate and criticize this middle-class culture as a way to overcome it, to forget it, to kill it. Paradoxically, to archive "is to forget and to memorialize in the same act; it is to preserve and to place under house arrest."[17]

While the archive thus allows those who see themselves or their cultural variants reflected in its collections to feel at home, it is also "usually a place of 'privilege': a physical space set off from the main library and with more luxurious appointments, invariably with some kind of limited access to keep out the rabble. You are a specialist, by intent or by interpellation, if you are there at all."[18] This is what Puig and Sarduy counter. They rework the archive such that what is within it is both what belongs to "the rabble" and "the rabble" themselves. The power of the archon, which asserts itself at the very threshold of the archive, bestows privilege and law to the marginal and subaltern. This is not to say, however, that the archive, even Puig's archive, displays mimetic, limpid reality in "hard nuggets of irreducible reality."[19] By dint of merely being collected, this marginal and subaltern material is reified, essentialized, and made a metonym of the non-literary culture it represents. The seemingly ironic outcome is that Puig's archives are just as mediated and alienating to the people and cultures it purports to represent, because they are housed in the novel—the epitome of high literature.

To continue with Derrida's ideas about the archive, we can consider what he calls "the violence of the archive itself."[20] To create order within the archive is a kind of violence since the newly instituted order created by bringing in individual entries deracinates and denatures the individual entries. On the one hand, the archive consists of collecting—a traditional act—while on the other hand, it also consists of putting things in an unnatural order—a revolutionary act. In the end, however, Puig (and Sarduy, for that matter) is not really creating an archive *for* the marginal and subaltern. Instead, he is creating an archive *of* these groups and cultural variants for readers of novels. In Lidia Santos's view, Puig creates a type of archive that is counter to the national archive, one that opposes [the national-popular aesthetic].[21] She adduces, among other forms of evidence, an explanation of the *cabecitas negras* [little brunettes, or literally, little black heads] who populate Puig's novels. This [mass of inhabitants from the Argentine interior . . . moves to the country's capital . . . , in the nineteen forties. . . . Most mestizos . . . became workers upon arriving in the city. . . . The phrase was reused by the Peronism of the nineteen forties as the foundation of the mythology of the popular party. In the 60s it is reevaluated (and thereby its mythical function returns) by the Peronist youth's national discourse].[22] Puig's archive, populated with the culture of the "cabecitas negras," creates a stylized Argentina that is quite different from "the national-popular aesthetic" of Puig's day. Ultimately, Puig's novels substitute [the mythology of the urban culture's marginalized, incorporating it into popular culture, after sanitizing its marginal aspects].[23] This is how Puig rewrites Argentina's cultural mythology.

The form of Puig's *Boquitas pintadas* is a parody of "consumer-oriented, mass-produced pulp literature"—a vehicle through which marginal and subaltern cultures enter the archive.[24] *Folletín* is the subtitle of Puig's second novel. While studies of the serial novel in the 1990s have disputed previous systematic studies that claimed the serial was "paraliterary" and "subliterary," I am here not interested so much in resolving the debate of whether a serial novel is an example of high or low culture, as it were, as I have already said in this book's introduction about this and other such debates.[25] Instead, I am interested in Puig's use of the serial novel as camouflage for a work that was clearly intended to compete with Boom novels and to be of their ilk.[26] The serial's socially recognized genre—its stereotype or reputation for being subliterary and pulp fiction—has the effect of creating an alternative archive.

As I have shown, the archive figures as a central trope in contemporary Latin American fiction and especially in Boom novels that searched for the essence of Latin American identity. These novels of the latter half of the twentieth century bring together the major discursive modalities through which Latin America was previously narrated. Boom novels showcase the history of Latin American narrative as they try to fashion their own modern myth of the beginning of that narrative, by reasserting Latin America's legal origins.[27] Their endeavor takes them back to the first narrative modality—the discourse of the law in the Spanish empire during the sixteenth century as represented by the figure of the archive. As González Echevarría asserts, "The law figures prominently in the first of the master-stories the novel tells. . . . When the Latin American novel returns to that origin, it does so through the figure of the Archive, the legal repository of knowledge and power from which it sprung."[28] Carpentier's *Lost Steps* takes us back to that putative beginning of writing. What he shows us there "instead is a variety of beginnings at the origin, the most powerful being the language of the law."[29] In *One Hundred Years of Solitude*, García Márquez also takes his reader through the several narrative modalities through which Latin America has been written about. While the scientific discourse of nineteenth-century travel books has a marked presence in the novel—Alexander von Humboldt is expressly mentioned—"the most tenuous presence [in *One Hundred Years of Solitude*] is that of the legal text, but one can infer it from the allusions to the chronicles that were in fact *relaciones*, and particularly in the founding of Macondo."[30] Patiño, in Augusto Roa Bastos's *I, the Supreme*, supervises documents that are contained in the Paraguayan Archives of State. These Boom writers therefore rehearsed the previous Latin American narrative vehicles in their own novels as part of a gesture both to subsume and to surpass them.

I do not suggest that Puig and Sarduy, or post-Boom writers for that matter, are the first to include popular culture in their writing in general, but they do exhibit "a particularly strong preoccupation with this material . . . , [as] skilled mimics of the artifacts of advertising and mass media . . . , [whose] novels and short stories resemble such popular forms."[31] While Boom works are "large, ambitious" and seek "to create a complete, autonomous world within the fiction," works by younger writers, who are certainly not literary epigones, "often [view] the quest for the totalizing novel as pretentious."[32] Boom novelists try to create mini-archives of Latin American history out of each novel, while post-Boom writers try to comment on that implicitly by suggesting that archives are open-ended, as they pretend to create archives of the marginal.

As I explain in the previous chapter, the archive is defined by González Echevarría as the repository containing the legal origins of Latin American narrative and, ultimately, of Latin America itself. The origins of today's Latin America, after all, are prefigured in legal documents negotiated by the Catholic Monarchs and Columbus prior to the Europeans' encounter with the "New World" and subsequently through a proliferation of other legal and notarial documents between Hapsburg Spain and its subjects in the Americas. This vast Spanish bureaucratic machine provides a discursive formula for addressing the crown. Rhetorical privilege is afforded all those who take part in the archive's scriptural economy, since it recognizes those who are able to simulate its discourse. In turn, according to this view, the Latin American narrative tradition is born out of the derivative relationship between power and writing issuing from this epistolary intercourse. The contemporary Latin American novel is linked to these early American chronicles through its own penchant for discursive simulation. In particular, this simulation manifests itself in "the novel's persistent disclaimer of literary origins and its imitation of other kinds of [nonliterary] discourse."[33]

Despite such a disavowal of the literary, both the contemporary novel and the early chronicles of the New World presume a literate subject who may access dominant forms of writing. Manuel Puig's *Boquitas pintadas* implicitly expands (and even questions) the theory holding the archive as the master-frame in which to search for the origin of Latin America's beginnings and historical identities. This search is commonly undertaken by Boom writers in their epic-like novels that approach culture deferentially, as something removed from common experience. In the lettered worlds of the Boom novels, culture and origins are contained in manuscripts and archives, which hold out the possibility of interpretation or enfranchisement.

Puig's characters do not have access to such enfranchising discursive modes; the archive to which Boom novelists traced their literary lineage does not provide a locus for the intersection of writing and power in the Coronel Vallejos of *Boquitas pintadas*. Instead, this world functions through a different cultural economy. The writing of Puig's characters (when the characters are literate, that is) mimics discursive formulae and rhetorical gestures of popular culture and the mass media. Ultimately, writing in *Boquitas pintadas* is beholden to rhetorical models rife with maudlin hyperbole and social codes of behavior replete with clichés and platitudes. These codes are imitated by disenfranchised members of the larger Argentine society such as women, and men of the lower rungs of the social ladder. Puig's characters have no archival repository of their own cultural brand in their world.

The only collections of recognized cultural markers they may access are fleeting: the sounds of popular music, memories of their own thoughts and conversations, and letters. In order to enter the world of scriptural privilege, they must create their own collections, either by obtaining fixed recordings of music, by recording their thoughts in a diary, or by breaking the natural epistolary economy and collecting the letters they have sent in addition to those they have received. Such collections (and indeed Puig's pseudoserial novel), however, attempt to function as an alternative archive to the mythical archive that was posited by the typical Boom novel as the origin of Latin America and its narrative. The alternative archive is an attempt to provide scriptural models of simulation that might displace the oral/aural ones of popular culture as well as its subgenres of writing (the diary and the letter, for example).

Puig's new privileged centers, occupying the cultural, social, and political spaces from which to narrate Latin America, are ultimately as much a mask and as deconstructable as the traditional hegemonic center. The significance of his work is as much a function of his reformulations of the cultural canon (the creation of more than one focal point) as it is of any decentering of the patriarchy. Ironically, this strategy is very much in keeping with the Latin American literary tradition, since its very foundation.

The modern novel, it has been posited, "developed from the discourse of the law in the Spanish empire during the sixteenth century, with the Picaresque mimicking the documents through which criminals confessed their crimes in search of atonement and legitimacy from the authorities."[34] As I have already mentioned, many of the early documents telling the history of the New World assumed the same forms, originally furnished by the notarial arts. Thus, both the Boom novel and these first Latin American narratives imitate the language of authority. Latin American narrative emerges from writers' use of dominant nonliterary discourses that are particular to given historical moments (*la relación,* anthropological discourse, and the like). Latin American writers have constructed positions from which to enfranchise their own stories by simulating the rhetorical strategies of these hegemonic discourses and historical documents: "This process of constraint and imitation creates a 'simulacrum of legitimacy,' and constitutes an escape from authority by revealing the conventionality of writing and its complicity with power and by providing ways for new stories to be told."[35]

What is referred to as a novel throughout different times in history "imitates such [hegemonic] documents to reveal their conventionality, their subjection to strategies of textual engenderment similar to those governing literature. Through this counterfeit of legitimacy the novel makes its contradictory and veiled claim to literariness."[36] Puig's novel is a counterfeit subgenre. Here, the novel is making claims to subliterariness. The novel is here "legitimized as a bearer of authentic stories by its association with those texts that tell" the stories of popular culture and not those of the first, hegemonic texts.[37]

Manuel Puig's novels also negotiate alternative figures, such as women and nontraditional males, into an Argentine and, ultimately, Latin American tradition. Puig provides these figures their own type of discursive venues, such as letters and serial romances, which allow them the type of rhetorical privilege generally reserved for a patriarchal male. In Puig's work, patriarchal males have a difficult time exerting their privilege.

Manuel Puig's novel, *Boquitas pintadas*, has an appreciation for the marginal. In it we find mixtures of various genres and cultures. Puig returns to rediscover and to conserve the familiar but virtually forgotten art forms and idioms formerly excluded from the realm of "literature." In his narratives, Puig employs the "vulgar" *géneros menores* and the frame narrative, thus eschewing closure. Moreover, the official family patriarch (the husband, father) is not directly present in Puig's works. We learn about him in *Boquitas* through women's narrations.

Through his engagement with the languages of quotidian reality in his work, Puig reminds the reader of Latin America's heterogeneity and discursive confrontations—its dialogue with various models and registers of language. His texts reveal that these models are themselves "embattled networks of dialogues among forms of discourse that comprise [them] among the languages that make up Spanish American reality itself."[38] In Puig's writing, fictional reality emerges from the interplay of heterogenous discourses, through which a complicated and contradictory assessment is made of the languages from which that fiction is drawn. He implicitly questions certain hierarchies of literary, subliterary, and nonliterary forms, themes, and languages. His work calls attention to and implicitly comments upon the hierarchies of value that inform and generate production and reception. However, within his novels, it is ultimately not clear exactly what (if any) model, language, or figure is unequivocally supported. That is, "the apparent assertion of equality among diverse narrative techniques, generic forms, and languages seems also to deny that same democracy."[39]

BOQUITAS PINTADAS

Boquitas pintadas (1969), *Heartbreak Tango* (1973) in English, advertises its subgenre and frame in its subtitle, "*folletín*" (a serial). Serial fiction is open-ended. This text, which pretends to replicate the generic model of the serialized novel, therefore suggests the possibility of regenerating itself out of control.[40] The "plot" in the text is labyrinthine, because it exists within Chinese boxes, or different, but related, levels of embedded narration. The most complex parts of *Boquitas pintadas* are those that mimic ordinary registers, while intercalating text and manipulating narrative planes. These generically disenfranchised registers reveal, or veil, the missing patriarchal protagonist—the town's Don Juan, Juan Carlos, who is already dead when the work opens. The novel's third episode, for example, begins with a nonnarrative, detailed description of a collection of photographs in a picture album. We "see" old images of Juan Carlos and other townsfolk over a couple of decades. Puig's generically hybrid text negotiates the patriarchy in a fragmentary work, without a continuous first-level narrator responsible for the whole text. In the end, all of the traditional men in the novel's world are dead or dying, and women hold their memories within marginal genres (ephemeral letters) in their hands.

Boquitas pintadas helps reformulate a tradition of Latin American narrative in which women and other subaltern figures are provided limited or bipolar spaces within which to function. Puig's novel does not attempt to destroy this tradition, but provides an alternative that is perfectly in keeping with one of the oldest traditions of Latin American narrative—the use of a master-frame to give voice to and enfranchise marginal figures. *Boquitas pintadas* is a heterogeneous collection, mainly of letters, but of other types of nonliterary and certainly noncanonical discourses as well, within which women speak freely and where traditional men must negotiate a nonpatriarchal and popular venue, ultimately relying on female voices.

Severo Sarduy has called *Boquitas pintadas* an [almost perfect serial novel . . . , the derisory double of a serial novel].[41] As we have already seen, Manuel Puig gives his second novel an alternative identity—*folletín*—as he continues to reformulate the Latin American cultural canon. As I have examined earlier, a traditional trope of Latin American narrative has been the use of a legalistic or notarial frame (a frame invested with truth value by a patriarchal society's zeitgeist), within which a writer would seek legitimacy for his work, often a tale of defeat or failure. *Boquitas* rearranges the hierarchy such that the novel is now a simulation of a popular, subliterary form, within which there is a narrative about the traditional patriarchal male (Juan Carlos), for which its author seeks enfranchisement, and the story of a woman (Raba) who crosses her society's bipolar space, who commits an act of violence against the patriarchy, but goes unpunished by it.

The title of Manuel Puig's *Boquitas pintadas* at once evokes women's mouths and their simulation.[42] This title primes the reader to expect a story about women; in fact, it is about marginal figures. Puig apparently subtitled the novel *folletín* because he originally intended to publish it in serial form in a Buenos Aires magazine.[43] He clearly chooses to keep this subtitle even after the work is not published in serial form. The serial itself is a marginal genre, considered subliterary. Although he uses mass cultural forms traditionally addressed to women, and the traditional serial usually relies on the audience's passive reception of the narrative, Puig's virtual serial requires the reader's active participation. As I mentioned above, Severo Sarduy has "pointed out that a genre that turns and looks at itself manages to go on existing while at the same time becoming a copy, perhaps even a parody of itself."[44] In his own words: [The device ends up identifying itself].[45] As Sarduy points out, Puig creates an "almost perfect" serial. This is no failure on Puig's part, but a purposeful device.

Like the female impersonator/male drag performer (so popular in Sarduy's novels) whose performance depends on the slippage between the seamless signification of "woman" and the deliberate spectacle of a man who is performing "woman," Puig's *Boquitas pintadas* relies on the reader's recognition of the simulation. Puig is not writing a real serial, since he publishes *Boquitas* as a whole unit, not in installments. The novel does, however, retain the sense of fragmentariness that defines a serial. As Jonathan Tittler has noticed, "Contrary to works that are materially unified in time, the whole is never as important as the isolated effects of its parts."[46] This means that, in *Boquitas*, each part of the serial, while connected to every other as part of a collection, has to stand alone in and of itself, providing enough information per se while piquing the reader's interest to attract him or her to the next section. This type of fragmentation dilutes the discourse and rhetorical formulas inherent in the voice of the patriarch such as those in Boom novels. As we will see in chapter 4, through the work of Carol Gilligan, the voices of women (and marginal figures) do not necessarily follow the same type of expositional logic that men's voices follow.

At this point, it would be useful to give a rough synopsis of the plot of *Boquitas*. The novel opens with a notice in the town newspaper of the death of Juan Carlos Etchepare, who we quickly learn is the local Don Juan. The novel ends with the death of Nené, one of Juan Carlos's girlfriends and a local shopgirl, who had eventually married up within her middle-class world. The final scene of the novel shows Nené's collection of love letters between her and Juan Carlos falling down a chute, where they are incinerated; fragments of their texts are illuminated in the flames before they burn. In between, the novel basically follows two love triangles: one involves Nené and Juan Carlos, and the other results in the unpunished murder of Pancho by one of his jilted female lovers, Raba.

Boquitas literally opens with a first installment, "PRIMERA ENTREGA," which starts with a fragment from an Alfredo Le Pera lyric.

As an epigraph, the musical fragment sets a popular tone and introduces a text that, in the chapter and the novel as a whole, mixes generic forms. Puig thus suggests that the reader need not have any specialized type of formal, traditional learning to read his text—if anything, the reader must have a certain degree of familiarity with popular culture. *Boquitas pintadas* mixes fragments from newspaper articles, letters, gossip, musical lyrics, police blotters, priestly confessions, and telephone conversations. There is scant trace of the traditional omniscient narrator. These myriad generic forms are normally considered subliterary, nonliterary, or paraliterary, but certainly not canonical. They convey the voices of marginal figures, such as middle-class women, because they purportedly represent the venues that these marginal figures traditionally use in reality.

The tradition of Latin American narrative that uses the trope of an enfranchising legalistic or notarial frame reverberates through *Boquitas pintadas*. The idea of narrative frame and its content are central to the novel. As I mentioned earlier, the title itself evokes the image of a frame (the painted lips) that contains the voice that will deliver the message. The painted little mouths are signified as those of women because of the use of the diminutive marker and the reference to lipstick, but are otherwise indistinguishable from those of men. There is no definitive reference to their genders. Men's mouths can also be described by using a diminutive suffix and can also wear lipstick. I am not just saying that Puig is veiling a reference to drag or cross-dressing, but rather suggesting that the novel's title evokes a type of ventriloquism in general. The framing component—the discursive and chemical cosmetics—mask a content that could be male or female. Even if we are dealing with female lips, they may still be masked. After all, lipstick is artificial. Puig does make reference to "boquitas"—more than one mouth; and his novel is about women of various types and classes and temperaments, not just one archetypal woman. They do all have in common, however, roles by which they seem constrained in their provincial society.

On a generic level, *Boquitas pintadas* is clearly not a serial: all of the episodes appear at once and are collected in the novel's traditional packaging. As a novel, however, it is a hodgepodge collection of genres and registers. As such, Puig's second novel is really a series of Russian dolls or frames. The traditional denomination of "novel" is here applied to a series of marginal, nonpatriarchal and noncanonical discourses and genres, which themselves frame marginal and marginalized figures. Puig maneuvers his work within the traditional scheme of Latin American narrative by having his novel pretend to be something it really is not—a serial. The serial, however, and as we saw above, is typically regarded as a disenfranchised and popular genre. Therefore, Puig is reformulating the tradition by having one of the most canonical of narrative types—the novel—pretend to be a disenfranchised popular form—the serial. This way, his women's voices do not seek legitimacy from a patriarchal frame; instead, his male's voices (or their echoes) seek to be communicated through the marginal venues, and thus themselves become marginalized.

The men, the logos, in *Boquitas pintadas* are at the mercy of the women who articulate them and of the narrative vehicle of which they are a part. The only significant male characters are Juan Carlos Etchepare, Pancho, and Nené's husband. Some of the other men, whom I will not examine, are Nené's emaciated and dying father and Juan Carlos's nonexistent (but alluded to) father. The narrative proper opens with an obituary notice for Juan Carlos, the town's heartthrob and womanizer. This supposedly virile figure is already dead at the very beginning of *Boquitas:* "La desaparición del señor Juan Carlos Etchepare acaecida el 18 de abril último" [The disappearance of Mister Juan Carlos Etchepare, took place on April 18 last].[47] Although we get to know a bit about him throughout the novel, he is really only an aura of a traditional male figure: we know of his ultimate demise in the first page of the novel and we know throughout most of the work that he suffers from tuberculosis. We learn about him mostly through the voices and letters of women. The first such series of letters or voices is from Nélida Fernández de Massa, also known as Nené, and makes up the first and second installments (*entregas*) of the novel. In expressing her condolences to Doña Leonor Saldívar de Etchepare (Juan Carlos's mother), Nené invokes and reanimates the memory of Juan Carlos. This is how the reader perceives him after reading the opening obituary notice. Nené is a former love interest of his who, although now married with children, longs for their unconsummated love. She actively tries to idealize him: "Está ya en la gloria del Cielo. Ay, sí, de eso tenemos que estar seguras, porque Juan Carlos nunca le hizo mal a nadie" [He is already in Heaven's Glory. Oh, yes, we must be sure of that because Juan Carlos never harmed anyone] (12). Perhaps unwittingly, however, Nené's letters give a deeper insight into Juan Carlos's personality and affect, as reflected in some of her comments: "¿Qué van a hacer con todas esas cosas de Juan Carlos que son personales? Yo sé que él una vez guardó un pañuelo con rouge, me lo *contó para hacerme dar rabia, de otra chica*" [What are you going to do with all of those things of Juan Carlos's, which are personal? I know that he once kept a handkerchief with rouge, he *told me it belonged to another girl to make me furious*] (emphasis added) (14).

Yo siempre me quedé con una espina, porque un día, poco antes de distanciarnos para siempre, lo pesqué a Juan Carlos en una mentira. . . . Tenía un pañuelito escondido en el bolsillo del saco, bien metido en el fondo, de mujer, perfumado, y no pude alcanzar a leer la inicial, bordada con muchos adornos, pero segura segura que no era "E", y la viuda Di Carlo se llamaba Elsa. *Me dijo que era de una chica que conoció en Córdoba, que él era hombre y tenía que vivir.*

[I always remained with something stuck in my craw, because one day, shortly before we parted forever, I caught Juan Carlos in a lie. . . . He had a little handkerchief hidden in his jacket pocket, tucked away deep inside, a woman's perfumed hanky. I was not able to read the initial, embroidered on it with many decorations, but for sure, for sure, it was not "E," and the Di Carlo widow was called Elsa. *He told me it belonged to a girl he met in Cordoba, that he was a man and had to live*] (emphasis added) (35).

Nené's letters reveal him as a person who treats women as love objects and not as individuals, despite her protestations of Juan Carlos's virtues. Mabel, a former love interest of Juan Carlos, confirms for the reader the syphilitic Don Juan's behavior toward women, in a conversation with Nené:

—¿Ahora se cuida más [Juan Carlos]?
—Estás loca. Se pasa la vida buscando mujeres. Lo que yo no me explico es cómo ellas no tienen miedo de contagiarse.
—Y . . . algunas no sabrán.

[—Does he take better care of himself now (Juan Carlos)?
—You are crazy. He spends his life looking for women. What I cannot understand is how they are not afraid of catching something from him.
—And . . . some of them probably do not know] (207).

We hardly hear directly from Juan Carlos, but we do get letters he writes Nené in *SÉPTIMA ENTREGA* and *OCTAVA ENTREGA*. *Boquitas pintadas* translates the traditional male through this nonpatriarchal epistolary genre, through which he cannot adequately communicate. He must use generic sections in his letters to various women: "Este parrafito lo he puesto igual en todas las cartas" [I wrote this same little paragraph in all of the letters] (107). Moreover, the voice of the traditional male is reduced to idle threats: "Y vos rubia mejor es que te cuides bien porque yo allá dejé mis bigías bien apostados, nada de malas pasadas porque me voy a henterar ¿vos te creés que no? Si la llegás a hacer un paquete con muchos firuletes a algún desgrasiado de allá lo voy a saber más pronto que ligero. No, de veras, yo no sé perdonar una jugada sucia, de eso no te olvides nunca" [And you, blondie—it's better that you take good care of yourself, because I left my lookouts well placed—no missteps because I'm gonna find out. You think not? If you end up giving some bastard from over there the time of day, I'm gonna find out quicker than quick. No, really, I don't know how to forgive a dirty trick, never forget that] (108); and "Te aseguro que me la van a pagar" [I assure you that they are going to pay] (114). Juan Carlos is an impotent communicator. He may fancy himself a Don Juan with the ladies, but he is a consumptive who cannot use standard language to write his letters (as can be seen in the passages above), despite the fact that he has an old proofreader at the hospital who goes over them for him: "Es una persona de mucha educación, ex-professor de la Universidad. A mí sí me dice que soy un animal para escribir" [He is a very learned person, former university professor. He does tell me that I am a brute of a writer] (116). "Más que corrección de ortografía solicit[o] ayuda para redactar la carta en cuestión" [More than spelling corrections, I ask him for help in composing the letter in question] (120). So Juan Carlos is not only a poor writer, but a poor communicator as well, since his proofreader ends up composing much of the letters for him. While most of the women described in *Boquitas* are trained as school teachers (which is called a woman's profession in the text), and they write letters well, the traditional men of Vallejos are clearly shown as incompetent communicators in the epistolary genre.

Letters and collections of letters are important frames in Puig's novel. As we saw earlier, *Boquitas* opens with a series of letters that Nené has written to Doña Leonor. Here, Nené asks Juan Carlos's mother for the letters that Nené and Juan Carlos had exchanged roughly a decade earlier: "Entonces yo pensé que si Usted no piensa mal y encuentra esas cartas que él me escribió a mí, a lo mejor me las manda" [So I thought that if it is all right with you and if you find those letters that he wrote me, maybe you will send them to me] (14). Since the novel's time is not linear, the reader does not immediately know that Nené has actually gotten the letters, until the very last section, when she wants to dispose of them and says she has had them for twelve years. Nené had Juan Carlos's letters tied with a blue ribbon and had requested that he tie hers with a pink ribbon, to differentiate between the genders. Through this, we see the trite and stereotypical division of genders and essentialized respective colors, as well as the difference in treatment of this nonpatriarchal collection by a woman (she keeps them neatly contained) and a man: "Él cuando me devolvió las mías estaban sueltas en un sobre grande, yo me enojé tanto porque no estaban atadas con una cinta rosa como se lo había pedido" [he, when he returned mine, they were loose in a big envelope, I got very angry because they were not bound with a pink ribbon as I had asked him to do] (14). Ironically, it is in these noncanonical letters that the memory of Juan Carlos is contained and disseminated, since his relationships have no issue. He is not a proper custodian for the letters, as the women are. If these collections of letters are seen as corporeal collections, in which people and their voices figure as signifiers or discourses on a page, then we see that Juan Carlos (like Pancho, earlier in the novel, and as I will examine shortly) keeps women fragmented and loose. Nené, on the other hand, keeps Juan Carlos (and his memory) integral, tied together. Ultimately, this collection is what carries his memory, and his memory is at the mercy of women (his mother, Celina, and Nené).

Nené is Puig's archivist in *Boquitas pintadas*. She represents the provincial person who "marries well" and moves to Buenos Aires, the distant city. The act of collecting and organizing writing is symbolic of Nené's self-awareness as an interstitial cultural subject, perhaps even a hybrid cultural subject. Her goal of possessing an archive of letters is her way of bridging the epistemological gap she perceives between a cultural register deriving from ephemeral (mass media) models and one enfranchised by the lettered culture of writing, into which she transitions when she moves to the capital city. Popular culture is the master-frame from which both collections (Puig's serial novel and Nené's letters) originally sought rhetorical camouflage. However, Nené's act of collecting the letters between her and Juan Carlos in discrete organizational units, as she decides to do after her move to Buenos Aires, is an attempt to reinscribe popular ephemera within the frame of dominant forms of writing. These letters are no longer fetishized metonyms of Juan Carlos but are "in-corporated" as whole collections of masculine and feminine units, ultimately guarded by Nené's lawyer, an allusion to the archon and the legal origins of the myth of the archive.

Puig is representing realms of Latin American culture that are not inscribed within the myth of the archive as origin of Latin American narrative. The characters who inhabit these alternative realms exist in personal spaces they negotiate, because they cannot be enfranchised or accurately represented by official authoritarian legal discourse in their society. Puig's characters simulate the world of the serial romance, of the tango. Women are the keepers of the alternative archive here and know how to negotiate its rules. (Celina can simulate its discourse and pretend to be her mother when she corresponds with Nené as Doña Leonor.) Men need help from members of the dominant institutional and lettered world (the former university professor). But even the university professor cannot ultimately function well within the letter's discursive rules (he wants to use too "novelistic" a discourse). Similarly, in *Boquitas pintadas,* Puig's presumptive lettered reader cannot find the novelistic formulae to which he or she is accustomed. Instead, he is made complicit by Puig in the voyeuristic and transgressive act of reading other people's private thoughts and letters without being guided or preceded by an omniscient narrator whose ultimate knowledge and imprimatur of organization and plot seemingly sanctions the reading of a more traditional text (such as a Boom novel) as fit for a reader's consumption. Puig's collection of very personal and private writings are not usually framed by narratorial mediation.

Although out of a traditional time sequence, the letter motif functions as a true letter would. There is a time lag from the moment a letter is conceived and sent until the moment when the recipient gets it. Although *Boquitas* opens with references to Juan Carlos and Nené's letters, it is not until the very end of the novel that the reader knows Nené has the letters in her possession. These letters represent a temptation for her to remember her youth and single life, now that she is married and miserable. Although by the standards of her townsfolk, Nené has done well for herself by marrying a respectable man, having two boys, and living in Buenos Aires, the capital, she feels trapped again: "Estoy sola en el mundo, sola. . . . Ayer me encerré en la pieza y mi marido la forzó, yo creía que me mataba . . . y yo como una loca le escupí en la cara. Me dijo que se la iba a pagar, pero se aguantó de pegarme. Yo creí que me iba a romper la cabeza . . . No aguanto más esta vida, todos los días lo mismo" [I am alone in the world, alone. . . . Yesterday I locked myself in the room and my husband forced it open, I thought he was going to kill me . . . and I spat in his face like a crazy woman. He told me I was going to pay, but he kept himself from hitting me. I thought he was going to crack my head. . . . I cannot stand this life any more, the same thing every day] (27–28; 30). She hates her husband and children, since they are all ugly, and they certainly pale by comparison to the beautiful Juan Carlos of her younger memories. These are obviously romanticized memories, as we readers recognize the phrase "He told me I was going to pay" as something Juan Carlos used to write her, too.

Nené's collections of letters are a feminine collection. For her, they provide the space for privacy and fantasy that she does not otherwise have in life. The outside world, the world of society, is a world of action for men in this novel, but a world of danger and traps for women. To be seen dallying with a man in public would send the gossips' tongues wagging, and a woman's reputation could be irreparably damaged. The privacy of letters offers the space within society's interstices for women to communicate with their lovers and others. Puig substitutes these private and nonpatriarchal venues for the traditional venue of the novel in *Boquitas*. But Puig is also aware of the danger in letter writing: the danger that the private letter will be intercepted by an intruder who will read it and possibly even simulate the voice of the recipient in a return letter.

Such is the case with Celina, Juan Carlos's sister and Nené's sworn enemy. We, the readers, do not know it until the end of *Boquitas pintadas*, but Celina is actually the person who had been responding to Nené's letters all along: "Se apresura a escribir el sobre antes de ser descubierta y sale rumbo al correo después de decir a su madre que va a la farmacia" [She rushes to write out the envelope before she is discovered, and she goes out to the post office after telling her mother that she is going to the drug store] (233). Only another woman, Celina herself, could co-opt the venue and simulate the voice of Doña Leonor.[48] In fact, we find out at the end that Juan Carlos's mother never received one single letter from Nené. As a member of the subordinate group (women), Celina is able to enfranchise her voice under the guise of a letter's rhetorical strategies. In the end, the letter—a marginal discursive venue—proves to be no purer a mode of enfranchisement than traditional Latin American narrative's hegemonic frame. In the end, however, it does prove to be a frame that is controllable by marginal figures such as women, and not by the traditional patriarchs or the representations of the logos. Ultimately, Nené has her collection of letters incinerated, annihilating the only remains of the patriarch's voice.

The nonpatriarchal and noncanonical venues in *Boquitas pintadas* also serve as a vehicle for the clarification of the truth regarding a murder in the novel. Antonia Josefa Ramírez, also known as Rabadilla or Raba, for short, kills Francisco (also known as Pancho), the father of her child. The women in the novel see Pancho as someone who betrays Raba, having promised her his love and marriage, but leaving her after finding out that she is pregnant with his child. Raba, who is at the bottom of Vallejos's socioeconomic ladder to begin with, suffers even more marginalization by some in her society. To Pancho, women are not individuals, but interchangeable: "Las piernas blancas de Nené, los muslos oscuros de las muchachas de La Criolla, el pubis negro de Mabel, el trasero oscuro de la Rabadilla, Nené, la Rabadilla, el pubis sin vello y blanco de Nené" [Nené's white legs, the dark thighs of La Criolla's girls, Mabel's black pubis, Rabadilla's dark rear end, Nené, Rabadilla, Nené's white and hairless pubis] (79). In fact, he sees them as fragmented and interchangeable body parts. Pancho, having abandoned Raba, is having an affair with María Mabel Sáenz, his social superior. This creates a web of relationships, since Raba ends up working for Mabel's family as a live-in housekeeper, yet does not initially know that Pancho is sneaking in at night to have relations with Mabel. After finding out, Raba plans Pancho's murder and ends up stabbing him to death.

Boquitas pintadas shows two different modes of communicating the facts surrounding the murder: the first, the official police report, in *DUODÉCIMA ENTREGA* [*TWELFTH INSTALLMENT*]; and the second, Mabel's confession to a priest. The official police document is a patriarchal document, allied with the deceased, who was a member of the municipal forces. It records information in an official and notarial language, with definite rhetorical formulas and expressions:

ACTA INICIAL (Extractos)
A los dieciocho días del mes de junio del año mil novecientos treinta y nueve . . .

[INITIAL RECORD (Extracts)
On the eighteenth day of the month of June of the year nineteen hundred thirty nine . . .] (181).

This official report also seeks to express time in a linear and logical progression, in an effort to make causal connections. Raba confesses to the violent act as a crime of self-defense: "Confesó haber dado muerte al suboficial de Policía [Pancho] con una cuchilla de cocina" [She confessed to having killed the warrant officer (Pancho) with a kitchen knife] (186); "[Pancho] la amenazó con su revólver y dijo que se le entregara allí mismo. . . . La [Raba], plena de rencor . . . le mostró la cuchilla para ahuyentarlo, pero [Pancho], ebrio, no dio importancia a la amenaza, por el contrario" [(Pancho) threatened her with his revolver and told her to submit to him right there. . . . (Raba), full of anger . . . brandished the knife to scare him off, but (Pancho), drunk, did not heed the warning, on the contrary] (186–87). This confession is tidy and eventually gets Raba acquitted of murder charges due to self-defense, even though there are still some unanswered questions that may taint her innocence: "En cambio una curiosa observación del Cabo Lonati arroja dudas sobre la no premeditación del hecho sangriento" [However, a curious observation by the Sergeant Lonati sheds doubt on the lack of premeditation of the bloody act] (188).

To be sure, this fairly straightforward story of self-defense is not the entire truth, but a version that the patriarchal society and its venue can appreciate. The "real" truth comes out in Mabel's confession to her priest in the *DÉCIMOCUARTA ENTREGA* [*FOURTEENTH IN-*

STALLMENT]. Mabel recounts that Raba had figured out that Pancho and Mabel were indeed having an affair right under her nose. Infuriated and confused, Raba "había tenido el atrevimiento de esperarlo y le había dado dos puñeladas" [had had the courage to wait for him and had stabbed him twice] (217). Afraid that her affair would be discovered, Mabel fabricates the official story for Raba and then gets her to repeat it convincingly. Mabel's confession to the priest, a dubiously enfranchised male, shows that Raba's actions were premeditated and that Mabel herself was an accomplice after the fact, in hiding the severity of the crime.

Raba, the subordinate of the subordinates—an abjectly poor woman—ultimately goes unpunished by the official patriarchal society. She is able to kill one of its members—a man and a member of the police force. As Mabel says, Raba is not judged by society's traditional laws, but by a higher divine justice: "¿Y Dios no tendrá otro modo de castigarla? ¿Tiene necesariamente que castigarla la Justicia?" [And will God not have another way of punishing her? Does Justice have to punish her necessarily?] (218–19). The official world of the patriarchy would not have recognized the injustice that Pancho had done to Raba. Her situation would have had to be inscribed within an official hegemonic frame, which would not have enfranchised her. In *Boquitas pintadas,* however, that frame—the police report, both in itself and as a metonym for the patriarchal system of justice—is only a minor one, sandwiched between frames of marginal discourses (letters, diaries, and the like) and within the masterframe of the virtual serial romance. In Puig's novel, women must create, appropriate, and champion their own discursive spaces. It is only in this way that they can resist the patriarchy's impulse to fragment them, translate them, elide them, and, ultimately, erase them. Moreover, in Manuel Puig's novels, the patriarchy is dependent on the marginal discursive venues for expression.

Puig reformulates the Latin American narrative tradition by having one of the most canonical of narrative types—the novel—pretend to be a disenfranchised popular form—the serial. This way, his women's voices do not seek legitimacy from a patriarchal frame; instead, his men's voices (or their echoes) seek to be communicated through the marginal venues, and have thus become marginalized themselves, within the larger tradition of Latin American literature. Recall that González Echevarría's theory of the archive evoked at the beginning of this book holds that the novel pretends to be a nonliterary text, but one invested with legitimacy and authority. The serial novel does not fall under this description. The serial itself is a marginal genre, and may even be considered subliterary. Although Puig uses mass-cultural forms traditionally addressed to women, and the traditional serial usually relies on the audience's passive reception of the narrative, his virtual serial requires the reader's active participation in order to piece together the complex narrative jumps. Moreover, in ending with death, *Boquitas pintadas* breaks with the typically happy ending of the Latin American serial.

The image of the archive is clearest in *Boquitas pintadas*'s final moment, when Nené's husband throws the love letters between her and Juan Carlos, which she had collected decades before, down an incinerator chute, to be destroyed, after Nené's funeral. These letters had been kept by Nené's lawyer—the figure of the *archon*, the law, and a reference to the law's role in the traditional view of the archive—to whom she entrusted the letters in the latter part of her life. In these letters, Juan Carlos tries to speak, with the patriarchal male's most unctuous and manipulative rhetorical privilege and authority. As we saw before, however, we learn at some point that Juan Carlos is functionally illiterate and actually had a professor write the love letters for him. Juan Carlos has to resort to the simulation of clichés and the style of popular culture, which is reproduced by a higher-ranking member of society. In the end, the novel is devoid of the discourse of power. The ephemeral love letter can easily be discarded. Nené keeps the letters tied together in two separate bundles, using pink ribbon for hers and blue ribbon for those belonging to Juan Carlos. These sentimental and essentialized gender conventions reveal the rules, as it were, that may govern the archive in Puig's novel. The letters' conflagration represents the archive as something that is finite in Puig's world, and not as a transcendental institution or meta-narrative. Archiving is, as Derrida derives from Freud, an act of forgetting, an impulse toward death. At the very end of the novel, we are left with random words and phrases that we read in flashes of light from the fire as they burn: "'nada de malas pasadas porque me voy a enterar,' 'te besa hasta que le digas basta, Juan Carlos,' 'Muñeca, se me termina el papel'" ["no dirty tricks because I am going to find out," "kisses until you say enough, Juan Carlos," "Doll, I am running out of paper"] (257).

The rules of the archive in *Boquitas* are not allied with power; instead, they are the conventions of bourgeois popular culture, a culture very much a part of Latin America and, certainly, of Puig's own world. *Boquitas pintadas* begins by announcing the absence of the traditional voice of power and ends by emptying its archive of power's simulated discourse. Puig constructs a sub-version of the archive, a counterarchive of popular and unsanctioned materials, thereby tracing his legitimate literary origins to the ephemeral voices of popular culture and the mass media.

In *Boquitas pintadas,* epigraphs, the mass media, and popular cultures are among the master-frames that legitimize the letters and the discourse of the characters that populate the novel's world. The sentimentality of the popular cultural forms is a touchstone for Puig's marginalized characters. This is Puig's alternative archive of popular culture—the repository of the subgenres. The metafiction (the epigraphs) are the myths Puig erects in the clearing left by identifying the traditional archive with the lettered and the cultured. The characters in *Boquitas* seek legitimacy from these epigraphs by writing equally sentimental letters and by trying to create their own collections (Nené's letters).

The novel opens with the death of the traditional male to create a clearing in the popular cultural archive for women's epistolary genre. By simulating a serial romance, Puig's novel enfranchises popular culture. Otherwise, the marginal people who are reflected in the novel would not have the cultural capital with which to enter or dialogue with the traditional archive, and would therefore remain elided from it. In the end, however, there is still a mimetic displacement of these people, from their oral, uncultured, unlettered societies to the lettered and written ones represented by those who truly read Puig's novel, which is not a serial romance after all. Similarly, at the end of the novel, Nené does not want to enter or dialogue with the archive, as she has her cache of letters burned.

The serial is composed of installments, which helps to mix generic elements, and to leave lacunae, just like the traditional archive. Seen this way, the serial is also an archive, then—it collects subgenres and subaltern voices. However, only women can seek legitimacy from the serial—it offers Raba a form of justice with impunity that she would never have gotten otherwise from other, official archives (represented in the novel by the police report). Mabel's confession to her priest also enters an archive of sorts, a subarchive because it represents the Church, an epistemology for the masses or underclasses.

Nené's collection of letters creates a *mise-en-abyme* effect relative to the whole novel. As the characters—women—enter the serial through their letters, so do they enter the larger, traditional archive as characters in the novel. Anyone can enter the alternative archive (like Juan Carlos's sister), if he or she knows how to simulate its language. Juan Carlos, however, does not, because the sentimental genres (music, the serial, and the like) are generally aimed at women. Juan Carlos can only communicate in and is trapped by stock clichés. Even when he turns to a scribe—the professor in the hospital—the latter cannot write within the economy of the subarchive. His letter is "muy novelesca" [very novelesque], according to Juan Carlos (120). Puig makes popular culture and the mass media the master-frame, the latest discourse, to be endowed with truth-bearing power. His characters try to simulate popular culture, just as his novel does.

The Buenos Aires Affair

If the serial romance is the archetypal genre of marginalized women, or of women in general, then the detective novel is that of men, or subaltern men, because of its overreliance on rational thought and detective work while not being high literature. Of course, these generalizations and oversimplifications are false, because all kinds of people enjoy both serial fiction and detective novels, but these stereotypes do exist, and Puig writes within their conventions. Certainly he means to analyze the discursive formulas used by these subgenres and to push their boundaries. In *The Buenos Aires Affair,* a pseudo-detective story, Puig, as in *Boquitas pintadas,* writes a novel that pretends to be subliterary. The novel contains a series of archival images through which Puig is able to capture and represent the culture of marginalized groups.

The *Buenos Aires Affair*'s subtitle is "Novela policial" [A Detective Novel], but Puig's third novel is merely virtual detective fiction. Although the work evidences some elements of the typical subgenre, [in this atypical detective novel, the case is precisely an absence of a case; well, it is never proven that a crime had taken place].[49] There is no detective, no typical murder, and no resolution at the end. Once again, as in *Boquitas pintadas,* this novel's subtitle prepares the reader for a specific generic model that never truly materializes. Once again, Puig's novel pretends to be a subgenre for textual—or paratextual, more accurately—camouflage.

The first thing readers notice about this work is its bilingual title. We are held up almost immediately by the main title's last word— "affair." We believe we are offered a clue in the subtitle's generic designation—"detective novel." However, as with *Boquitas*'s ambiguous and multivalent title, *The Buenos Aires Affair*'s title could mean various things. It could refer to a situation, to a romantic affair, or to a matter. We do not know which one, but are certainly persuaded by the subtitle that we will read about a mystery that unfolds in Buenos Aires. The novel's alternative identity will house a series of archives that contain marginalized cultures.

The most general archive in the novel is the novel itself, which contains various discourses; it is itself a narrative collage. The first type of discourse we encounter is the cinematographic, by way of epigraphs. Every chapter of *The Buenos Aires Affair* begins with a snippet translating a scene from a classic movie, along with dialogue and direction. Every epigraph features a different diva, usually from Hollywood's golden age of cinema from the 1930s and 1940s. The epigraphs do not always relate directly to the chapters' action, but they do set a particular melodramatic mood that often highlights the psychological treatment to which the characters submit themselves and also frame the chapter through mediation.

We readers are obviously not watching the scene unfold on celluloid, and we are not in a movie theater. Instead, we are put in the position of the actors, and we are shown their motivation and screen direction. Therefore, the epigraph is an impostor of sorts, a virtual film experience, just as the novel we are reading is only a virtual detective story. In both cases, novels (or a novel's literary device, in the case of the epigraphs) are pretending to be nonliterary media. The fact that the epigraphs are translated into Spanish and that the actual scene's action is condensed for us readers adds to the artificiality of the literary device. Moreover, as Derek Frost has pointed out, "Some of the epigraphs betray their fraudulent quality openly by altering or inventing important story elements."[50] In fact, some scenes are concocted altogether.

In the end, the epigraphic frame makes us mediate artistic genres. We seek filmic representation on paper, and we try to read the plot of a detective story in a novel. We must also translate the epigraphs, not just for content (not just to remember that they were originally written in English), but also for cultural context. After all, these movies were set in the U.S. and written for a U.S. audience.

A similar type of mediation is experienced by the main characters in *The Buenos Aires Affair.* We know from their names and their family backgrounds that we are often dealing with a generation of people whose parents are not native born. Emigrant culture in Puig's novels is not limited to movement from Europe to Argentina, however, because we often also see Argentines themselves move either from the interior to Buenos Aires or from the capital to the pampas. In all of these cases, we see a displacement and an accompanying negotiation of culture as characters seek new discursive and cultural models that fit them better and that replace their ancestors' or earlier lives' systems: [The Argentine protagonists of (Puig's novels), second generation European emigrants, have grown up uprooted and lacking linguistic and cultural models their parents were not able to provide for them. In order to resolve this deep identity conflict, these characters have had to latch on to the cultural models of a society that was debating with itself between the search for an individual identity and the adoption or the adaptation of imported models, of a second class in most cases] (Colmeiro, "Lenguajes propios y lenguajes apropiados," 167).

Puig's characters often turn to foreign—specifically U.S.—cultural models as a result of their search for new cultural idioms and templates. Puig's novels show the pervasiveness of the mass media—which are really beginning to become an archive of world culture at the time of the post-Boom, and which will spread through the technologies of globalization in the following decades. Puig's characters' fascination with U.S. cinema in particular, in several of his novels attests to this use of secondhand discourses, as he tells Rodríguez Monegal.[51] Many of Puig's characters, especially these displaced ones, resort to the archive of foreign discursive models.

The characters in *The Buenos Aires Affair* learn to speak, to carry themselves, and to think about themselves through these foreign films and magazines. When Gladys thinks of the way she would like to imagine herself, she dreams up an interview with a reporter from New York's *Harper's Bazaar*. At one point, she tells the reporter that she yearns to

> "pasar por mi piel el perfume corporal polinesio que recomienda una página entera de su revista, porque esta noche quiero sorprender a alguien con una nueva fragancia. . . . El dibujo de muchachas polinesias, se las muestra frescas como la brisa que nace de la marejada, como suaves también son los pimpollos que caen en la arena húmeda, y cálidos los llameantes atardeceres de las islas. Perfume de esencia de perla para el cuerpo.
>
> [rub on my skin the Polynesian body perfume that an entire page of your magazine recommends, because tonight I want to surprise someone with a new fragrance. . . . The drawing of Polynesian young women shows them as fresh as the breeze that is born from the swell, as soft also as the new shoots that fall on the moist sand, and as warm as the flaming evenings of the islands. A perfume of pearl essence for the body.][52]

This popular magazine serves as a nexus of knowledge and desire for Gladys, among Argentina, the U.S., and Polynesia. Gladys derives the discourse of her self-image and social projection through the language of this globalized archive of popular culture. The orientalized image of the East's indolence, opulence, and surface beauty is mediated by a U.S. perspective and sold to Latin America. So, when we hear the words of Puig's marginalized figures, we are often really hearing them through the preexisting discursive formulas of U.S.-dominated mass media.

Pierre Bourdieu's work on distinction and judgment of taste is a significant lens through which to understand better these characters' [cultural bilingualism].[53] Bourdieu's monumental *La Distinction* (1979), translated into English as *Distinction* (1984), analyzes how those in power define aesthetic notions such as taste: "Because they are acquired in social fields which are also markets in which they receive their price, cultural competences are dependent on these markets, and all struggles over culture are aimed at creating the market most favourable to the products which are marked, in their manners, by a particular class of conditions of acquisition, i.e., a particular market."[54] He explains how social class is likely to decide people's interests and likes, and how distinctions based on social class get reinforced on a daily basis.

In direct opposition to Kantian aesthetics, Bourdieu observes that even when subordinate classes seem to have their own notions of good taste, "it must never be forgotten that the working-class 'aesthetic' is a dominated 'aesthetic' which is constantly obliged to define itself in terms of the dominant aesthetics."[55] For Bourdieu, Kant's standard of the impartiality of the natural aesthetic gaze is fundamentally a middle-class phenomenon, predicated on the ability of this class to separate itself from daily manual labor. Kant's proposition of the naturalized "Analytic of the Beautiful" becomes for Bourdieu a matter of the difference in how culture is acquired. Therefore, for Bourdieu, the aesthetic gaze is far from an expression of subjectivity. Taste is for him [the internalization of class struggle].[56] The educational system is what trains and inculcates people's taste.

As we see above, in *The Buenos Aires Affair,* many of Puig's characters are educated as to a new sense of taste. Gladys is embarrassed when Fanny disdains her predilection for popular culture. She quickly learns from Fanny and others that the aesthetic of the mass media— fashion magazines, the radio, and the like—provides one with very little cultural capital in this new world she is entering. Similarly, Leo chooses to remake himself, by seeking psychotherapy, in order to be up to assuming the new role as head of the art journal. What is truly fascinating about Puig's work is that in his novels, he is creating the vehicles for teaching taste. He is allowing popular culture to stand next to "good taste" and to compete with it for enfranchisement in literature.

Similarly, marginalized and subaltern characters mediate themselves in this novel through the language of psychoanalysis—a discourse imported to Latin America from Europe and, often, through the U.S. *The Buenos Aires Affair*'s medical and psychological case histories are archives of people and their social worlds. In fact, "the process of detection in which we are invited to participate is not criminological but psychological."[57] The vehicle of the case history attempts to contain and explain the human being's entire psyche, just as the medical history/autopsy attempts to document the person's entire physicality. Jonathan Tittler, however, identifies this novel as an "insurrection against the 'Father of Psychoanalysis' [Freud]."[58] He points out that *The Buenos Aires Affair* contains "a superficial appropriation of Freudian doctrine, in which, on the thematic-characterizational level, all the right questions are implicitly asked and then satisfactorily answered."[59]

If psychoanalysis is not a key to understanding the characters better in this novel—and certainly we see instances when Leo lies to his doctor and to himself—then what is its purpose in *The Buenos Aires Affair*? Here, it functions as another of Western culture's masternarratives. It is supposed to hold out the promise of a better self-understanding. It is a formula to which subaltern and marginalized people such as Gladys and Leo turn in this novel, as they seek to reinterpret themselves in the new societies to which they move: they can only avail themselves of this treatment once they have money and time. When Leo assumes the position as head of a new and important art journal, he feels compelled to reinterpret himself: "Para asumir plenamente la responsabilidad que ese prestigio implicaba, Leo decidió iniciar tratamiento psicoterapéutico, en nombre de la revista más que para beneficio personal" [To assume fully the responsibility that that prestige implied, Leo decided to begin psychotherapeutic treatment, more for the magazine's sake than for personal benefit] (102).

We also see the adumbration of the archive through psychoanalysis in the figure of the psychoanalyst himself. The doctor, invested with power by the discipline, becomes the judge, the law, the archon. He is the writer and keeper of the case study, and the interpreter of tests as well. As Leo tells his doctor, "En el sueño yo estaba aquí y Ud. me mostraba esas láminas con manchas de tinta impresas, que antes se usaban para tests, simétricas, ¿se acuerda? . . . Y yo buscaba la mariposa que tuviera rota un ala sola. Y no había modo de encontrarla pero Ud. se enojaba" [In the dream I was here and you were showing me plates with ink blots printed on them, which were used for tests before, symmetrical blots, remember? . . . And I was looking for the butterfly with only one broken wing. And there was no way to find it, but you got angry] (122).

Neither psychoanalysis nor the psychoanalyst is effective in this novel. Although Gladys is told that "un tratamiento psicoanalítico lo arreglaría todo" [a psychoanalytical treatment would fix everything],(46) she becomes addicted to medication, which keeps her in a stupor most of the time, and Leo makes no headway in understanding or curtailing his psychopathic tendencies. The latter is actually able to lie to his doctor and to try to concoct an alibi for his violent behavior.

As I pointed out above, *The Buenos Aires Affair* is replete with a variety of discourses. There are more than a dozen narrative methods in this novel, "ranging from quasi-cinematic visual descriptions and documentary collages to interior monologues . . . to dialogues in which the speech of one of the two interlocutors is suppressed. All this . . . is a way of defining and making available for experience a human reality that would be inaccessible from other narrative angles."[60] This novel is Puig's alternative archive, which gathers together these many different ways of telling the same story and of approaching the same characters.

The narrative collage is also reflected in Gladys's artistic work— itself an archive of other work. Her great artistic discovery is a creative work in the form of a collage that is literally made up of remnants: "La obra era ésa, reunir objetos despreciados" [That was the piece, to bring together neglected objects] (108). There is no theoretical frame, as Leo says, to her work. Instead, [the result is a hybrid and heterogeneous pastiche . . . with knick-knacks].[61] This is a miniarchive of dross and flotsam, of subaltern, if you will, artistic idioms, and Leo is the archon who guards it. After all, it is up to him whether Gladys gets to show her work in the great international exhibition in Brazil: "Leopoldo Druscovich . . . decidió . . . convocar la presencia de la artista plástica que había resultado finalista [María Esther Vila]—a continuación de la ganadora Gladys Hebe D'Onofrio—en el concurso para representar a la Argentina en la Muestra de San Pablo" [Leopoldo Druscovich . . . decided . . . to summon the presence of the artist who had turned out to be the finalist (María Esther Vila)—followed by the winner Gladys Hebe D'Onofrio—in the contest to represent Argentina in the Sao Paulo Exposition] (136). Leo controls access to Gladys's archival work, much as her first crush at the Instituto Leonardo da Vinci does when he disdains her and her work for winning the school's top prize over him. Gladys feels that the worth of her work and her own self-worth are controlled by that eighteen-year-old boy.

We see smaller canons or subcultures' collections as vehicles for social transitions among immigrant groups. Gladys meets Fanny in school when they are both young. Gladys suffers an embarrassing moment when she reveals that instead of reading grand novels, she routinely listens to the radio at home. She is then given a cultural education by Fanny, who embarrasses her for not having read "Hermann Hesse, Thomas Mann y Lion Feuchtwanger" (30). Fanny, whose last name is Zuckelmann, is Jewish and promotes European works. Her last name is one among others—D'Onofrio and Druscovich—that denote foreignness. We are reminded of the many foreign names used by Borges in his short stories and of the cultural canons these characters carry with them and must negotiate in their new world, Argentina.

Overall, *The Buenos Aires Affair* is a discursive archive holding many different ways of narrating the same story about the evolution/devolution of marginalized people. There is no third-person omniscient narrator to serve as archon, but there is a semblance of an organizing voice in the footnote device Puig uses. This creates the effect of a metatext that is attempting to organize the main work, much as Borges's "inquisidores," librarians or archivists who live in the library, might try to shed some light on the archive's contents. The use of so many different discursive formulas, often to narrate the same scene or to describe the same character, creates [a complicated game of mirrors, in which all reflections point toward the artificiality of the preceding model, as they simultaneously produce the optical illusion of authenticity. Once again, parody begins with self-parody. The text becomes self-reflexive, constantly questioning its own essence].[62] We see here the archive trying to contain itself, much as the ultimate metalibrary in Borges's Total Library, or his "catálogo de catálogos" [catalogue of catalogues], the log of all the other books giving its reader omniscience, contained in the "Hexágono Carmesí" [Crimson Hexagon] in his Library of Babel.

However, just as in these two examples in Borges's stories, Puig's meta-archive leads to no greater understanding of either the characters or their lives. Leo dies at the end, but in a random accident that does not reveal his guilt to the world and does not mete out any punishment for his crimes, and Gladys is a shell of a person at the end of the novel, who might attempt suicide once again. In fact, just as in Borges's stories about the attempt to create a Total Library, there are self-destructive elements in Puig's archive-novel, which are analogous to Freud's death drive, as Derrida identifies them. Here, we see clearly the death and destruction of the main characters and the lack of resolution of the subplots—did the man raped by Leo die? Who was the person killed by the police for his political activities? This supposed detective novel never reaches a climax; there is no resolution, and the genre's plot conventions just unravel into loose ends.[63]

Nominally a detective story, *The Buenos Aires Affair* is a novel of simulacra. It is an archive of disguises, of discursive formulas, a [heterogeneous mosaic] similar to Gladys's artistic oeuvre.[64] The novel's characters are free to pick and choose among several discursive modalities to express themselves, and often to camouflage themselves. Puig is laying bare the process of writing novels. He presents a smorgasbord of Bakhtinian heteroglossia. These characters, originally from lower rungs of society, negotiate their way through their worlds by employing and manipulating discourse. The archive through which they rummage for their rhetorical masks contains linguistic formulas from the lowest classes of "cabecitas negras"—*lunfardo*—to the most rarefied theories about sculpture. These characters do not necessarily seek enfranchisement from hegemonic discourses, as in González Echevarría's archival paradigm. Instead, they seek to manipulate discourses such as the psychoanalytic one in their favor. They send up these master-narratives as they show their ineffectiveness—neither the psychoanalytic discourse nor the detective-legal discourse of the police can "capture" these characters.

4
Manuel Puig:
The Patriarch Betrayed: The Archive's Alternative Voices in *La traición de Rita Hayworth* and *El beso de la mujer araña*

MANUEL PUIG REFORMULATES LATIN AMERICAN NARRATIVE BY INvesting alternative discursive venues with canonical power. As we saw in chapter 3, Puig's *Boquitas pintadas* abounds in nonpatriarchal discourses through which the figure of the traditional male protagonist, or patriarch, is articulated: "Puig pertains to the scheme of countercultural writing in Argentina."[1] In fact, this traditional male figure rarely, if ever, appears or speaks directly in Puig's first two novels—*La traición de Rita Hayworth* and *Boquitas pintadas*. This radial portrayal of the patriarch serves to decenter his narrative prerogative. What replaces the authoritative discourse of the traditional omniscient narrator is an array of voices, arranged in no definite hierarchy, that enter into a complex, shifting dynamic. The patriarch's identity is at the mercy of the women, nontraditional males, and children who may or may not allude to him. Although he seems to be a center *sous rature,* an invisible force around which much of the two novels' action takes place, he remains an elided force, which allows the marginal figures to speak unencumbered and outside of his omniscience and gaze. These marginal figures are allowed to speak within the interstices of a novel—spaces created by "subgenres" and "nonliterary" discourses such as letters, diaries, gossip, films, and music.

The interplay of voices that hews to these interstices occurs when the discourse of one chapter is juxtaposed to that of another, when writing appears next to spoken language, or when a specific figure or character is compared intertextually with an established type or literary genre. The result of this verbal montage, just as in *The Buenos Aires Affair,* is a decentered, heteroglossic novel in which truth is relative, in contradistinction to the absolutism of society's dominant patriarchal structures. Puig's novels dismantle patriarchal culture's process of producing and reproducing consensus—a process that assumes that there exists a legitimate center (a superior and unique position) from which to establish control and to determine hierarchies. Nelly Richard says that the supposedly legitimate center has been the privilege of Western patriarchal culture, "whose representational apparatus has been the source of those homogenizing categories which apply to both language and identity."[2] She concludes that patriarchal discourse suppresses any notion of "difference" that might challenge the dominant model of subjectivity.

In *La traición* we see several different registers of society, often within the same realm of existence. This is similar to the several different social classes we see in *Boquitas pintadas*, as well as the fluid movement between classes that some of that novel's characters, such as Nené, accomplish. The use of some notions of Pierre Bourdieu are useful here for developing a better understanding of how these dynamics work within Puig's novels. We have already seen my initial treatment of Bourdieu in the opening chapters of this book, but now we will be able to apply some of his ideas directly to the literature in question.

Many of Puig's characters are able to move between or among traditional social classes, and many more of them are able to appreciate or, at least, have access to cultural registers of all sorts. Bourdieu's theories of cultural and social stratifications based on aesthetic taste in his work *Distinction* reflect precisely this kind of fluid ability and not an ossified profile of culture or access to it.

In the kind of cultural analysis proposed by Bourdieu, individuals inhabit a multidimensional social space rather than being defined by an attachment to a social class that is recognized as relative to all of the other social classes within a given society's order. Individuals are defined instead by the amounts of each kind of capital they possess: "Differences in cultural capital mark the differences between the classes."[3] More significant, there is no single, overarching social ladder recognized by everyone. According to our philosopher-theorist, each division of the dominant class develops its own aesthetic measures; "each fraction of the dominant class has its own artists and philosophers, newspapers and critics, just as it has its hairdresser, interior decorator or tailor."[4]

With Puig's characters, however, we are hardly ever talking about elites or patricians—Bourdieu's "dominant class." Instead, his novels are populated by a range of social actors, from the dregs of society—Raba, for example—through the rising and falling lower-to-middle classes—such as Nené and Leo—to the solid middle and possibly upper-middle classes exemplified by Mabel. As a variation on Bourdieu, we see in Puig's novels that there are subclasses within each social group or class, that the boundaries between these classes are porous (as we see individuals migrate between classes), and that each class has its own microstratification. We may extrapolate from Bourdieu's assertion that each division of the dominant class develops its own aesthetic measures, and say that within subaltern classes, there are also dominant positions and hierarchies.

Furthermore, in a world rife with the globalized culture of the mass media—as are the worlds of Puig's novels (and of Sarduy's, for that matter)—people of all social strata have access to, and develop an appreciation for, not just the same things, but for each other's culture (both high and low) as well. That is why, in *La traición,* characters have access to and appreciate letters, diaries, gossip, films, and music from several different social classes, except for those items from the dominant class. What individuals are exposed to and what they engage in, in Puig's novels, depends on the concept Bourdieu calls "field." This social theory seeks to explain differences in cultural preferences within the same social class, without analyzing all choices simply in terms of economic classes and ideologies. A field, or (in French) "*champ*," according to Bourdieu, is a social arena in which individuals "struggle for control over valued resources, as David Swartz tells us."[5] This notion can be applied to the characters in Puig's novels to reveal that they value culture differently and they value different cultural variants depending on either the field in which they are maneuvering or their relational position in a field or social space. This is different from saying that each of these characters belongs to a rigid social class and that he or she, therefore, may only value and recognize cultural variants from within that class. Puig challenges the notion that individuals have static and rigidly stratified access to culture.

Puig's novels also challenge the dominant view of critical social theory of the 1960s. As Lidia Santos identifies, popular culture was, in the main, considered illegitimate, or spurious, at that time.[6] Edward Sapir's work of the first half of the twentieth century, grounded in anthropological relativism, dominated the 1960s view of popular culture. Sapir considered spurious culture that which can be characterized as inherently not "harmonious, balanced, but self-contradictory"; that which is prone to sudden changes, immediacy, and fragmented productions, resulting in a "spiritual hybrid of contradictory patches."[7] This certainly describes popular culture as it is inflected by the mass media. Sapir's ideas set up the dichotomy of genuine culture and spurious culture. Puig, and Sarduy for that matter, create archives of spurious culture. By including these supposedly inauthentic and counterfeit voices and ideas, the two writers raise popular alternatives to the level of "culture" and supply other writers with legitimate literary models to be followed.

We may bring in our previous discussion of Maria Lugones's ideas about impurity as resistance here, in reference to how Puig's novels' heterogeneity challenges the traditional archive. *La traición de Rita Hayworth* is a novel in which nonliterary discourses abound. We readers seemingly overhear gossip, read letters, and perceive extraneous voices within what we may try to identify as the dominant narrative form in the novel. Where the traditional theory of the archive posits that the novel pretends to be a single form of hegemonic nonliterary discourse—that of the law, science, anthropology, and the like—at any given moment throughout history, Puig's version of the archive escapes that need to be pure, that method of modeling only one form of discourse, the one presumed to be superior to the novelistic one. Instead, Puig's novel purposely mixes discourses, especially nonliterary ones.

Marginal figures such as women and indigenous people have also been part of the Argentine literary tradition for centuries, but not in its novels. Especially in the nineteenth century, the country's literature reflected the tension that would be inherent in any nascent nation's struggle to define itself and its "others." The *género gauchesco* has already been the object of much study. Work on this latter tradition focuses on literature's relationship with the state in the co-optation of the gaucho's voice when his body was needed for political purposes during Argentina's struggle to define itself as a nascent nation.[8] The voice of the captive has also been co-opted in Argentine literature, such that this figure represents a traditional or stock discursive space that is manipulated by the dominant national culture.[9]

In the middle twentieth century, the typical Boom novel embodied the search for the totalizing novel, able to create its own complex and detailed world. Some general characteristics of Boom writing are the following: jumps in linear time (forward or backward); narrating the story from the present backward; prolepsis; flashback; the simultaneous use of dialogues from different temporal planes; and a grand ambition of historical synthesis. These works exhibited an extreme intricacy in their novelistic construction and narrative innovation. They strived to "create major works of fiction whose innovative force would drive art forward into the future and secure a place in the history of narrative."[10] Often these ambitious novels mixed realism and social commentary with myth and magic, in an effort to confront inexhaustible issues. A number of them sought to create a complete, autonomous world within the fiction.

Moreover, the aesthetic of the Boom novel has been likened to elements of the "traditional" novel: "characters that follow mimetic conceptions, a temporality that is recoverable despite fragmentation, and an implicit faith in the authenticity of local color as a source of truth about culture and the propriety of language."[11] The gender of the characters may also be tied to traditional schemes, "prescribed by the cultural tradition to which they belong, who have biographies that explain their actions in the novel, and who speak and think in the Spanish corresponding to their nationality and social class."[12] Overall, the Boom novels sought to be complete and substantial, while eschewing traditional narrative continuity.

Post-Boom works, if such a concrete epoch can be delineated, assume a less authoritative presence than those of the Boom.[13] They allow fiction to be explicitly incomplete and insubstantial. Post-Boom fiction exhibits a strong preoccupation with popular culture, advertising, and mass media, and simulating popular forms such as the serial and crime novel. In comparison with Boom novels, post-Boom fiction is not governed by any strong program or any central narrator. In fact, the absence of a privileged narrator ultimately precludes an objective truth.

Regionalism gains a centrality that had not existed during the Boom because of, ironically, more universal concerns. There is a greater interest in individual cultures: the vanishing populations, peasants in a new urban setting, and Afro-Hispanic peoples. By extension, the marginalized, in general, are brought to the fore and collocated at the center of these new narratives. There exists an inherent appreciation for cultural heterogeneity and the contingent nature of knowledge and reality. What is at stake is no longer truth. Readers are denied basic orienting information about either the narratives' internal truths or real-world truths. Consequently, the post-Boom aesthetic, generally speaking, highlights the contingencies of the formulations of literary canons—contingencies with which Puig and Sarduy's novels abound, as they reproduce teleological gestures of cultural knowledge only to distill language, the novel's ultimate and leveling reality.

La traición de Rita Hayworth

Manuel Puig's first novel is *La traición de Rita Hayworth* (1968), *Betrayed by Rita Hayworth* (1971). This is a work that is denied widespread critical praise, but one that does put Puig on the map as a new and revolutionary writer, especially for the more progressive critics. Language, and its diverse manifestations within gender characterizations, is an important aspect of *La traición*. Puig, unlike nineteenth-century Argentine writers and even some twentieth-century writers, allows marginal figures in the Argentine world to speak as they are, without having to conform to the norms of patriarchal and enfranchised discourses. In *La traición*, women gossip and characters discuss aspects of popular culture. That is not to say that Puig confines women, for example, to a hermetically sealed space. Instead, he recognizes from empirical observation (as Carol Gilligan has) that women, and other marginal groups for that matter, often speak "in a voice of their own." In Puig's novels—"grand narrative" collections—dominant figures and discourses may have an identity that is alternative to the patriarchal one, yet framed within a traditional venue.

Carol Gilligan's *In a Different Voice* (1982) provides the theoretical underpinnings for much feminist gender-role theory in psychology, literature, sociology, and even law. Gilligan, who wrote her influential work when Puig and Sarduy were publishing their novels, begins with the basic premise (borne out by empirical research) that there are essential differences in the world views and moral reasoning capacities of men and women.[14] Men, she argues controversially, are more analytical and concrete, and have a preference for detached, objective, and rational reasoning, whereas women are less analytical, more subjective, more connected to others, and more contextual in their reasoning abilities.[15] Gilligan's suggestion is not one that would hierarchize one gender as superior over the other, but says that men and women have essential differences in analytical reasoning and moral judgment capacities. Moreover, Gilligan does argue that our cultural and societal systems at large place a greater premium on the analytical and reasoning skills that men are more apt to exhibit. Rather than seeing these gender-specific characteristics as different and complementary, however, patriarchal culture has traditionally defined them as hierarchical, with men supposedly exhibiting a higher level of development.[16] Gilligan concludes that for centuries the voices of women have been muted by the voices of men, which have been presented as the central and universal voice. The failure to see the different reality of women's lives and to hear the differences in their voices stems in part from the assumption that there is a single mode of social experience and interpretation.[17]

La traición de Rita Hayworth does not translate women and other marginal figures through the language of the patriarchy. This novel, instead, presents alternative narrative venues such as the diary and the letter. Puig's novels, in general, "assimilate diverse forms of so-called subliterature. His novels all involve intertextual relationships with cultural phenomena beyond the written word. He uses material from the mass media movie spectacle."[18] The alternative narrative venues in Puig's works not only transmit nontraditional discourses but also eliminate any one center of official emission. The narrative authority that may be conventionally concentrated in an omniscient author figure is diffused among several characters in *La traición*. None of these narrating characters can claim prerogative with regard to any one "truth." The reader is not guided by a strong patriarchal monologue. Instead, he or she reads a nexus of intersecting voices not usually heard in literature: the young, the poor and provincial, the female, and the sexual "other." The one glaring absence is the father/husband authority figure.

Although *La traición* does include many situations of everyday life, the novel itself is not a part of popular culture. Its construction demands a greater scrutiny from the reader, far beyond that appropriate to pulp fiction or popular narrative. The novel is divided into sixteen sections, or chapters, with a symmetrical division of the novel into two parts of eight chapters each. In the work's first chapter, "En casa de los padres de Mita, La Plata 1933" [At Home with Mita's Parents, La Plata 1933], the novel opens with a domestic setting (*en casa*, at home) and starts off by discussing a domestic task: "El punto cruz hecho con hilo marrón sobre la tela de lino color crudo, por eso te quedó tan lindo el mantel [The cross stitch made with brown thread over beige-colored linen fabric, that is why your tablecloth turned out so pretty].[19] The first image of the novel is that of fabric being woven, the effect of which is to announce the interwoven texture of "trivial" voices throughout the work. There is no traditional identification of the characters, who turn out to be townspeople and family of the protagonist, Toto, who is a newborn in this scene. The characters chat about everyday life, yet also function as indirect narrators, since the reader is put in the position of observer. We are not told things directly by the characters, nor is there a central narrator who delivers information. It is as if we were to have entered the room unnoticed where these conversations were taking place. We are even put in the position of eavesdroppers, who learn information without being able to ask questions or otherwise control the direction of the conversation. We miss out on details, as a child in a room of talking adults would. Like a child, we read information without being able to differentiate as to age or sex. Ideas also undergo a blending and leveling, such that things having to do with shopping and cooking run into and carry the same weight as those relating to emotions and morality. The vernacular and familiar language used throughout represents accurately the rhythms and regional peculiarities of the spoken language:

>—¡(Amparo, vení!
>. . .
>—Quería que matara una araña que iba por la pared. . . . Si le echás un poco de agua salen las arañas de mierda del escondite y les doy un zapatillazo que se quedan reventadas contra los ladrillos.
>
>[—Amparo, come!
>. . .
>—I wanted you to kill a spider that was crawling on the wall. . . . If you throw a bit of water on them those damn spiders will emerge from their hiding places and I will stomp on them until they are splattered on the bricks] (24).

This scene includes regional language and common, everyday expletives. But this familiar scene is denatured and presented to the reader as "Literature"—a generic characteristic of which he or she is aware before picking up this or any "novel" to begin with.

Sex roles tend to be rather rigid in *La traición*. Women are preoccupied with their physical attractiveness, marriage, and family, while men feel pressure to perform to the standards of *machismo*. Paquita, who touts her promising fiancé, is envied by other women, while Herminia, an educated woman, falls into desperation at not being married by age thirty-five: "Tengo treinta y cinco años y ya estoy arrumbada en un rincón. Creo que a los cuarenta perderé el poco de esperanza que me queda y eso será la oscuridad total" [I am thirty five years old and I am already discarded in a corner. I think that at forty I will loose what little hope I have left and that will be total darkness] (267–68). Even the protagonist, Toto, can begin to gauge the difference in the sex roles: "Mamá pega cachetadas que no duelen mucho y papá pega cachetadas que deshacen" [Mother's slaps do not hurt much, and father's slaps destroy] (37). Moreover, Herminia believes him to be effeminate and vain; Toto is more interested in going to the movie theater with his mother than spending time with his father.

Toto is the novel's young protagonist, and Berto's son. *La traición* is a nontraditional *bildungsroman* in that it does trace Toto's maturation and sentimental education, except that it does not indoctrinate him within a traditional patriarchal scheme. In fact, Toto develops a much greater interest in the cultural spaces of women in the novel, especially in that of his mother. These spaces are generally in the movie theater and the home. Toto's first substantive chapter is the third one, "Toto, 1939." It opens with a description of what seems to be a doll collection that fascinates the young boy. We are given a typical scene of a boy playing with dolls, which foreshadows his growing up socially marginalized. The chapter is composed mainly of Toto's stream of consciousness, in which his father hardly appears, except as a looming character who causes anxiety, figuratively castrates him, and punctuates the chapter with an ominous refrain.

One of the first images Toto gives of his father, Berto, is: "A papá no le gustan las cosas dulces" [Father does not like sweet things] (31), right after taking delight in remembering an experience he shared with his mother of eating sweets: "Mami te comiste un muñequito [*de dulce de leche*], yo me comí otro" [Mommy, you ate a little cake doll, I ate another] (31). He immediately forges an alliance with his mother and recognizes his father as different. Afterward, Berto is a source of anxiety and ultimately of a figurative castration for Toto, at an eatery, when the boy has to go to the bathroom to urinate: "Papi: ¡ganas de hacer pis!" [Daddy, have to pee!] (33). Berto sends him off by himself, but Toto replies that he cannot reach the light switch in the bathroom. His father then asks an older girl to accompany him to the ladies' room. The boy does not want to go. He fears the girl and feels awkward about using the ladies' room, but feels trapped by the situation. At this point in the chapter, Toto contemplates escaping, but describes his fears and anxieties about being taken captive by a gypsy man, "un Gitano malo malo cara de carbón con brazo peludo que roba a los chicos que están bien vestidos y se han escapado . . . queda [un gitano] que roba los chicos . . . la cara parece negra como de carbón y le pega a los chicos con el rebenque, como a los caballos. [a bad, bad, coal-faced gypsy man with hairy arms, who steals children who are well dressed and who have run away . . . there is (a gypsy man) who steals children . . . his face is as black as coal and he hits children with the lash, like horses] (33–34). As in the traditional Argentine captive narratives, the gypsy here functions as the "other," who looks different and is a delinquent. Toto is the captive of his own fears, ones that are inspired by the myths and "old wives' tales" prevalent in his provincial Argentine town of Coronel Vallejos. The town itself may be seen as a captive of its own superstitions and popular culture.

Toto is forced to go with the older girl to the woman's bathroom, but he does not manage to urinate, since he is afraid the girl might betray his own or his father's trust: "Pero si la nena estira la mano y apaga la luz antes de que yo termine de hacer pis" [But what if the girl stretches her arm out and turns off the light before I finish peeing] (34). When the two children return to Berto, Toto is embarrassed, symbolically castrated by his father and by his father's proxy: "¡Escondo la cabeza entre los pantalones de papi!" [I hide my head between daddy's legs!] (34). He must defer to his father and hide behind a locus of Berto's masculinity—his crotch. We see another manifestation of this traumatic embarrassment return toward the very end of this chapter, in one of Toto's stream of consciousness narrations: "Pero yo me escondo en el baño de las mujeres y la nena me alcanza y de penitencia me pone una pollerita por haberme metido en el baño de las mujeres" [But I hide in the women's bathroom and the girl catches up to me and makes me wear a little skirt as my penance for having hidden in the women's bathroom] (46). Toto feels feminized in a way that his conscience tells him he should not feel. He fantasizes that what he feels must be accompanied by a physical, sartorial signifier *qua* stigma—he would wear a girl's skirt.

Toto's anxiety about his father is also made manifest by Berto's ominous threats, which punctuate the chapter. We do not really see the father in this chapter, but only hear echoes of his voice and the promise of patriarchal action: "Nunca te he pegado pero el día que te ponga la mano encima te deshago" [I have never hit you, but the day I lay a hand on you I will destroy you] (37). He does not necessarily control Toto through physical action, but through the prolonged threat of eventual annihilation. Toto has internalized this fear and is prone to self-policing: "Mamá pega cachetadas que no duelen mucho y papá pega cachetadas que deshacen" [Mother's slaps do not hurt much and father's slaps destroy] (37). Berto's threat functions in the way that the Foucauldian panopticon might—by causing the object of discipline (Toto) to internalize the subject's gaze (Berto's). In this chapter we first hear Berto's threat, as remembered by Toto. Then, the second time, we hear Toto declare his father's threat as a generality, as something that Berto does. The third time Toto refers to the threat, further along in the chapter, he has clearly visualized himself as the victim of the annihilation: "No me dieron una cachetada, papá si me pone la mano encima me deshace" [They did not slap me, if father lays a hand on me he will destroy me] (44). Berto's voice and rhetoric of violence function in the way that the traditional voice of the Latin American patriarch *qua* dictator has done. His power is derived not so much from his physical presence, but from his voice and its constituent rhetorical position. Berto is not physically present in most of the text, but his voice can be heard sporadically.

Toto's castration plays itself out further in a sexual role-play in which an older girl, Pocha, engages with him. Pocha wants to pretend that she is "taken" (in effect, raped) by a pubescent boy. Toto does not understand either puberty or sexual relations: "Pocha decime qué quiere decir cogía: 'no podemos jugar a eso, tiene que ser un muchacho grande, con pelos en el pito' [Pocha, tell me what 'taken' means: "we cannot play that, it has to be a big boy, with hair on his pecker"] (42). And Pocha, who understands sexual relations as something to which a woman must not acquiesce, but which she must instead pretend to have forced on her, obviously understands them as rigid roles to be acted out: "Si un muchacho se subía a la azotea mientras yo estaba dormida, me sacaba la frazada y me cogía . . . es una cosa mala que no se puede hacer, se puede jugar nomás, porque si una chica lo hace está perdida, está terminada para siempre" [If a boy went up on the roof while I was sleeping, he would remove my blanket and would take me . . . it is a bad thing that one must not do, one may only play it, because if a girl does it she is lost, she is finished for ever] (42). Because he is told that he is not yet physically capable of playing the part of the pubescent boy, Toto decides that he will play the part of the girl who is "taken" and that Pocha can play the role of the boy. He is learning a sexual initiation, not from his father, and not from a girl with whom he is intimate, both of which would conform to traditional heterosexual modes of sexual initiation for boys. Instead, Toto is learning a transgendered heterosexual initiation of sorts. He is neither learning from the patriarch nor mimicking his actions. He is instead learning from a nonpatriarchal figure investing herself in the role of the traditional male. Toto learns of heterosexual relations by simulating the role of the woman in the relationship. Toto learns yet another lesson, as he is unaware that Pocha's aunt is spying on their little game: "Me acuesto en la alfombra como que estoy durmiendo en la azotea y la Pocha . . . viene de atrás caminando despacito y quién está espiando por la puerta un poquito abierta? ¡la tía de la Pocha se está riendo de mí!" [I am lying down on the rug as if I were sleeping on the roof and Pocha . . . comes from behind walking slowly, and who is spying through a crack in the door? Pocha's aunt is laughing at me!] (42). He learns that to be effeminate, or to play the role of the woman or girl, is to risk ridicule.

Once again, in a moment of virtual transvestism, Toto is castrated. He perceives that playing the role of a woman (or girl, in this case) is not allowed of a boy. Pocha's aunt laughs at *him* ("se está riendo de *mí*"), and not at Pocha. Toto's angry fantasy of retaliation toward Pocha involves acts of cutting and sublimated sexual violence: "No le puedo pegar porque soy más chico, que si no le cortaba los rulos con la tijera de recortar artistas y después le hacía meter en la boca los rulos que se los comiera" [I cannot hit her because I am smaller, otherwise I would cut off her curlers with scissors I use to cut out movie stars and later I would make her stick the curlers in her mouth so she would eat them] (42). By cutting off her curled hair, he would be excising part of her feminine charms that are in the process of developing (she is working on her physical appearance). He also fantasizes about shoving the phallic and "hairy" curlers (two motifs that dot this chapter) in her mouth—perhaps "taking," or sodomizing her, as she has taught him is proper for a boy to do to a girl. Toto learns about sexual relations as part of a violent act, but not from a male. In this scene, women are the ones who, veiled in patriarchal roles, impart the traditional male's lessons that they themselves have internalized.

Perhaps the most significant veil for the patriarchal male appears in the very last chapter of *La traición,* "Carta de Berto, 1933" [Berto's Letter, 1933]. This chapter is surprising, if not shocking, on many levels. First of all, we are enticed by the promise of hearing at length from Berto, the patriarchal male who, until now, has been virtually absent. He has been present mostly in the conversations and writings of the novel's marginalized characters. We are also surprised to see that Berto would communicate in the epistolary genre—one usually considered subliterary or marginal and not patriarchal. Lastly, it is surprising that the date of the chapter is 1933, not only because, until now, every chapter has been in chronological order through 1948, but also because 1933 is the date of the novel's first and second chapters.

The traditional center of the novel is tacked on at the very end of *La traición,* at the margin of the novel's world. What we actually get are mediated forms of the patriarch, not a direct address. Berto communicates with his older brother, Jaime, and sister-in-law, Adela, through the rhetorical and indirect venue of the letter. Berto is unable to address his frustrations and resentment to them personally. The reader, also, is given an indirect address from the patriarch. We read his letter at the very end of the novel, but we remember that it was written in chapter 2, "En casa de Berto, Vallejos 1933" [At Berto's House, Vallejos 1933]:

> —Amparo, después me tenés que llevar esta carta al correo. . . .
> —Me lo llevo al nene conmigo al correo, señor.
> —Amparo, acordate que me juraste no decírselo a nadie.
> —Yo no se lo dije a nadie. Por Dios que me caiga muerta.
> —Nunca le digas a Mita que tenemos un secreto.
> —No, señor.
> . . .
> —No tengo que ir al correo porque el señor rompió la carta que estaba escribiendo.

[—Amparo, you have to take this letter to the post office for me later. . . .
—I am taking the boy with me to the post office, sir.
—Amparo, remember that you swore to me that you would not tell anyone.
—I did not tell any one. May God strike me dead.
—Never tell Mita that we have a secret.
—No, sir.
. . .
—I do not have to got to the post office because the gentleman tore the letter he was writing] (27–28).

When we finally see the patriarch, he is an aura, not the original. Like the letter he might have sent, the manifestation of the patriarch is delayed, from the moment the message is emitted to the moment it is received. But Berto never does send his letter: "The social transfer of information ideally associated with the postal service is here shunned by the embodiment of manliness. . . . The strong and silent Berto reverts to strict conformity with the macho ethic."[20] Not only does Berto never communicate his feelings to his family members directly, but he is also unable to use successfully a venue of the marginal—the letter. Although he does write the letter and puts his feelings on paper, he cannot send it: "Esta carta va al tacho de la basura, para vos no pienso gastar un centavo en estampillas" [This letter goes in the wastepaper basket, I do not intend to spend a penny on stamps for you] (299). He is constrained by his sense of tradition. Although the reader has access to the letter, he or she is not able to read it until fifteen years in the novel after it is written.

La traición de Rita Hayworth defers the voice of the patriarch until the very end of the story line. At this point, his actions and words are impotent, since they are conveyed many years after they are first meant to have effect. We see that, like an inverse of Carol Gilligan's notion, the traditional male's "voice" has been supplanted by that of marginal figures in the novel. The next patriarch-in-waiting, Toto, is not enfranchised within the role of his father. He must learn to negotiate his masculinity within the frame with which he is most comfortable—his mother's. As with the captive in the Argentine literary tradition, Puig's work creates discursive spaces for marginal figures. And like the use of the captive figure toward the contemporary end of the tradition, Puig's marginal figures are not dependent on the patriarch for a narrative venue; they can signify for and in themselves, despite limitations of class and sex.

El beso de la mujer araña

El beso de la mujer araña (1976), *Kiss of the Spider Woman* (1979), is Puig's best-known novel because it was turned into a play, a film, and a musical. This work literally brings together popular culture and the mass media with politics, in the persons of Molina and Valentín, in a dialogical rewriting of sorts of Cervantes's *Don Quixote* and "El coloquio de los perros." Puig lays bare the creation of archives as being politically inflected and a product of memory—the latter an idea in Derrida's *Archive Fever* I have already examined. Lastly, the contrast between Molina's self-projection as an effeminate and gay man and the long footnotes about theories on homosexuality provide two discursive models about sexual orientation and gender that are at odds. The meta-text's patriarchal authority is vitiated by the insistence on highlighting popular culture. This novel is an oral archive, such as that of marginalized, illiterate people. It is an archive of bodies—imprisoned by the state—and a heterotopia of memories.

The mass media, although not a common or "proper" main focus for a novel in Latin America in the first half of the twentieth century, were certainly a fixture of Latin American culture and politics prior to their use by Puig and Sarduy. At least as far back as the 1930s and 40s, the mass media were used by politicians in Latin America to seduce the populace: [Radio had been, at that time, the vehicle par excellence of political propaganda and melodrama].[21] We need only think of figures such as Eva Perón who mixed popular culture and the mass media with politics. Television and film were both successful vehicles for reaching the people in Mexico and Argentina and were certainly exploited by these countries' populist governments in the first half of the twentieth century. As Lidia Santos notes, the respective governments of both Lázaro Cárdenas in Mexico and Juan Domingo Perón in Argentina maintained their propaganda campaigns on state-run radio stations.[22]

El beso clearly mixes politics and sexuality, more so than in any of Puig's previous novels. Benedict Anderson's analysis of the nation in *Imagined Communities* raises issues of gender and sexuality. As he observes, "In the modern world everyone can, should, will 'have' a nationality, as he or she 'has' a gender."[23] Although he himself does not further develop the idea, Anderson's comparison leads to the analogy that, like gender, nationality is a relational term whose identity derives from its inherence in a system of differences. In the same way that "man" and "woman" define themselves reciprocally (though never symmetrically), national identity is determined not on the basis of its own intrinsic properties but as a function of what it (presumably) is not. A nation is shaped by its "other." But the very fact that such identities depend on difference means that nations are forever haunted by their various "others."

It is these unelidible "others" that Puig brings to the fore. He has but to scratch the surface of national identity to reveal these ineluctable, if disavowed, others. National identities are defined in contradistinction to, and are therefore dependent on, their "others." Puig needs only exploit that inherent tension to reveal the unofficial cultures not enfranchised within literary traditions. The nations whose guiding fictions are based on "mythologies of exclusion" give individuals of a hegemonic stripe a sense of nation, peoplehood, collective identity, and national purpose while they marginalize those designated as "other."

One of the responses to this national ontological ambivalence is the representation of the nation as a community, based on gender and sexual norms—putative inherent touchstones. Therefore the homeland will often be depicted as a female body, and the rise of the nation will be based on the metaphorical myth of a heterosexual family romance. The idealization of what used to be the reproductive family unit entails exclusion of individuals or families without issue from the myth of the nation. In the Argentina in which *El beso* is presumably set (although the movie version is set in Brazil—proving the story's more universal appeal), being gay and being a leftist revolutionary certainly exclude one from the myth of the nation.

Molina and Valentín are prisoners of the Argentine state. They are deviants according to the world and time in which they live: the former is a social or sexual deviant, while the latter is a political or philosophical deviant. Molina's crime is love and Valentín's crime is sedition. Although their bodies are imprisoned, their ideas are expressed dialogically, within the apparent frame tale of Hollywood movies. This is certainly a fiction that, at first blush, correlates to Scheherazade's life-granting telling of tales in the *Thousand and One Nights*.[24] As we read further, however, we quickly realize that there is indeed a frame to this narrative of melodramatic movies, but that it is the conversations that Molina has been forced to have with the "Director," the prison official who is coercing Molina into beguiling Valentín, who, in turn, would issue a confession of sorts, which Molina would then report back to the prison guards. The heterotopic space of this prison, as Foucault would deem it, is an archive of both oral culture and mass media, as well as revolutionary philosophy and seditious planning—not unlike the fiction of Cervantes.

Foucault's concept of heterotopia is an important idea through which we can understand the setting and context of my reading of *El beso de la mujer araña*.²⁵ This notion is based on his study of the way modernity sees the confluence of space and time. The important terms in Foucault's concept are utopia and heterotopia—two unique sites that are linked to other spaces. The utopia is basically an unreal space. In contrast, the latter term, my focus here, is linked to, yet in tension with, those other spaces. Let us concentrate specifically on heterotopias, which Foucault says are simultaneously mythic and real.

Foucault defines heterotopias as spaces and places that have meaning in nonhegemonic conditions and that are coeval with society's origins: "There are also, probably in every culture, in every civilization, real places—places that do exist and that are formed in the very founding of society—which are something like counter-sites."²⁶ Foucault gives the example of the mirror image as a heterotopia. Ideal and unreal, the image one sees of oneself in a mirror is a utopia. The mirror is also a heterotopia, however, as Foucault describes: "in so far as the mirror does exit in reality, where it exerts a sort of counteraction on the position that [I occupy].... It makes [that] place that [I occupy] at the moment when [I look] at [myself] in the glass at once absolutely real, connected with all the space that surrounds it, and absolutely unreal, since in order to be perceived it has to pass through this virtual point which is over there."²⁷ The mirror is an easy metaphor to understand—a utopia because the image one sees in it does not exist (in fact, it is the inverse of the person or object before it) and a heterotopia because the mirror is a real object that forms the way one relates to one's own image. This is an example that is probably common to everybody's experience, but Foucault goes on to describe other real-world examples of hetertopias that are more germane to *El beso*.

In an effort to define heterotopias further and to give concrete examples of them, Foucault creates systematic descriptions that he terms a "heterotopology," having six principles. The prison and the archive are described in two such remarkable ones: the first and the fourth. Within the first principle, he categorizes our modern society as having heterotopias of deviation, "those in which individuals whose behavior is deviant in relation to the required mean or norm are placed. Cases of this are . . . psychiatric hospitals, and of course prisons."²⁸ The prison is heterotopic because it is a space parallel to normal society—in it, yet not engaging it—where undesirable bodies are kept. Foucault's fourth principle discusses time. These heterotopias "begin to function at full capacity when men arrive at a sort of absolute break with their traditional time."²⁹ These are institutions "of indefinitely accumulating time, for example museums and li-

4 – MANUEL PUIG: THE PATRIARCH BETRAYED 115

braries," and "a sort of general archive."[30] These places enclose objects of all styles and from all times in one location. They exist within time, but also outside of it, as they are erected and conserved to be physically resistant to the ravages of time.

Both heterotopias, the prison and the archive, are therefore similar in several ways. The prison collects all kinds of bodies considered undesirable in society at large for different reasons—different crimes and different sentences. The archive, or museum and library for that matter, also houses corpuses of books (or other items)—usually desirable books, but also banned, censored, or otherwise undesirable books. Both spaces sequester their contents and risk their contents' oblivion. We will remember that archives contain so many books that it often is difficult to find any one item. We will also remember Derrida's notion of the archiviolithic power—the drive to destroy the trace of memory without any remainder—and the way things that are archived, whether in one's memories or in a real building, are likely to be forgotten or destroyed. There is a risk that a book will be forgotten or even lost in the archive. For example: "A persistent criticism of the Escorial was, precisely, that it ingested books, swallowing texts whole, burying them in a paradoxically remote center: 'magnificent sepulcher (*magno sepulcro*) of books where the cadavers of manuscript codices are conserved and rotted' [Magno sepulcro de los libros donde se conservan y se pudren los cadáveres de los códices manuscritos]" (Spanish in brackets in the original).[31] Human prisoners are also sequestered from society. They lose their social identities inside their cells and also risk being killed in prison. Time, another similarity between prisons and archives, is not linear in either place. The archive may be read in any order, and any web of connections among books may arise. In prison, one's memories and thoughts are re-created outside the need for linear time. In *El beso de la mujer araña*, for example, time flows in several directions when Molina recounts his movies. We sometimes see flashbacks or forward time leaps, or a mixture of both. We hear him narrate what often turn out to be forbidden movies—Val Lewton's *Cat People*, with its obvious lesbian subtext, and the Nazi propaganda film. Puig gives us an archive of the forbidden in that prison cell.

The most salient aspect of Puig's *El beso de la mujer araña* is its dialogical narrative structure, with which the novel opens. Readers of the Hispanic tradition might immediately think of Cervantes's *Don Quijote* [*Don Quixote*] and "El coloquio de los perros" [variously "The Dialogue of the Dogs" or "The Colloquy of the Dogs"] from his *Novelas Ejemplares* [*Exemplary Novels*]. The dialogues of Don Quijote and Sancho Panza, and of Cipión and Berganza, respectively, are among the most memorable features of each work and animate the readings as they play with the limits of narrative. Puig's fourth novel is a heterotopic archive—a prison—for what cannot be unfolded or told in the Argentine society of his time, a prison for sexual and political outlaws.

Undesirable books and undesirable bodies come together in the act of censorship, especially in the time of Cervantes. Georgina Dopico Black studies both textual and historical scenes of book burning and censorship, and the censorship and destruction of undesirable others—*moriscos* [Spanish Muslilms who converted to Catholicism] and crypto-Jews—in Cervantes's Spain as well as in his works. At the time of the consolidation of the Spanish empire, the new nation was seeking to purge itself of those whom it considered "other" and to expurgate socially and politically dangerous material from its books. The Inquisition (and its corollaries of Philip II's 1567 ordinances of cultural repression against the *moriscos* and Philip III's 1609 decree of expulsion of the same group), as well as several new laws—such as the *pragmática* "passed at the Cortes de Valladolid ordering, under penalty of death, that all books printed in or imported to Spain be licensed by the Consejo de Castilla"[32]—symbolically bring together books and bodies.

This relationship between books and bodies is, in fact, substantiated semantically as well as historically. As Dopico Black notes, "The practice of referring to books as bodies was common enough in early modern Spain: *cuerpo* [body] where books were concerned referred in the first place to the materiality of the book—a materiality that was given the contours of a body—with face [*carátula*], spine [*lomo*], and even fingers [*índices*]."[33] Many early modern texts used this language: the censor referred to a text's composition as a body of sorts, according to an Aristotelian model of proportions, and rhetorical and philological texts spiritualized the same language of book as body.

The rise of censorship in early modern Spain, on both the mainland and in the colonies, gave rise to stratagems by which printers sought to elude the Holy Office of the Inquisition as well as civil authorities. One common subterfuge was to create a textual transvestism of sorts. Prohibited books were sometimes published with false covers, "so that what on the surface appeared to be a prayer manual might actually have contained a text by one of the Valdés brothers whose entire *corpus* was placed on the 1559 index [of prohibited books]."[34] This textual illusion proved to be a successful ruse, especially when it came to books that were shipped to the Spanish colonies, where there were other factors to take into consideration:

4 – MANUEL PUIG: THE PATRIARCH BETRAYED   117

native readers, with different community standards. In particular, "books of romance, vain and profane histories, and books of chivalry" were feared too dangerous for the colonies.[35] Judging a book by its cover, therefore, was often no easier than judging persons by their "covers." This textual "passing," to use Dopico Black's term referring to "books pretending to be what they were not in order to avoid the flames," "has striking resonances in a society in which passing was an everyday affair."[36] Spain and its colonies were home to crypto-Jews, *moriscos, mestizos,* and *mulatos* (just to name a few "others"), many of whom passed for what they were not—*limpios de sangre,* blood-pure.

Why is there then such an obsession in literary texts of early modern Spain—in several of Cervantes's works alone—with book censorship or burning, and especially while using language of the body and corporeal metaphors? As Dopico Black suggests, the emergence of secular authorship is related to the rise of institutional controls. Books could be more dangerous than bodies or spoken words because they could spread messages far and wide (to the "New" World, as we see above) and contained a much broader semantic field to be interpreted, or misinterpreted, by readers. Ultimately, Dopico Black surmises that books are "assigned (symbolic) bodies because bodies are somehow more pliable—more readily disciplined—than words."[37]

Puig's *El beso de la mujer araña* does not focus on books per se so much as it does on films. Films, and foreign films at that, are comparable to the *novelas de caballería,* or chivalric novels, prohibited in early modern Spain from crossing the Atlantic to the Americas for fear of an undue influence on native readers. The two men in prison are influenced by the telling, or the retelling, of these movies that are full of exotic danger. Their bodies are more pliable than their ideas. Even when Molina is coerced into extracting information from Valentín and informing on him, he is eventually seduced by Valentín's belief in and love for his ideas. Puig is no stranger to making his novels "pass," or pretend to be what they are not. This textual transvestism (*Boquitas pintadas* as serial fiction and *The Buenos Aires Affair* as a detective novel, for example) avoids hegemonic culture's censorial judgment about subliterary forms. Molina, who also cross-dresses, in prison, pretends to be things he is not—a woman as well as Valentín's ally and friendly interlocutor (at least at first).

Dialogue in *Don Quijote* is catalyzed by "los libros, autores del daño" [books, authors of harm], which are kept in Quijote's library.[38] In *El beso,* much of the dialogue is catalyzed by films Molina recounts or names: *Cat People, The Falcon's Brother, The Enchanted Cottage, Dracula, The Wolf Man,* and *I Walked with a Zombie*—foreign films and dangerous ones, at that. These are Hollywood films from the 1930s and 1940s—an archive of popular culture from abroad, which overwhelms autochthonous cultural models: [Hollywood not only invades Puig's novels with its atmospheres' and narrative forms' seduction, but also with its *stars,* stereotypes who model feminine experience and define its objects of desire].[39] The fact that Molina is so preoccupied with U.S. movies, and not with Argentine, or even other Spanish-language, films reflects the mass media's reaches, both geographical and ideological: [Hollywood is not only the well-known space of consolation and consumption of popular myths, but a possibility close to mass consumption of liberating introspection].[40] In any case, Hollywood films are, to Molina and Valentín, what *novelas de caballería* are to Don Quijote and Sancho Panza, and the knight errant is to Quijote as "the wife of a traditionally heterosexual man" is to Molina.[41] We readers are asked to empathize with, as Molina does, the (heterosexual) woman and not with the voice of the patriarch.

El beso de la mujer araña begins with dialogue, although readers do not immediately know who is talking or anything else about setting and characters. We quickly realize, however, that the quoted lines in the novel denote two different speakers, as we are drawn in more and more by what will turn out to be Molina's seductive recounting of *Cat People,* the 1940s B-movie. His interlocutor, Valentín, is also being seduced into trusting Molina, of course. Puig is therefore fictionalizing the effects of fictional narrative, of literature, on readers. The representation of dialogical interaction is seductive in the novel.

No author is more seductive through dialogue than Miguel de Cervantes Saavedra, of course. Love and the law, in Cervantes's works, "is the pith of his creativity, at the intersection of discourses issuing from those drives, a crossroads at which stories take shape in language."[42] Cervantes, who himself spent time and wrote in prison, often situates his most important characters and works at the junction of love and the law: consider *Don Quijote,* Ginés de Pasamonte, "El coloquio de los perros," among others. The new kind of narrative in early modern Europe, the novel, emerges at the same time as the modern state develops, and therefore mirrors concomitant social and legal changes: "The new developing social structure consists of an incipient leveling of classes, the feeling that through the law commoners and peasants can appeal to codes and kings that will protect them from the powerful, and at the same time that the new laws identify them as potential transgressors. . . . This identification . . . literally comes from the development of the notarial arts and the organization of record keeping and archives."[43] The same can be said of the mass media and popular culture for the commoners and marginalized people in Latin America. In Puig's novels, and certainly in *El beso,* characters feel that they can turn to "codes and [queens]" of these nonliterary genres and culture, as the early moderns felt they could turn to the law.

I have looked above generally at how Don Quijote and Molina are similarly inspired by obsolete and "dangerous" pre-texts, but there is another work by Cervantes that is worth analyzing as a way to see *El beso.* "El coloquio de los perros" is also a picaresque dialogical tale. We can see many surface similarities between Puig's and Cervantes's works. As Guy Thiebaut points out, there are several main points of contact: "a certain similarity between Cipión and Valentín (last syllable is stressed; a connotation of a determined personality, sure of himself, let us say masculine) and between Berganza and Molina (a more feminine connotation with last vowel 'a')"; "another more obvious similarity is found in the role played by both pairs: Berganza/Molina are the ones who narrate; Cipión/Valentín, the ones who listen."[44] Valentín says, "Pero, si no te parece mal, me gustaría que fuéramos comentando un poco la cosa, a medida que vos avanzás"[45] [But, if it is all right with you, I would like us to analyze the thing, as you go forward], and Cipión says, "Habla hasta que amanezca, o hasta que seamos sentidos; que yo te escucharé de muy buena gana, sin impedirte sino cuando viere ser necesario" [Speak until dawn, or until we are overheard; for I will listen to you very eagerly, without getting in your way, except for when it might be necessary].[46] Thiebaut adds, "Another similarity is found on the level of the atmosphere conducive to dialogue; it takes place at night and in a secluded place."[47] In both works, the dialoguing pairs engage in critical analysis of the narrations—"comentando" [critiquing] and with "planteo" [an exposition], as Valentín says, and "con discurso" [with reason and logic], as Cipión insists.

Cervantes's works—*Don Quijote* and "El coloquio de los perros"— explore the nascent genre of the novel within the framework of picaresque tales involving prisons and love. Puig's *El beso* betrays the inner working of the novel—the way love weaves a seduction through dialogue and the way readers are pulled into a story. Puig's novel is ultimately motivated by coercion, however, as prison officials have forced Molina to befriend and debrief Valentín. The dangerous pre-texts that seduce the latter are from the archive of Hollywood's classical age of cinema. Dialogue—the novel—here actually seems to result from a coercive relationship with power: the power of the patriarchal voice or of the state to subjugate its undesirable others.

The marginalized others have their own archive of popular culture that is different from the patriarchal discourse of the traditional

Boom novel. Molina has stored in his memory a vast archive of classic Hollywood films. The synopses he narrates to Valentín are framed by the men's colloquy, extending from bowel movements to political philosophy, until it is this colloquy that really becomes the substance of the novel. Readers will also take special note of the strand of metatext, the footnotes that echo intellectual discourse and language.[48] These notes seem to intrude upon the rest of the novel and to attempt to exercise authority over it. They often convey an archive of psychoanalysis and theory about homosexuality and other subjects relevant to the situation at hand in the novel's plot. These notes, together with Molina's memory lapses, conversations with the warden, the direct presentation of the characters' subconscious via the use of italics, and so forth, create a structural disorder in the novel that challenges readers' impulse to read time, and to read generally, in a linear fashion. Instead, the novel, like the archive, must be rummaged through and pieced together.

As in Cervantes's texts, Puig's *El beso* "covers up—paradoxically, by putting in full view—the strategies designed to keep the text moving, the reader reading, and the characters talking until the end. The talk between the two prisoners is not unlike the 'talk' between author and reader, that is, the textual dialogue that runs throughout the novel's body as well as under it, at its feet."[49] Both authors, Cervantes and Puig, perform the mimetic representation of the readerly process in their works. Through the *mise-en-abyme* created through these basically dialogical structures, they are able to incorporate the archive of popular culture as material worthy of critical analysis. This archive is safely displayed in the heterotopic prison space, which is shaped—contained—by power. In the case of both Cervantes's and Puig's works, "the exercise of power and the experience of pleasure seems tied together through the production of discourse, through language.... That language often originates in or takes everyone toward the world of popular culture, the realm of popular experience, establishing the common ground between these apparently polarized subjects [homosexuality and Marxist political discourse] or the theories and practices they suggest."[50]

Dialogue in *El beso* reveals the inner workings of the novel because it also establishes the main characters' identities as interrelated and relational. In other words, these characters, Molina and Valentín, and their identities are complementary. The novel starts with unidentified interlocutors. In fact, *El beso* opens as though it were a Platonic dialogue of sorts, using the Socratic method and at times even the dialectical method of inquiry. The first four lines attributed to the character we will come to know as Valentín are questions spread throughout more than a page's worth of dialogue at the very beginning of the work: "—¿Y los ojos?" [—And her eyes?], "—¿El animal no la puede oler antes?" [—Can the animal not smell her before?], "—¿No hay gente en el zoológico ese día?" [—Is there no one in the zoo that day?], and "—¿Y ella no tiene frío?" [—And, is she not cold?] (9–10). Valentín's next line contradicts Molina's description of the action in *Cat People,* the movie he has been narrating, and forces Molina to define his terms and reconsider his characterization of the film's star: "—Si está ensimismada no está como en otro mundo. Ésa es una contradicción. —Sí, es cierto, ella está ensimismada." [—If she is absorbed in her own thought she is not in another world. That is a contradiction. —Yes, it is true, she is absorbed in her own thought.] (10).

This unmediated narrative, this unmediated opening, is at odds with the patriarchal voice of both the footnotes and the warden who coerces Molina. The footnotes seem to convey a scientific and, therefore, authoritative legitimacy that clashes with the personal and nondidactic dialogue between the main characters. These metadiscourses would seem to be trying to contain the dialogue, albeit unsuccessfully.[51] Outside of the diegesis, they may be seen as analogous to a novel's frame (the serial or the detective fiction), which does not accurately describe the content (*Boquitas pintadas* and *The Buenos Aires Affair,* respectively) or to the building housing the archive itself, guarded by the archons; and inside the novel's plot, they are analogous to the prison walls, which, as heterotopic, are both within society and outside of society at the same time, which remove homosexuality and certain political philosophies from society but cannot eradicate them within the prison cell. There is a battle in this novel between discourses of different valences. There is "fiction friction" when the nonliterary yet hegemonically discursive and patriarchal footnotes vie for primacy, both on the page and in readers' minds, with the novel's narrative proper. The dialogical structure, then, extends to the discourses within the novel itself—the footnotes' colloquy with the narrative proper and the recounted films with the characters' lives in prison.

The movies Molina narrates also help to erode the patriarchal discourse of the traditional Latin American Boom novel. Much of the substance of *El beso* derives from [the Hollywood movie industry, whose **mythical imperialism** extends beyond the Argentine and Latin American borders].[52] The point of the seemingly incessant dialogue in the novel is originally, in fact, to draw out and ensnare Valentín, as per the warden's demands—we will remember that the final image of Molina is that of the spider woman herself: "—Vos sos la mujer araña, que atrapa a los hombres en su tela" [You are the spider woman who snares men in her web] (265). The archive of the marginal that is unfolded in the prison cell, the foreign movies that are narrated, are actually masks donned as a device that can be "manipulated by the figure of authority who seems to orchestrate things from above and behind the entire novel"—is this the warden, the creator of the footnotes, or the novel's author himself?[53]

Similar to the dynamic that motivates the origins of archival fiction within González Echevarría's conception, there is an illusion created in *El beso* through which power has to don the mask of popular culture in order to be recognized and enfranchised, as it were, in this context. In González Echevarría's archival notion, the socially marginal person is able to borrow the mask of legitimacy, often through the rhetorical formulas afforded him by the *relación* and wielded by a scribe, and thereby to speak to power. In this novel, as in Puig's other novels, the mask of legitimacy that is donned is that of popular culture and the mass media. That is the formula required to enter the archive of the marginal.

In *El beso*, Molina, the sentimentalist maven of popular culture, acts as the scribe for Valentín, the rational thinker who is tortured and poisoned because of his politico-philosophical beliefs: "Me gustaría dictarte una carta para ella. . . . —Sí, en borrador, porque no sé bien qué le voy a decir. Tomá mi birome" [I would like to dictate a letter to you for her. . . . —Yes, in draft form, because I do not know exactly what I am going to say to her. Take my pen] (181). When Molina takes and uses Valentín's pen, there is an obvious phallic exchange, or borrowing, to be more accurate, which solidifies the bonds between the two men. Molina, however, is also acting as scribe because it is his sentimental rhetorical style, as showcased through his recounting of the films, that would work best in this "love letter" to Marta from Valentín—the hard-line rationalist—who tries to exert self-control at all times. In fact, the revolutionary regrets having "written" the letter, once it is completed, and therefore destroys it: "—¿Por qué la rompés? —Está mal dejarse llevar por la desesperación. . . . —Pero está bien desahogarse. Vos me lo decías a mí. —Pero a mí me hace mal. Yo tengo que aguantarme" [—Why are you destroying it? —It is bad to allow oneself to be driven by desperation. . . . —But, it is all right to vent. You used to say that to me. —But it is bad for me. I have to control myself] (185). Valentín is therefore not adept at wielding the codes and formulas of popular culture, despite being proficient in Marxist rhetoric and philosophy.

El beso is a series of Chinese boxes or Russian dolls ultimately governed by codes from popular culture and the mass media. Although the voice of authority, the voice of the patriarch, is present in the novel—it often punctuates the novel (via the footnotes) or is looming in the background (the warden as panopticon of sorts)—it must compete with and often give way to the marginalized voices of women's desires (in the Hollywood films) and to the dialogical structure that dominates most of the novel and that resists and even explodes the univocal authority of meta-text and of the penal system of an oppressive nation. We readers are ultimately seduced, not by *El beso*'s meta-textual or other patriarchal authorial devices, but by the dialogical recounting of melodramatic films, just as Valentín is. We are seduced by the imitation of the subliterary reality of popular culture.

El beso de la mujer araña puts into practice Puig's archival project, through which popular, subliterary culture speaks to power.[54] The dialogue within the prison cell's walls—this oral archive of popular culture—resists the state's power to coerce and to disappear. Although the dialogue is originally motivated by an external and patriarchal force, it ultimately becomes important per se, ends up buying time for the victims of the oppression, and is ironically used against the state's penal mechanism that inspired it in the first place. This rhetorical and artistic move is very much in keeping with the Latin American, and especially Argentine, tradition of using the mass media "to denounce the State's manipulation of information . . . , collective actions against the state's power."[55] Puig's fourth novel wields the power of the archive of the marginal in a more historically relevant manner than he did before.

5
Severo Sarduy:
Monstrorum Artifex: Cultural Compendia as Alternative Archives in *De donde son los cantantes* and *Cobra*

SEVERO SARDUY'S NOVELS REEXAMINE THE CUBAN CULTURAL TRADItion as elaborated in some of its most canonical texts. These canonical Cuban works project a cultural imago—a cultural archive, which they construct from elements they call distinctly Cuban. What is Cuban, however, is already a mixture of U.S. popular culture and mass media as well as African, European, East Asian, and, of course, native elements. This study examines how Sarduy simulates these grand gestures of building an archive for cultural patrimony and shows them to be simulations themselves. Sarduy is able, therefore, to negotiate alternative figures, such as different racial groups, women, transvestite males, and so forth, into a Cuban and, ultimately, Latin American narrative tradition.

In this chapter on Severo Sarduy, I will explore the voices and/or discourses that replace the patriarchal male figure in Sarduy's texts and ultimately co-opt the grand genre of the novel, emptying it of truth-bearing power. In *Myth and Archive,* González Echevarría hypothesizes that "the novel, having no fixed form of its own, often assumes that of a given kind of document endowed with *truth-bearing power* by society at specific moments in time . . . [in order] to show [such documents'] conventionality, their subjection to strategies of textual engendering similar to those governing literature, which in turn reflect those of language itself."[1] For Sarduy, the forms that his novels assume are nominally those that patriarchal culture has canonized as truth-bearing documents. Ultimately, however, rife with popular culture and clichés, his works are touchstones of the subaltern. In this chapter, I wish to explore the possible uses of a foundational, patriarchal, and self-legitimating genre (which the novel ultimately is) as a vessel for the formation and communication of either dominant or, in our author's case, subordinate cultures. Indeed, Sarduy cross-dresses his work, so that subordinate genres pass for a patriarchal one. This chapter will focus on two novels. First, I trace the Cuban intellectual and cultural history that Sarduy reformulates, and I follow the failed attempts of the traditional patriarchal figure in *De donde son los cantantes;* second, I examine the history of cultural collections and their motivations as I deconstruct *Cobra*, both the character and the text, as a corporeal Cuban collection—a home for a Neobaroque monstrosity. This section also notes points of contact between Fernando de Rojas's *La Celestina* and *Cobra*'s constructions of "home" and women.

Puig and Sarduy invest their characters—traditionally marginalized and unenfranchised entities—with the privileged discursive position usually monopolized by patriarchal figures. This discursive transvestism allows the marginalized entity a position within canonical culture, because this entity establishes its ability to speak the same way as the patriarchy—the possessor of the phallus and the logos.[2] Sarduy and Puig suggest that canonicity is related to the degree to which one has access to rhetorical formulas that are already enfranchised.[3] This is how the master-narratives of patriarchy have always worked. They are "inventions which nevertheless powerfully controlled interpretation."[4] The subordinate culture that these writers foreground is explicitly as artificially constructed as the dominant one. Therefore, patriarchal privilege is shown not to hinge on essence, but on simulation.

In Severo Sarduy's novels, *De donde son los cantantes* (1967) and *Cobra* (1972), the author is discredited, not only as creator, but also as an indispensable, authoritative figure who controls the meaning of the texts.[5] As González Echevarría notes, [Sarduy's oeuvre parodies the *Boom* novel's reflexivity, which is based on the all-powerful figure of the author, that projection of romantic irony].[6] Sarduy also rejects the notion of a natural language [belonging individually or naturally to language].[7] For him, language is already a translation, since he rejects the notion of a privileged central transmitter. It follows, then, that literature is already also a translation, with more than one gravitational center, not as the *grands récits* had suggested. The elision of authorial legitimacy, and his view of literature and translations, are two defining aspects of Sarduy's work. The traditional patriarch proves impotent, as he is unable to know any of the creatures he pursues. He first intends to consume them, but ends up absorbed by them.

The quest for cultural knowledge in Cuba presents a special situation, given the radical changes occasioned by the Cuban Revolution of 1959. The revolution seeks to redefine the notions of Cuban nationality and even Hispanic identity. It provides the basis for a thorough questioning of Cuban culture and its traditions. Two of the most significant mouthpieces of Cuban culture and literature are Cintio Vitier (1921–2009), in his *Lo cubano en la poesía*, and José Lezama Lima (1910–1976), in his essays and *Paradiso*.[8] They and others try to articulate Cuban culture, in the earlier tradition of Jorge Mañach's *Indagación del choteo* [An Inquiry on Choteo] (1928) and Fernando Ortiz's *Contrapunteo cubano del tabaco y el azúcar* [Cuban Counterpoint of Tobacco and Sugar] (1940), as it was being transformed around them. Vitier and Lezama work with grand narratives to forge the new repositories of Cuban culture and bequeath a new cultural imago to the Cuban nation. Ironically, they also represent their work as the true embodiments of Cuban tradition.

Sarduy works within this tradition of convoluted or fungible frames. His object of scrutiny, however, is the whole tradition itself, or the archive of Cuban literature. He prefers to invert the frame and the subject. Rather than create a break between frame and subject, his work synthesizes one continuous artifact. He offers the Möbius strip as a visual model, where "outside" and "inside" surfaces blend into one another, eliminating bipolar nomenclature. Another visual metaphor for Sarduy's approach is the Chinese boxes. One would expect a box to contain something, but in this case each box contains a smaller box. There is a series of containers containing, well, nothing. Each box is both the outside and the inside—the contained itself. The surface and the interior are one and the same; signifier and signified are one; yet they are dependent on one another for relational identity at any given moment in time.

Sarduy's work accomplishes a paradigm shift. His work is not only *about* simulating discursive frames, it is itself subject and object of simulation at once. He recognizes that Latin American literature is sui generis in that it has always pretended not to be what it truly is, but instead to be something it is not; to wit, Columbus's *Diary*, Cabeza de Vaca's *Naufragios*, and the like. In lifting up the veils of Latin American literature, Sarduy reveals that they mask nothing essential. These trappings are themselves the substance. There is nothing beneath the discourse except a tradition of masking. Consequently any narrative about literature (metadiscourse) figures into the same economy as another unit of currency, but never figures as intrinsically valuable. By focusing on transvestites and other objects of such simulation, Sarduy mimics the frame *and* content of traditional Latin American literature.

In essence, Sarduy is not communicating through discourse, but creating a cultural artifact that can enter the economy of the archive. By appealing to the cultural/national archive's authority, Sarduy is able to enfranchise these nonpatriarchal elements while revealing the archive's contingent value and self-perpetuating myth. In today's world of eroded reverence for grand narratives and the canonical aegis, there is a greater chance of extending official recognition and memorialization to that which has been traditionally marginalized.

While nonpatriarchal subjects are included in works of the *modernistas*, they are kept at a safe distance and analyzed in relation to patriarchal norms. As Oscar Montero points out, "*Modernismo*'s aesthetic sublime" eschews erotic deviance, pushing and keeping it outside of its "closed circle."[9] It would not be much different until Latin American writers such as Lezama and Sarduy, among others, "begin to crack [the circle]."[10]

In *De donde son los cantantes* and *Cobra*, crossing over implies more than just a sartorial shift. Visually, apparel can "disguise, reveal, determine, erase, or dynamize a particular moment in time and place."[11] An appropriation of archival trappings, on the other hand, effects a paradigm shift, at once enfranchising nonpatriarchal elements while demystifying the archive itself.

Works of literature, like political entities (personal subjects) can be enfranchised within cultural or political canons. In his collection of essays *Escrito sobre un cuerpo: Ensayos de crítica* [Written on a Body: Critical Essays] (1969), Sarduy ultimately explores the similarities between the human body and the text. He points out a text's structures and what supports it. He is interested in the textual surface's inner workings. A reality outside the text does not exist, according to him. In fact, especially in his later work, Sarduy elides the concept of the author altogether, and, as we will see later on, the figure of the patriarch. What is left? Simulation. That is the substance. Sarduy will express simulation and *choteo* as the basic characteristics of Cubanness—*lo cubano*.

Choteo (*chotear*) probably has a familiar ring to most Cubans, so much so that it has been the subject of critical inquiry. Jorge Mañach wrote on the cultural phenomenon in his *Indagación del choteo*. Mañach calls *choteo* "relajo"—a type of disorder and subversion. This type of chaos results in a leveling and a nullification of the hierarchy."[12] It situates everything on the same plane, lending all things familiarity and removing oppositions.

Sarduy's semantic field is not one of oppositions, as structural linguistics postulates, but a more fluid conception of meaning derived from the tensions in simulation: [For everything to signify, it is necessary to accept that duality does not inhabit me, but an intensity of simulation that constitutes its own ends, beyond what it imitates instead].[13] Sarduy thus interrogates systems of knowledge and classification.

In the essay "Dispersión: Falsas Notas/Homenaje a Lezama" [Dispersion: False Notes/Tribute to Lezama], Sarduy lauds Lezama for creating a collage in his work, or "mirage," as Sarduy calls it.[14] In Lezama's work, things are juxtaposed, creating a gnostic space.[15] Sarduy refers to this grouping of disparate things as a dialogic presence: "The *French, Latin, culture* texture takes into account the chromatic scale value, the stratum signified by the vertical cut of writing, in its unfolding of parallel wisdom."[16] Sarduy also comments on Lezama's use of metaphor, a component of his baroque style, which [creates infinite connections].[17] Since metaphors are cultural in nature and are extremely wide in reference, [Cubanness . . . appears in disguise, read through all cultures: defined as a superposition of these cultures].[18] For Sarduy, all of Lezama's work, his *oeuvre*, is an imaginary "era": [Sarduy found in Lezama the static visionary, the one who, by hardly leaving Havana, restates Cubanness through an imaginary and textual pilgrimage based on a necessarily bookish and literary teleology].[19]

Sarduy sees that Lezama reconstitutes Cuban space as a difference of cultures. Lezama does not see Cuba's makeup as a synthesis, a syncretic culture, but as a palimpsest. Sarduy, along the lines of Lezama's work, believes that the Cuban novel must highlight the various levels—the [archeological planes][20]—of the palimpsest. As we shall see shortly, Sarduy does just that in *De donde son los cantantes*. He represents these planes in separate tales (one Spanish, another African, another Chinese) in order to [bring about Cubanness with the meeting of these [tales], with their coexistence] within one textual body, or volume.[21] Sarduy responds to ontological projects and traditions such as Lezama's and Cintio Vitier's by rewriting these. Lezama achieved this same coexistence profile of Cuban reality [in the structural unity of each metaphor, of each line].[22] Sarduy achieves it in a textual whole, a collage, without margins and centers.

The last factor in the equation leading to Cuban reality is what we saw earlier as *choteo*. According to Sarduy, *choteo* results from the impact in collage itself. It is [an element of laughter, of discreet mockery] inherent in *lo cubano*.[23] In fact, *choteo* is a form of simulation. Sarduy traces the roots of this palimpsest of simulation—Cuban reality/*lo cubano*—back to Silvestre de Balboa's *Espejo de paciencia* [*Mirror of Patience*] (1606), Cuba's "first poem." He quotes Cintio Vitier's appraisal in *Lo cubano en la poesía* of Balboa's poem in respect to what is usually considered an extravagant mistake: [the mixture of mythological Greco-Roman elements with indigenous flora, fauna, instruments, and even clothing].[24] Vitier believes this element to be what truly links the poem with the history of Cuban poetry. This proto-*choteo*, [*An elemental feature of Cubanness*, . . . is the soft laughter that shatters the pompous, the illustrious, and the transcendental in all of its closed forms].[25] Sarduy's use of Vitier is an explicit appropriation of Vitier's voice in *Lo cubano en la poesía*. This appropriation is also a seizing of Vitier's canonical discourse. Instead of contradicting or openly challenging the rhetorical thread that runs through *Lo cubano en la poesía*, Sarduy unravels it and uses it to stitch together different texts. For Sarduy, the tradition of collage, on which he has Cintio Vitier weighing in, reaches its ideal form in Lezama's *Paradiso:* [With *Paradiso*, the tradition of the *collage* attains precision, settles itself, and defines itself as an 'elemental feature of Cubanness'].[26] Sarduy values Lezama's juxtapositioning of heterogeneous phenomena as a violent encounter that manifests Cuban reality. This violent encounter allows for the recovery of [all strangeness, all exteriority].[27] This kind of fortuitous confrontation produces *choteo*.

Besides José Lezama Lima, Sarduy considers José Martí the other pinnacle of Cuban writing. Cintio Vitier famously considered Martí to represent a fullness of spirit. Martí is the historical pivot in Vitier's Hegelian narrative in *Lo cubano en la poesía*. For Sarduy, the language of Martí's *Diary* is the Cuban essence. This essence consists of not only the use of individual Cuban words, but the discourse and musicality of the work. It is on this latter level that in both Martí and Lezama, "synthesis has totally taken place."[28] That is the synthesis of meaning and being.

The body also is a locus of signification. The body as signifier, like the text as signifier, may be perceived as pure rhetorical artifice or simulation. Only the form signifies; but there is no such significance behind/beneath the form. Sarduy extends his concept of simulation to human gender. As we will see, many of his texts feature cross-dressing protagonists and cross-speaking characters (characters whose speech is made up of bits and pieces of different discourses). Not only is the text itself heteroglossic, but, in many instances, heteroglossia appears as characters.

The idea of collage (text) that I examined earlier may be a springboard to Sarduy's more complicated idea of transvestism (body).

Moreover, a more elaborate transformation of body into signifying text is performed by the transsexual/transgendered character, so much associated with Sarduy's novels. His discussion of Dadaist collages, in particular, sheds light on his use of characters in the novels I will soon examine. These collages, he says, separate the sundry objects they use from their utilitarian values. The objects are not integrated, but instead are made themes of the paintings. These objects [take over plastic space and blaspheme it at the same time, in their emanation and mockery].[29] The object is thus the subject, yet obviously still the object.

In *La simulación* (1982), Sarduy once again takes up the subject of *Escrito sobre un cuerpo* but revises his ideas on transvestism. He states that [the transvestite does not copy; he simulates].[30] To copy would suggest that there is an original. This concept of original "woman" does not exist; according to Sarduy: [*à la limite*, there is no woman].[31] How do we interpret *à la limite*? Does it refer to anatomy and organs that some people have and others do not? This will certainly turn out to be a complicated question, given the fact that Sarduy's characters are not bound by the genitals with which they are born. Sarduy's work of art in the age of mechanical reproduction truly gives Walter Benjamin a run for his money. Sarduy does not need to resort to an operation to deconstruct the idea of "woman" as a Platonic form. As he says, [*she* is an appearance, . . . her realm and the strength of her fetish hide a defect].[32] The reason the male transvestite can simulate "woman" is because "woman" is a performance to begin with, one that even females simulate. Sarduy reasons, [the inexistence of the copied being is rather what constitutes the space, the region, or the underpinnings of that simulation].[33]

Without delving too deeply into the differences between "gender" and "sex," and "woman" and "female," we see not only the chicken-and-egg conundrum fast approaching, but a mire of signifiers beyond which there is no precisely agreed-upon meaning. The purpose here is not to flesh out or extrapolate theories, the likes of which have been the backbone of feminist studies, queer studies, and cultural studies in general.[34] Instead, the significance here is the instability and insubstantiality of gender; the lack of essence behind sexual signifiers, other than referential, performative, and contextual essences.

Sarduy's work concerns another grand narrative—that of the essence of gender roles and their support of much of Latin American literature, from nineteenth-century romances to dictator novels.[35] In Sarduy's novels, the main character is often multiple in many ways. He does not represent a central univocal narrator or patriarch. Instead, he metamorphoses and/or splits into other characters, exhibits gender changes, and cross-dresses. Sarduy's protagonists can pull this off because they are sheer discourse. The characters simulate discourse, and discourse simulates the characters. If Sarduy can dislodge gender as a touchstone of the social and natural orders, then the binary bulwark supporting the patriarchy vanishes.

De donde son los Cantantes

De donde son los cantantes has been called "novel, antinovel, or pastiche of a possible novel . . . , an emptying of the traditional novel into a new balancing of the world by the word."[36] Sarduy's work situates itself and the reader at the crossroads of various patriarchal master-narratives: the anthropological, the ethnographic, the historical, and the general ontological. Ultimately, Sarduy challenges the legitimacy of any one narrative that sets itself up as hegemonic to the exclusion of others. On the surface, *De donde* simulates the type of cultural touchstone proffered by Sarduy's predecessors (Cintio Vitier, Lezama Lima, and others). In this text, however, all narratives are leveled, as they vie for supremacy as master-discourse. *De donde* announces itself as an archival project, promising to contain, to ask and answer, Cuban cultural and ontological queries. What we see in the end is the enfranchisement of cultural fetishes. Sarduy thus reveals the contingent value of cultural artifacts.

Sarduy begins his second novel with a *Curriculum cubense,* the stuff of archives, but he ends it with what, at first blush, would seem to be an ancillary section he calls "Nota," or Note. This meta-textual ending simulates the rhetorical strategy of using nondiegetic material to explain or legitimize fiction in a patriarchal voice. The inscrutable message of Sarduy's Nota, more akin to Borges's use of footnotes, however, sheds no light on this "curriculum" we have supposedly just learned. I will begin my analysis of this novel with its last section—Nota—as a way to frame my reading of the novel.

This "Nota" is the very last part of *De donde,* tacked on as a coda. This section contains an ironic *excusatio propter infirmitatem* and a discussion of the content of all of the text's previous sections in a direct and self-conscious address to the reader. Rhetorically, it functions as a generic marker, indicating that the preceding is the subject and that *it,* itself, is part of the frame. It does this, in part, by pointing out in a footnote (which creates a Chinese box effect) the previous use of notes as well as the authenticity to which they attest: "*Nota.* Las 'notas' de autor al final, o a veces al principio, de novelas, son comunes. Alejo Carpentier, por ejemplo, incluye notas al final de sus novelas *Los pasos perdidos* y *El siglo de las luces,* en ambos casos tratando de dar fe de la autenticidad de los paisajes descritos, o la historicidad de los acontecimientos relatados." [*Note.* Authors' 'notes' at the ends, or sometimes at the beginnings, of novels, are common. Alejo Carpentier, for example, includes notes at the ends of his novels *Los pasos perdidos* and *El siglo de las luces,* trying to be accurate in both cases about the authenticity of the described scenery, or about the historicity of the narrated events].[37] With Sarduy, however, we realize that these distinctions have no currency—as in the Möbius strip, inside and outside are one. If we read further on in the footnote, we hear Sarduy's ironic voice: "Pero, por supuesto, no podemos sin más asumir la autoridad de estas notas, que más bien son absorbidas por la ficción, máxime en una como ésta en que el autor habla a veces con los personajes, y se incluye en la novela" [But, of course, we cannot just rely on these notes' authority, which are more properly absorbed by the fiction, more so in one such as this in which the author sometimes speaks with his characters, and includes himself in the novel] (235). In fact, we may see the "Nota" as just another section of the narrative of *De donde,* which is one of the reasons it can be discussed first. By incorporating a meta-discourse in the text, Sarduy once more comments on the hollowness of the linguistic sign. An appended "Note" of this type seemingly makes us privy to the intentions and interpretations of a text's author. But instead of providing an overarching and authoritative interpretation of *De donde,* the *Nota* only elucidates the moods, perspectives and motivations of a group of thespians: "Aquí todo es mirada, contemplación, realidad evanescente" [Here, everything is gaze, contemplation, vanishing reality] (235). Because of its patent attempt at simulating (in the guise of an authorial afterword), the "Nota" serves to demystify the conventions/trappings of discourse; it therefore emancipates the supposed text from its supposed frame, making everything a readable text. By analogy, because *De donde,* weaves much of Cuban iconography into its fabric, it also emancipates these artifacts—Lezama Lima, Cintio Vitier, and ultimately, *lo cubano*—from any hegemonic discourses that may coopt them.

The title itself of *De donde son los cantantes* is an utterance *sous rature:* it is both a speech act (performing the text's function of defining an origin) and a query that disavows the speech act. The text's pseudoanthropological search is mock-scientifically engaged in cataloguing and recording flora and fauna, as well as "culture"—myth, ritual, customs. *Curriculum cubense,* the first section of the novel, announces itself in the patriarchal Latin nomenclature of science/social science (master-narratives) and opens the work with a vertiginous description, if not haphazard catalogue or archive, of texture, color, telluric elements, sounds, and body parts—in short, flora, fauna, and geography: "Plumas, sí, deliciosas plumas de azufre, río de plumas arrastrando cabezas de mármol, . . . colibríes y frambuesas . . . y Auxilio rayada, pájaro indio detrás de la lluvia" [Feathers, yes, delicious sulfur feathers, river of feathers dragging marble heads, . . . hummingbirds and raspberries . . . and striped Auxilio, Indian bird behind the rain] (91). Where does the place described exist? Perhaps it is the answer or complement to the novel's title. Where it exists, literally, of course, is on the text's page; as Sarduy says to Lezama, [On this homeland that is the page].[38] I do not say this prosaically. I mean that language appears as the first protagonist of this novel, it is *de donde son los cantantes*.[39] Let us note that "Plumas," the first word of the text and Auxilio's theatrical garb, means both feathers and *pens*. "Her" *señas de identidad* [signs of identity] is language—writing, on the otherwise blank page. Auxilio does appear as language, but as "plumas" suggests, she is written language, already a translation of the oral tradition. She appears as a simulated woman (already a simulation, according to Sarduy). The introductory Latin nomenclature quickly gives way to an aggressively proliferating vernacular.

On this chaotic archive-canvas of images, which seems to offer a totalizing if indecipherable surface, we glimpse the nebula from which the three main sections of *De donde* will emerge. Sarduy's *Curriculum cubense* opens as if after a synecdochic explosion of amorphous parts and elements dissociated from their wholes, but seen in the act of coming together, before things begin to take on definite shapes.[40] The elements contained in this opening collage are pure language, mere words, without a discursive frame. *De donde* proffers a discourse about personal and literary identities that comes out of fragmentation. Sarduy is fragmenting literature, specifically that of the Boom: [*De donde son los cantantes* fragments literature because it goes beyond the Boom, because it abandons itself to the cultural being beginning . . . with writing and with its formal operatives].[41] What most distinguishes Sarduy's work from Boom literature is his insistence on bringing together the banal with rarefied literary and scientific knowledge. *De donde* engages these latter discourses as well as a national patriarchal discourse: [*De donde son los cantantes* is a fragmentation of literature, a new space that, since the Boom, wants to go beyond].[42]

Throughout the *Curriculum,* characters will be outlined by the signifiers on the page, will transform themselves, and will finally reunite in the section called "Self-Service." These characters are discernable because of the discourse that contours them. Changing discourse transforms the characters into new characters. Auxilio and Socorro (a cry for help, in Spanish) resonate identities back and forth. These characters may freely associate/bond with other characters, much the same way that certain chemical elements may freely and temporarily associate and bond with other elements, given the right circumstances. In the "Self-Service" section of the novel we see some sort of black hole—Auxilio (Socorro)-General—subsuming a black woman and a Chinese woman: "Así el binomio Auxilio-General chupó todo lo que había alrededor, y claro está, chupó a una negra y a una china: así se completó el curriculum cubense" [That is how the Auxilio-General binomial sucked in everything that surrounded it, and, clearly, sucked in a black woman and a Chinese woman: that is how the Cuban curriculum was completed] (101).

This opening section of *De donde* implicitly announces itself as the type of work undertaken by Cintio Vitier in *Lo cubano en la poesía* and José Lezama Lima in *La expresión americana* and *Las eras imaginarias*.[43] Sarduy's *Curriculum* clearly is a rewriting of the racial/ethnic aspects of *Lo cubano en la poesía*. Where Vitier elides African significance in distilling a "Cuban" essence, Sarduy presents a Cuban culture that has been leveled to the signifiers on the page—all of marked significance. Sarduy is quite aware of the different contingencies that come to bear on the value and use of texts and culture. Within his pseudocultural compendium, he helps to refocus the lens of the culture machine, which processes literature to churn out literary history and literary "classics" within a grand narrative or archival frame. Thus, in *De donde* we see unstable personal and gender identities, as well as a Cuban cultural amalgam composed of Spanish, African, and Chinese elements.[44] The text is a celebration of heterogeneity, metamorphosis, and contingency. Although the great significance Sarduy attributes to the population of Cubans of Chinese origin is disputable, the point is not whether or not they made up a minuscule percentage of all Cubans.[45] Rather, their inscription within a text, especially within one purporting to define anything cultural, draws attention to the mechanics and power of master-narratives to enfranchise and lend value to groups.

Sarduy also inherits the tradition that Fernando Ortiz examines in his *La cubanidad y los negros* [Cubanness and Blacks] (1939). Like Sarduy's nebulous primordial *Curriculum*, Ortiz's metaphor for the cuban nation is "el ajiaco" ["the stew"]—a symbol of racial and cultural mixtures studied by Gustavo Pérez Firmat, where all of the elements that converge there may be identified.[46] Ortiz, however, is intent on denying that there is such a thing as a "race." His "ajiaco" slowly erases all differences, leaving only identities. Ortiz is best known, after all, for his concept of "transculturación," or "transculturation." Ultimately, this process creates "la cubanidad." This too is an argument that elides racial difference. What seems most significant for Sarduy's purposes is that Ortiz believes that the Cuban nation is not already made, but is continuously making itself. Sarduy's characters too, are continuously making themselves, always in the process of becoming, like language.

The first section of the tryptic that follows Sarduy's *Curriculum cubense* is "Junto al río de cenizas de rosa" ["Near the River of Rose Ashes"]. Sarduy focuses on Cuba's Chinese cultural heritage in this section. The Spaniards who took the Columbian voyage across the Atlantic sought the proverbial better sea route to the East—to China, India, and their neighbors. They thought what they had found was the "new world" and that its inhabitants were of the "East." When this "discovery" is first described, it is (mis)named with European signifiers and with Asian signifiers. The Hispanic desire to reach and attain the East manifests itself in the various place names and early misunderstandings. Thus it is said that "Cubanacan," the indigenous name from which the name "Cuba" derives, was assumed to be a reference to the great Khan. Moreover Cuba's easternmost province, from which Spanish colonization began, is named *Oriente*. The Spaniards in the Columbian voyages never do reach the East, and their wanderlust is never fulfilled. However, they do manage to marry their discursive understanding of the East to the reality they behold in the New World. Columbus's and Spain's intended expedition is a failure. They never attain the East, or what they fantasize is the East.

Sarduy's tale recasts this foundational fiction of Latin America as a tale of failed patriarchal exploits and unfulfilled goals: the real tales that the early Latin American chronicles mask under fictional and enfranchised elaborations within rhetorical master-frames. Flor de Loto [Lotus Flower]—Eastern sensuality, luxury, and fetish—is pursued by el General—the nominal Spanish authority, who wishes to "colonize" her. El General, however, turns out to be a voyeur, "un mirón," who is not able to possess Flor's image any more than her body: "Da un salto Flor de Loto, y, como el pececillo que al saltar fuera de agua se vuelve colibrí, así vuela entre las lianas. Es ahora una máscara blanca que rayan las sombras de las cañas, es apenas el vuelo de una paloma, el rastro de un conejo. Mira a ver si la ves. No se distingue" [Flor de Loto takes a leap, and, like the little fish that upon jumping out of water becomes a hummingbird, she flies among the reeds. Now she is a white mask that the canes' shadows stripe, she is barely a dove's flight, a rabbit's trace. See if you can see her. You cannot make her out] (108). She is protean and cannot be fixed: "Ella es mimética" [She is mimetic] (109). What distinguishes her for the General is her physical features: "La denuncian sus ojos, dos ranuras doradas, ojos de encantador de serpientes" [Her eyes give her away, two golden slits, the eyes of a snake charmer] (108). He must seek her in her adumbrations: María Eng, and Auxilio and Socorro. They are never really "her."

Sarduy questions what identity is. Even if the General were to know Flor de Loto (biblically and otherwise), would he really know her? Is this kind of knowledge possible? Or can we really only know the surface? Perhaps the only thing we can know is the projection of the "Other" that we have erected to sustain our differentiated self-definition.[47] After all, even at the end of this section, when Flor meets her doom, the General is no closer to knowing her than before: "Por su sangre la reconocería" [They will know her by her blood] (136). She only ever appears as "pellejo pintado" [bedaubed skin] (115). Ultimately, Flor must metamorphose into pure desire, behind which there is no "real" substance. In fact, what remains unsaid is that Flor is a transvestite prostitute. Her "essence" remains unseen; she is an illusion. As we see in the General's trajectory, his voyeurism fueled by desire turns in on itself and manifests a streak of masochism. The General's Acteon-like contemplation of María Eng's sexual encounter with the North American sailor is punished by Carita de Tortura, who pulls out the General's fingernail. The representative of the patriarchy, of authority, and of law finds himself impotent to possess what he most desires. He must instead gaze upon it onanistically. He may only process its surface signs, for which he will ultimately be punished.

The surface of this section of the text, like the previous one, is alive with a collage of signs. When we first see Flor and, shortly after, the General, we see them as part of a natural landscape. Their bodies, but especially Flor's, afford them camouflage at times, while at other times they are just elements among the foliage and fauna. The passage mixes indigenous "Cuban" elements and descriptions of the bodies of the others. Flor's body, most of all, is at once foreign: "La denuncian sus ojos, dos ranuras doradas" [Her eyes give her away, two golden slits] (108) and a native amalgam: "Es . . . una flor podrida bajo una palma. . . . No la veo" [She is a rotten flower beneath a palm tree. . . . I do not see her] (109). Sarduy paints for us with the same brushstrokes of Silvestre de Balboa, as described in Cintio Vitier's *Lo cubano en la poesía*. As we recall, Vitier praised Balboa's poem for what had been considered a mistake: the mixture of Greek and Roman mythology with indigenous elements. Sarduy himself, however, designates Balboa's *Espejo de paciencia* as the root of *lo cubano*/Cuban reality, precisely because it is a palimpsest of simulation. It is this mixture in collage out of which *choteo* results. *Choteo* is the verbal/discursive and gesticulatory equivalent of collage. According to Sarduy, *choteo* is the basis of Cuban reality.

In "Junto al río de cenizas de Rosa" ["Near the River of Rose Ashes"], Sarduy opens the interstices of the archive of Cuban culture and inserts a Chinese component. This component recalls the object of the failed Columbian expedition. Sarduy suggests that this hybrid Chinese-Cuban culture can be known only on its surface. In fact, the theme of the theater that is present in *De donde*'s inaugural scene reverberates throughout the work and will be developed further in *Cobra*. Sarduy emphasizes the idea of performance and simulation.[48] He introduces the director of the *Opera del Barrio de Shangay* [Opera of the Shanghai Neighborhood] with the words "(¡Atmósfera china, muchachitas!" [Chinese ambiance, girls!] (110). In the theater, stage performances are all surface signification. In many of Sarduy's works, the stage is his characters' and readers' natural element. He does not work with the patriarchal dwelling (house or estate), but with the theater and stage. On the stage, familial relationships and identities can be improvised or simulated. Moreover, the implication is that all social discourse is done on stages of sorts. Even if the thespians do not wear artificial masks or even costumes, they wear the mask of performance or simulation, because there can be no other way of discerning meaning in their venue.

¿De dónde son los cantantes? [Where are the singers from?] They are "from" discourse; quite literally, they are discourse. *La Dolores Rondón* is the second section after *Curriculum cubense*, in which the central character is of African origin. This central character is actually "dialogue" and its function in communication.[49] The section is dominated by back-and-forth narrative sparring, each narrator trying to outdo the other in a style we saw earlier with Auxilio and Socorro. What comes through is not so much the virtuosity of *Narrador Uno* or *Narrador Dos* but the result of their interaction. Nonlinear and desultory, the basic story of the life of Dolores Rondón unfolds through dialogue. Sarduy suggests that the voices and cultures of the politically and scripturally disenfranchised are processed through their own method of memorialization. Sarduy thus further examines the politics of genre and archivization. Ultimately we see that in this story the patriarchal authority figure, Mortal Pérez, is decentered when he fails to communicate anything but clichéd rhetoric. Although

Dolores meets her doom, she lives on in the spoken or sung word. Sarduy presents another aspect of nonarchival Cuban culture while disenfranchising the patriarch from his vocal privileges.

Dolores is a recognizable descendant of *Cecilia Valdés*.[50] This and other nineteenth-century antislavery novels can be seen as the origins of "Cuban" literature: "Las obras antiesclavistas . . . por primera vez se hacen la pregunta sobre lo cubano" [The antislavery works . . . ask themselves for the first time about Cubanness].[51] Accordingly, Sarduy returns to the origins of "Cuban" literature. In many antislavery novels, however, the voices we hear are refracted through a canonical prism; they use hegemonic genres (the novel) and discourses: "The full version of *Cecilia Valdés* [is] more a panoramic novel of Cuban manners and mores than an antislavery narrative proper."[52] Sarduy's version of this origin of the island's literature *qua* Cuban identity is poetic and oral and is ultimately archived in Dolores's grave.

Dolores's story unfolds from a double narration, as we saw earlier. Although these narrators do not assume one consistent identity, as most of Sarduy's narrators do not, they do create an echo of Nicolás Guillén's poem, "Balada de los dos abuelos" ["Ballad of the Two Grandfathers"]. Dolores's story cannot be told from a singular perspective and is not remembered by hegemonic narrations, but in her epitaph. Her life story lives in oral, poetic, and even musical traditions. When the two narrators begin their dialogue, Sarduy places us on stage once more. We see a setting: "*En la provincia, época republicana reciente*" [*In the province, recent republican period*] (142) and several stage directions throughout. Various characters come in and out, but the story is punctuated by the narrators. This aspect of performance, and live performance, lends Dolores's story a certain freedom that is not possible in the standard novel form. In the standard novel, one is fixed by discursive frames. The stage performance is dependent on simulation and interpretation, so that different actors may represent a character differently. Dolores's voice is accompanied by music and sounds and other forms of popular culture, such as "guitarra y tambor obatalá" [guitar and obatalá drum] (144) and "el cha-cha-chá en los patios, al fondo" [the Cha-Cha in the yards, out back] (148). Her forms of communication (including the dream, which prophesies her doom) are those that are beyond language, used in a discursive way. Music and dreams, and even the synergy of a dialogue, operate at a liminal level, sometimes viscerally, effecting deeper communication.

In contrast, Mortal is unable to communicate with his audience during his political speech:

Mortal *(aspirante a concejal. La voz del primer verso se ha vuelto autoritaria):* Yo
. . . *(pero hay defectos en el micrófono, en la radio. Primero como "estática", a tal punto que se escucha una sola sílaba, luego el dial recorre todas las estaciones. Silbido agudo.)*
(publicidad cantada) Jabón Candado, deja la ropa *(hablado, vocecilla)* o en el Caballero de la R *(voz de intelectual)* Wallraf-Richartz-Museum *(hablado)* y de una situación interna ext *(cantado, Ella Fitzgerald)* in the moon.
Mortal *(continuando el discurso):* Yo, hij *(pero vuelve la "estática").*

[Mortal *(aspiring councilman. The first sentence's voice has become authoritarian)*: I . . . *(but there are problems with the microphone, on the radio. First as "static," to such a degree that only one syllable is audible; later the dial scans every station. Sharp whistle.)*
(sung commercial) Candado Soap, leaves clothes *(spoken, little voice)* or in the Gentleman with the R *(intellectual's voice)* Wallraf-Richartz-Museum *(spoken)* and from an internal situation ext *(sung, Ella Fitzgerald)* in the moon.
Mortal (continuing the speech): I, son (but the "static" returns)] (150).

Mortal's inability to communicate seems due to certain mechanical difficulties and other interruptions he is experiencing as he tries to get started. Narrator Two says, "Parece que los dioses están en su contra. No llega ni siquiera a comenzar su mensaje" [It seems as though the gods are against him. He does not even get to begin his message] (150). But as Narrator One mockingly suggests, there is no message: "(risita rápida): ¿Mensaje? Para que haya mensaje . . . " [(fast little laugh): Message? In order for there to be a message . . .] (150). As we see further along, when Mortal starts his speech from the beginning, he speaks in rhetorical flourishes that are devoid of true meaning: "Yo, hijo de la Provincia, en el día de hoy, he recibido la proclamación como candidato a concejal por Camagüey, la más bella que ojos humanos vieron, para ocupar un puesto en el gobierno de la República *(aplausos).* Para nosotros el poder no será un triunfo sino un sacrificio, como la Patria es ara y no pedestal" [I, son of this Province, today, have received Camaguey's nomination for candidate to the council, the most beautiful city human eyes have ever seen, to take a position in the Republic's government *(applause).* For us, power will not be a triumph, but a sacrifice instead, as the homeland is an altar and not a pedestal] (150). Mortal's speech is full of commonplaces and formulaic expressions. Communication is obstructed, since these frequently used phrases are platitudes, exhausted of real meaning. This is a clear parody of the political process and of the distortion of the "voice of the master"—generally a monologue or homogenizing discourse.[53] In this case, however, Mortal is interrupted by the other characters, who make fun of him, and he responds with more prefabricated rhetoric: "Narrador Uno *(burlándose de Mortal por haber empleado la palabra entusiasmo sin conocer su raíz):* "¡Oye eso!" Mortal *(que lo ha escuchado):* Sí, en un entusiasmado coro los vecinos ilustres de este glorioso y dos veces heroico pueblo. La voz mambisa" [Narrator Number One (*mocking Mortal for having used the word "enthusiasm" without knowing its root*): "Listen to that!" Mortal (*who has heard him*): Yes, in an enthusiastic chorus, the illustrious neighbors of this glorious and twice heroic town. The rebel voice] (151). Sarduy's comical scene demystifies the kind of rhetoric that might otherwise have contributed to a Foucauldian self-policing. The politician is impotent in controlling his own voice and the effect it has on his listeners. Sarduy shows us that once this discourse is open to dialogue, it fails.

The last major section of *De donde* purportedly is devoted to the Spanish component of Cuban culture. "La entrada de Cristo en La Habana" ["Christ's Entry in Havana"] however, pays special attention to Arabic-Spanish culture and thus parallels the ontological search that propels the entire text. Sarduy links tenth-century Arab Spain to twentieth-century Havana through his peripatetic characters. This proves interesting, since in the late fifteenth and early sixteenth centuries, when the Spanish arrived in Cuba and the rest of the Americas, and began to settle there, they had just officially expelled Spaniards of Semitic origin who would not convert to Catholicism, with further expulsions to come in the seventeenth century. The third component of Cuban culture is one indelibly marked by the Semitic worlds. Sarduy obliquely recovers these worlds through their contemporary Cuban manifestations. Cuba and the "New World" in general are the masks or simulations of the "East."

The itinerant Socorro wishes to insert herself within the traditional cornerstone of the Hispanic literary canon: the "national" Spanish epic tradition epitomized by *El Cid.* In her search for Mortal, Socorro casts herself in the epic hero's role: "Así quiso ser Socorro, conquistadora de Mortal y del mundo, nuevo Cid, bastión de Castilla, inquisidora de mahometanos y circuncisos" [That is how Socorro wanted to be, conqueror of Mortal and of the world, the new Cid, bastion of Castile, inquisitor of Mohammedans and of the circumcised] (176). Socorro's longing to simulate the *gestes* of an epic hero like the Cid engages this epic's problematic role in Hispanic letters. Although part of an oral tradition, the song of *El Cid* is passed on in the fixed written form of manuscripts. Textual variants were a natural and common consequence of the oral tradition; yet the idea of canonicity is based on the "ur" text—an original and single touchstone. In traditional Hispanic canons, the epic of *El Cid* stands at the beginning of the Castilian *qua* Spanish tradition. If, however, we recall the myriad Semitic characters in the epic—Raquel and Vidas and the various Arab friends and foes—we quickly see that much of the Spanish world was not at all homogeneous and that at times the Christians are portrayed as the foes.

Though clearly not about the medieval epic of *El Cid,* this section of *De donde* does set up a relationship between the worlds of medieval Spain and the "New World," specifically Cuba.[54] This relationship is a continuum in which medieval Spain and post-Columbian Cuba are simulacra of each other, as represented visually by the surface of the Möbius strip. As Spain was officially expelling "Eastern" elements from its land, it was also looking to sail East. It unwittingly covered over this new world with the names and images conceived in the old world. In Sarduy's Cuba, *lo cubano* is not homogeneous in the least. As Spain was "cleansing" itself of non-Christian elements, the New World was becoming more and more heterogeneous. Therefore, "La entrada de Cristo en La Habana" may also be seen as an ironic allegory of the evangelization of the New World by the Spanish Christians.

Sarduy juxtaposes elements from different times and cultures, as Lezama Lima and Silvestre de Balboa did. This way, he shows that Cuba is as much a cultural amalgamation as Spain is. For example, in the midst of talking about Socorro, Sarduy intercalates a slightly altered poem by a tenth-century Hispano-Arab, Mutanabbí. In this example of intertextuality, Sarduy sustains different contexts on the same plane and thus reinvigorates all of the texts involved. Moreover, Sarduy drops a note for his reader, letting him or her know that this poem is an "adaptación de un poema de Mutanabbí . . . número 175 . . . traducción de Emilio García Gómez" [adaptation of one of Mutanabbí's poems . . . number 175 . . . Emilio García Gómez's translation] (177). By referring to García Gómez, Sarduy is invoking the tradition of Hispanic medievalists and philologists who elucidated the Arabic origins of much of Hispanic culture. These scholars were instrumental in helping to refocus the cultural lens through which literary history is seen today. In this section of *De donde,* Sarduy also focuses on the transition from the Iberian Peninsula to the Cuban world. The central figure here is Christopher Columbus, or, rather, his diary/ship's log (*Diario de bitácora*). After all, this is the source of most of what we know about Columbus's first voyage. What is curious about Columbus's diary is that we have extant today only a *copy* of the original, in fragmentary form. Columbus mainly exists today as a simulacrum left by Fray Bartolomé de las Casas.

In Sarduy's text, Socorro meets up with Auxilio before they make their voyage from the port of Cádiz, in Spain, to Cuba. This was the port from which Columbus was to have set sail for the East. It was also the port from which many of the expelled Jews were leaving Spain, in October, 1492. With the numbers of Jews so great, Columbus's ships had to leave from the much smaller port of Palos. The Cubans, Auxilio and Socorro, embark on their voyage to Cuba and write their own *Diario de bitácora,* which appears in Sarduy's text. We note, however, that Sarduy gives us "*Fragmentos* del Diario de Bitácora de Auxilio y Socorro" [*Fragments* from Auxilio and Socorro's ship's log] (emphasis mine). Here Sarduy is simulating the endeavor of las Casas, who composes the currently extant *Diarios* from manuscript fragments. Furthermore, what Sarduy actually gives his reader is the inverse of the history of the "discovery" of the New World: originally alone, the Cuban Socorro wants to narrate the Iberian *canciones de gesta* [chansons de geste], taking on their roles; now together with Auxilio, she narrates the "discovery" in a Cuban idiom, *qua lo cubano.* Their diary is replete with *choteo*—"Un viento nos sopla de popa y al casco vienen a pegarse hipocampos. Auxilio cazó algunos y los frió en aceite" [A wind blows at our stern and sea horses come attach themselves to our hull. Auxilio captured some of them and fried them in oil] (192). When they arrive in Cuba, the narration takes on a Cuban inflection: "La realidad es nacer y morir. ¿Por qué llenarnos de tanta ansiedad? ¡El que no cambia se estanca, mi socio, así es que ni hablar!" [Reality is being born and dying. Why fill ourselves with so much anxiety? He who doesn't change falls into a rut, man, so don't even think about it] (194). This new Columbian voyage is narrated in a Cuban voice, not a European one, and all the more so because these are words from a Beny Moré song. We get fragments of this anachronistic voice that are narrated by Sarduy. In the age of conquest, the language of Spain was its medium for spreading its culture and dominion across the "New" World, and this new national language had just been standardized in March 1492 by Nebrija. But in contemporary times (when master-narratives have been debunked), the language that bears Spain's name has escaped its control. Both Auxilio's and Socorro's text and the text that we have of Columbus's Diaries are simulations, clothed in narratorial discourse.

Ultimately, this section of *De donde* follows the metamorphosing Mortal-Christ into Havana and into death. This is based on the Christian belief in resurrection after death: "La vida no comienza sino después de la muerte, la vida" [Life does not start but after death, life] (230). We see this Christ figure—the word made flesh—

decaying and falling to pieces. Auxilio and Socorro end up trying to piece him back together: "Lo fueron recogiendo, buscando en el fanguero. Pedazo a pedazo Lo envolvían en un paño, con amor, con cuidado" [They started gathering Him up, looking in all the mud. Piece by piece they would wrap Him up in cloth, with love, with care] (233). While earlier in this section we saw Sarduy making Auxilio's body into a textual object—"se estampó la primera letra en una nalga . . . los textos del Señor: con cuños de madera se los grababa encima. . . . Haré de mi cuerpo Tu libro, ¡leerán de mí!" [she stamped the first letter on her buttock . . . the Lord's texts: she engraved them on herself with wooden stamps. . . . I shall make of my body Your book, they will read from me!] (221–22)—now we see Christ's body (flesh) made word. Sarduy ends this section with the same synecdochic image of a dismembered subject on his literary canvas that begins the text in *Curriculum cubense*. The subject can only be remembered on the text itself, as it has been throughout *De donde*. While the Christian religion is based on the belief in the transcendence of the body to a spiritual realm, the body of Sarduy's Christ figure is tied to the text through the belief that there is no realm other than the page, or discourse itself.[55] The very last paragraph of this section exemplifies this belief: "Ya iban alcanzando los portales cuando, desde los helicópteros, llovió la balacera" [They were just getting to the gates when, from the helicopters, a hail of bullets came down] (233). After the body of the Christ figure has fallen apart and is carried away, we are left with language on the page and a sense of choteo—the helicopters and the hail of bullets.

Accordingly, Sarduy's representations of *lo cubano*, and by extension of ontological projects, are parodic inventories and itemizations of various components of the Cuban culture archive: race, sexuality, music, politics, and the like. As a straw man, *De donde* gestures at breaking binary categories in a search for answers that are unencumbered by methodology. Sarduy's approach to race, for example, distills three separate strands, which he subsequently proceeds to weave together. Clearly, matters of race are exceedingly complicated and racial identity is much more collapsed than Sarduy's parodic addition of a third, albeit attenuated, term—the Chinese—to a binary equation. Sarduy's probing into issues of Spanish "racial" homogeneity (*limpieza de sangre* [cleanliness of the blood]) already vitiates the triptych he paints. In his next work, *Cobra*, Sarduy will revisit many of the issues he explores here, and will further focus on issues of gender and sexuality. He will find an impetus in the Baroque concept of the monster—an amalgamation of disparate beings into one.

Cobra

De donde son los cantantes is Sarduy's simulation of an ontological archive of Cuban culture. His totalizing gesture, reminiscent of the previous cultural projects of Vitier and others, reappropriates this authoritative and patriarchal discourse and seemingly enfranchises Cuba's popular and marginal cultures. In *Cobra*, Sarduy's third novel, both text and main character—Cobra—are heterogeneous constructions that want to be canonical; they will control the discourses that define them. Severo Sarduy's *Cobra* endeavors to uncover some of the basic constructs that maintain a Cuban cultural imago and concomitantly a cultural archive. Sarduy examines the body as well as Latin America's mistaken founding identity. What Sarduy lays bare, however, is that neither one is a grand touchstone for Cuban culture. The Cuban cultural imago derives from a patriarchal collection of traditions and values that are organized around contingent and often binary projections (*machismo* and Columbus's mistaking the New World for the "East") and controlled by institutional discourse—the rhetoric of patriarchal power. Sarduy writes *Cobra* as a continuation of the Baroque tradition of bringing together a collection of disparate elements.

Severo Sarduy adopts the Hispanic literary tradition of the Baroque, which had been imported from Spain to Latin America but adapted to an American perspective. Sarduy's version of this literary movement is known as the Neobaroque, and he elaborates on some of its important notions in his work, *Barroco* [*Baroque*]. Twentieth-century Latin American writers turn to the Baroque and its American version—the Spanish-American or the Colonial Baroque—as the first literary "movement" to develop in what is today Latin America. It reflects the first Creole consciousness of being different, of being strange, of being a composite and accumulation of cultures. This so-called *Barroco de Indias* [Baroque of the Indies] probably took so well in American soil because it could appreciate the richness and multiplicity of the American reality, especially since Spain, the Hispanic Baroque's land of origin, had been "homogenized" relatively recently.[56] The Spanish Baroque of Calderón's *La vida es sueño* [*Life is a Dream*] (1636), but one example among many others, had already generated an aesthetic of strangeness and monstrosity, which was also metaphorically congruent with the hybrid reality manifest in the Americas (the mixture of European and indigenous elements).[57] The Neobaroque writers take up that thread of hybridity and monstrosity as the signature of their writing, throughout the latter half of the twentieth century.[58] *Cobra*, Sarduy's text and character, embodies

Neobaroque sensibilities: hybridity, monstrosity, excess, marginality, and performativity, to name just a few. *Cobra* fashions a cult around simulation in which the hegemonic is in search of legitimacy from the marginal—the inverse of the traditional archival formula in which the subaltern seek enfranchisement from the hegemonic. Ultimately, Sarduy takes apart the cultural archive and then stitches together a Baroque cultural monstrosity that includes marginal elements.

Although the so-called *Barroco de Indias* was imported from Spain, it was an artistic movement that developed in what today is Latin America as it adapted to an environment rife with dualities and pluralities (the Baroque Americas were a culture with large ornate European-like buildings and churches competing with native American edifices, for example), and, as I suggested above, even monstrosities. The rich cultural texture of the New World could be woven into Baroque literature. This culture, hybrid because of its numerous indigenous, creole, and European elements, could find literary enfranchisement within hegemonic forms of the day through the Baroque aesthetic.

In Latin America, José Lezama Lima declares the Latin American Baroque to be the "señor barroco" [Sir Baroque] in his *La expresión americana* [*The American Expression*], the origin of a personal and artistic consciousness from within Latin America.[59] Similarly, Alejo Carpentier's essay "El barroco y lo real maravilloso" ["The Baroque and the Marvelous Real"] champions the Baroque movement as the origin of an authentic American artistic expression: [our art was always baroque: from splendid pre-Columbian sculpture . . . to the best contemporary American novels . . . to physical love, which is made baroque in the Peruvian *guaco*'s curly obscenity].[60] Jorge Luis Borges, in his *Historia universal de la infamia* [*Universal History of Infamy*], characterizes the Baroque as a movement of excess and of a lack of restraint: [I would say that the Baroque refers to that style that deliberately drains (or wants to drain) its possibilities and that borders on its own caricature . . . the Baroque is the final stage of all art, when the latter exhibits and dissipates its media].[61] The Baroque manifests itself as a reaction against the singularity of focus in Neoclassical art. The Neobaroque appropriates the Baroque's heterogenous aesthetic as it integrates expressions of popular culture and privileges difference. Simulation—that is, representation—is treated on the same plane as reality in the Neobaroque: [it has expanded, making itself more complex, as it includes representation as a determining element in perception, eliminating the traditional hierarchy between reality and simulation. Theatricality, artifice and the representation of reality—whose saturation of significant codes takes it to hyper-reality—, these are in the end some of the paths toward knowledge and aesthetic enjoyment in our time].[62] Severo Sarduy appreciates the Baroque's excess as an aesthetic of contamination. For him, the Baroque allows noncanonical elements to combine with canonical culture, and thus to contaminate it: [to be Baroque, today, I think, means to threaten, to judge, and to parody the bourgeois economy, based on cheap administration—or as they say, 'rational'—related to goods, at the center and very foundation of that administration and of all of its underpinnings].[63]

In his *Barroco* (1974), Sarduy describes the origins of Baroque sensibilities and examines cosmological theories that were affected by and that influenced the Baroque artistic movement. Specifically, he elaborates on the Baroque's movement away from the classical circular figure to the elliptical figure (which is discernable in the works of Calderón, Góngora, and their contemporaries): [The step from Galileo to Kepler is that from the circle to the ellipse, that from what is traced around the One to what is traced around the plural].[64] For Sarduy, the Neobaroque is the rebirth of the "geometric figure ellipse, in addition to the corresponding rhetorical figure ellipsis, [which] is projected as the mechanism of the baroque."[65] In "El Barroco y el Neobarroco" ["The Baroque and the Neobaroque"] (1972), Sarduy focuses on the notion of excess. He calls Neobaroque excess what Fernández Moreno describes as [the apothesosis of artifice, the irony and the derision of nature . . . artificialization].[66] Here, excess is linguistically described as the literary displacement of the sign: [Literature gives up its denotative level, its linear enunciation; the sole center disappears in the stars' trajectory, which was thought to be circular until then, and becomes double when Kepler proposes the ellipse as the figure of that displacement].[67] The ellipse generates a second focal point, besides the singular one that is used to generate a circle, and so it is a metaphor for at least a dual perspective on reality, when it does not disperse meaning altogether: [the Baroque was destined, from birth, to ambiguity, to semantic diffusion].[68] Sarduy uses this philosophy in his writing to elide the univocal message found in literature before him. But let us not forget that an ellipse is drawn one circle at a time, after which the excess intersecting lines are removed to reveal the elliptical form. Therefore, although the elliptical form connotes excess and overabundance, it does so by sacrificing a part of each of the circles to create the new form. The resulting form may be that of a Baroque monster or diptych figure, which is a combination of seeming opposites. It manages both to upset the equilibrium of a patriarchal system based on binary categories and to incorporate itself into a canonical tradition as the progeny of the Baroque, a tradition that negotiates marginal and even iconoclastic elements that it ultimately incorporates. Sarduy's *Cobra* reflects these types of mixed cultural collections. We have already looked at the archive as the epitome of these collections, but let us examine some general types of major cultural collections whose raison d'être and history may help inform my subsequent analysis of Sarduy's *Cobra*.

One way to define culture, especially a national one, is by the sum of the nation's archival institutions and the artifacts of civilization they have chosen to enfranchise. Museums, libraries, encyclopedias, and literary canons place a value on the miscellany of their collections by electing to preserve these things and to exhibit them for their visitors' erudition. A hegemonic and supposedly autonomous national consciousness is born from and/or nurtured by these types of organizations. National literature (within the national archive), for example, helps to create an imaginary realm in which narratives and discourses mirror the nation and impart nationally important lessons and values, ultimately organizing a consensus about what is central to the nation and what is marginal. Literature and other collections may be amassed in one repository, which becomes the symbolic cradle of national culture. As we have seen in my study of the archive here, however, there are also destructive elements, sometimes latent elements, within archives that unravel national narratives.

The library, especially the national library, is a cultural arm of the state, whether or not it is directly funded by the government. As institution, public or private, the library directly mediates between society (culture) and literature (knowledge). As a concept, the library has both contoured and been shaped by literature. The idea of the library has often been inscribed as a constitutive moment in works of literature and in historical fact: in the earlier Hispanic world of Philip II's Escorial, the library was coeval with, if not causative of, decisive moments in the shaping of a Hispanic identity. The idea of the library is the organization and mobilization of issues—censorship, translation, manuscript versus print cultures, and canonicity, among others.

The library may be considered the literary cradle of a particular nation, since it is the repository of the actual texts that inscribe the idea of a nation before it actually exists, as well as works that define it and its values. The library may also be considered the anvil on which a national identity is forged, either through inclusion of other identities in the national mix or delimitation of the "other." Libraries have many projects underway other than just acquiring materials and cataloguing them—conservation, lectures, and policies regarding access and teaching. "Inventorying titles, categorizing works, and attributing texts [are] all operations that [make] it possible to set the world of the written word in order."[69]

The encyclopedia functions as a knowledge and truth-containing textual edifice. Unlike the library, however, it provides a supposedly unabridged repository of universal knowledge with the promise of continual replenishment and supplementation through printings of subsequent editions. Unlike the library's contents, those of the encyclopedia are easily and individually accessible; its alphabetization and finite number of volumes ensure this. This comprehensive work purports to present the universe in text, in one language, and in the random and unbiased order of the alphabet, "the certainty that *a* authoritatively leads to *b*, and *b* to *c*, and that *a*, *b*, and *c* deserve equal attention."[70] Legitimacy, here, is provided by inclusion, which supposes juxtaposition to other entries of similar value. We will remember, in Borges's "Tlön, Uqbar, Orbis Tertius," that the narrator and his friend cannot find the country Uqbar in any atlas, but do find it in a version of the encyclopedia. In Borges, we see a modern literary exponent of the encyclopedia and its purported ability to gather and organize discourses.

Borges's "Tlön, Uqbar, Orbis Tertius" focuses on the fabled aura of the encyclopedia: the universal leveler of vertical hierarchies and validator whose textual space imposes order based only on a horizontal arrangement in a traditional sequence. And, unlike the library, this repository is seemingly infinite, not constrained by physical space, since it can exist in an infinite number of volumes and editions. This heterotopia of knowledge and information is assembled on a page, in collage fashion, projecting a sense of chaos. Foucault's *Les mots et les choses* opens with Borges's Chinese encyclopedia to invoke such a heterotopia as we saw in chapter 2. The Borgesian list of animals "disrupts the familiar discursive framework within which knowledge finds its place in our culture: the history of the 'order of things' in the West is the history of the Same. When this order is challenged (when knowledge breaks down or mutates) then the very earth seems to move beneath our feet."[71] For Foucault, the encyclopedia "stages the dissolution of knowledge" because of the difficulty, if not impossibility, of comprehending and articulating all of its entries through one discursive field.[72] Foucault has stressed the long-range continuities in cultural practices (nondiscursive practices) in many contexts, but in *Les mots et les choses* he emphasizes abrupt changes in the structures of discourse of the human sciences, at several junctures in the course of history, displaying a conceptual discontinuity from the disciplines that had immediately preceded them.

The world in the encyclopedia of Tlön "is not a concourse of objects in space; it is a heterogeneous series of independent acts."[73] "[The] encyclopedia is predicated on synecdoche, only that [in Borges's story], the part can hardly be expected to produce a whole. The sum total knowledge about Tlön is hopelessly incomplete and is in need of further invention or investigation."[74] There is something suspicious, if not downright treacherous, associated with "syntactic concatenation" in Borges's story.[75] The encyclopedia dissociates entries from their discursive and patriarchal contexts and weaves them all into the same cloth. In fact, it does reorganize, if not maintain, a patriarchal frame, since it elects items on the basis of relevance (positive or negative value) to the culture of its readers—take, for example, the names of many of the major encyclopedias: "Americana," "Britannica," "Hispanica," and the like. These cultural entries are important to the minds of a nation or empire.

Cultural collections are ultimately gathered, organized, and displayed for educational benefit and/or because of the empirical profile of their viewers. The library, encyclopedia, and museum, alike, denature the individual items in their assemblages to put these on display as the epitomes of their kind. The museum is a repository of national culture, much like the encyclopedia and the library, except that it displays or exhibits its collections. Ultimately, the museum offers its visitors a performance of culture and artifacts. Ossified artifacts do not fulfill the function of the museum, unless they are able to do so performatively, as part of a collective narrative.

Traditionally, the museum, as a concrete idea and institution, tries to provide a cultural education, to inspire pride in national culture, and to maintain cultural continuity between generations and among social classes. To do so, it may extract objects from their everyday settings and coordinate them in an exhibit, where they are rendered archetypes yet immutable and idle, never to be used again for their original purpose. For a new state, the museum can provide an official catalogue of newly important objects or newly important ways in which to see, use, or remember old objects.

The nation achieves cohesiveness through a common language and culture, both of which share a common history that merges imperceptibly with a mythical past. A state, in contrast, is concerned with marshaling force, defining its borders (self versus other), and promoting material and social stability. A state's history is a question of documents and artifacts, which have to be authenticated, if need be through scientific methods. A nation's essence, on the other hand, is usually expressed in mythology and history, and in its various forms of artistic expression. The museum and its science, museology, are an aspect of the overall patriarchal endeavor to document, preserve, and understand a nation's and/or a state's development and experience. Museums are also simulations; that is, they denature objects and reincorporate them into a "natural" setting, where even copies or reproductions can be substituted for the real object. Museums can also reorder or hierarchize within certain groupings, or create collages of things, at will. Certain objects can be paid too much or too little attention.

Museums play an important role in the preservation, narration, and reformulation of history. They facilitate the recovery and reinterpretation of the past. The museum as an institution and idea enjoyed great promotion in Renaissance Europe (after the Americas had been "catalogued") to minister to the aesthetic tastes of the aristocratic classes—we have already seen the museumlike Escorial. Those who collected knew they were engaged in the preservation of elements of their own civilization for future generations, thus ensuring a kind of cultural Darwinism, where what survived would seem the "fittest." The museum's use was to store information and to illustrate with concrete examples the stages of development through which human beings had passed. In the sixteenth and seventeenth centuries, [a distinct period in the history of culture was initiated as it integrated itself with relative independence into the artistic and scientific fields].[76] The creation of museums and art galleries was coeval with the valuing of works of art without the coercion previously imposed by religious or political commissions. Artists now competed for cultural legitimacy, according to García Canclini, who uses the work of the sociologist Pierre Bourdieu.[77] Dwivedi's research shows that the eighteenth century introduced scientific and archaeological objects to other collections in gallery spaces, "owing to the progress in scientific experimentation and in archaeological studies . . . it also introduced a new type of gallery furniture in the shape of elegant glass-paned armoires which were used for displaying curios and instruments."[78] The nineteenth century would prove to be a century full of historical change and cataloguing. "Museums were flooded to the point of overflowing with products created by all kinds of human endeavors, by all peoples of all periods."[79] Let us not forget that the nineteenth century was the culmination of many European colonization enterprises, as well as the century during which most Latin American countries achieved their independence from Spain and thus could begin to project national self-images with official autonomy.

The post-structuralist period sparked remarkable criticisms of museums. A museum may be seen as a heterotopia or a discourse, and a display as an utterance within that discourse. Post-structuralist approaches—stemming from the work of Barthes, Foucault, and Althusser—have been inclined to emphasize the textuality of certain museological sites and to scrutinize the function of the reader or observer.

Scholars have analyzed Foucault's study of institutions to identify power-knowledge dyads embedded in museum display.[80] JoAnne Berelowitz uses Foucault's studies of surveilled space as a theoretical paradigm for reconsidering systems of monitoring and segregation in museums. Tony Bennett's work focuses on Foucault's studies of institutional expressions of power-knowledge to explain the function of the museum in shaping citizens. In contrast to Foucault's concept of the panopticon, Bennett says that such a corrective device is the opposite, bringing the show of power to the fore. For him it is the visibility of power in the display that turns observers into subjects instead of objects of control.

Cultural collections are ultimately gathered, organized, and displayed for the educational benefit of their viewers and users or to celebrate the values and culture that these people already share. The library, encyclopedia, and museum, alike, denature individual items by assembling them in displays as the epitomes of their kind. *Cobra*, the character and the text, also gathers and displays disparate elements in one body—both textual and physical. Cobra is a corporeal museum since she is a display of a cultural amalgamation. A snake and transvestite, transsexual, and transgendered male, Cobra combines both hegemonic and subordinate characteristics in such a way as to prove a monstrous spectacle. In *Cobra*, the phallus is emblematic of the hegemony, while the figure of the manufactured female body both collapses and conflates gender issues, homosexuality, and, generally, the marginal.

Cobra, both text and character, presents a sort of corporeal archive or museum, also because the text and Cobra him/herself are composed of many of the topics of the history and culture of the Americas (Cuba, especially) from pre-Columbian times to the present (the mass media, and so forth). Cobra's corporeal collection is an exhibition of this cultural history, a *tableau vivant*, since s(he) is essentially performance.

In a performance, however, what we see of it is already the actor's personal translation into motion, gesture, sound, and the like, of a previously composed script. Cobra's poses and discourses are scripted. They are reflections of reflections. Similarly, much of Latin American culture is said to be a reflection of European misreadings of other texts. *Cobra* offers us a Baroque sense of time, not a linear progression that we associate with industrial societies and their idea of deadlines and chronometry. *Cobra*'s time is a sort of spiral, also a Baroque figure. Baroque history is not linear.[81] It is made up of a series of repetitions that are not quite the same but that move in various directions—leaps, spirals, compressions and contractions—at the same time. This dynamic breaks up traditional notions of discursive hierarchy.

In *Cobra*, as in Baroque literature and cultural collections (the encyclopedia, the library, the museum, and the like), the marginal may usually be incorporated by simulating the canonical. The protagonist of Sarduy's *Cobra* is male, but not a traditional patriarchal male. As a transvestite male, Cobra not only dons the mask of a constructed woman, but also her discourse and the discourses of other marginal figures.[82]

Cobra opens in the *Teatro lírico de muñecas* [*Lyric Theater of the Dolls*], where the eponymous transvestite character agonizes over her overly large feet. Both Cobra and La Señora, the burlesque's owner, try to shrink Cobra's feet. Their success is ultimately hyperbolic in that they themselves are reduced to Cobrita/Pup and La Señorita, respectively. Without attempting to flesh out all of the doublings, square rootings, and returns to original states, I will note that initially Pup tries to replace the first Cobra (who has gone off to the "East"). The peripatetic one, however, returns to displace her double, Pup. Sarduy's novel opens in a performance space, with characters whose gender and relational identities eschew an inherent and essential origin.

Male transvestism is a performance of a construction of woman. It also eschews an inherent original "woman." Here, the notion behind transvestism is predicated on the belief that females learn to perform as women: they learn to dress, walk, talk, gesture, interact socially, put on makeup, and the like; and that the performance of "woman" is that of a marginalized character within a cultural setting. I would argue that the male transvestite may perform two different types of cross-dressing. In the first type, his success ultimately depends on his audience's recognition of his performance as simulation. His goal is to perform a man performing a woman. The second type of cross-dressing, however, is successful only if the illusionist, the male, is able to pass for a woman without anyone being the wiser. Regardless, what Sarduy will ultimately argue is that the transvestite's [máscara nos hace creer que hay una profundidad, pero lo que ésta enmascara es ella misma: la máscara simula la disimulación para disimular que no es más que simulación] [mask makes us believe there is depth, but what this mask masks is itself: the mask simulates a disguise in order to hide that it is merely simulation].[83] A brief look at scholarship on transvestism may further clarify this issue and shed more light on its performative function.

Judith Butler has suggested that drag is not a departure from gendered identity, but rather *is* gendered identity in its fundamental performativity.[84] And in *Vested Interests: Cross-Dressing and Cultural Anxiety* (1992), Marjorie Garber argues that the transvestite functions in culture to indicate the place of a "category crisis"—"a failure of definitional distinction, a borderline that becomes permeable, that permits of border crossings from one (apparently distinct) category to another."[85] In its undoing of the false symmetry of binary oppositions, its crossing of borders and its exposure of the performative imperative at the core of identity, the transvestite emerges as a fitting figure for Sarduy's deconstruction of national identity.

The metamorphoses of Sarduy's transvestite characters showcase the artificiality of gender, just as Sarduy's representation of national identity as a mosaic of different elements showcases the plasticity of the nation. Both gender and national identity in *Cobra* are suffused by the artificiality of *pacotilla* [kitsch]. As *pacotilla,* gender makes no pretense to depth or essence but remains a surface phenomenon, a complex play of visible signs (hair, costume, makeup, gesture). To consider national and cultural identities as forms of *pacotilla,* we must turn to Sarduy's representations of the East in *Cobra* as a pastiche of texts, icons, and rituals.

Cobra's journey to Tangiers is a crucial point in the narrative, both because Tangiers is the geographical site of Cobra's "castration" scene, which appropriately enough divides part I from part II, and because Tangiers is a geographical hinge between Occident and Orient in the novel. In Dr. Ktazob's Tangiers clinic, Cobra and Pup undergo surgery, Cobra losing a penis and Pup gaining the pain of the operation, in a parodic literalization of psychoanalytic transference. Tangiers and Casablanca operate both surgically and semiotically; castration takes place in cities rich in association with what Garber calls "the Western fantasy of the transvestic, pan-sexualized Middle East, a place of liminality and change."[86]

In seeking surgery, Cobra moves from transvestite to transsexual. In *La Simulación,* Sarduy distinguishes between the former, who effectively abolishes the distinction between man and woman by moving between the two categories, and the latter, who reifies the man/woman opposition by remaining within its terms, only leaping from one side of the pair to the other.[87] Whereas the transvestite Cobra destabilizes the dichotomous logic of gender, the postoperative transsexual Cobra in some sense restabilizes binary logic. At this point locale becomes all-important, since Tangiers, Tibet, and India take up where transvestism left off. Transvestite space, in which distinctions are impermanent and binary oppositions are permeable, becomes Oriental space. In Oriental space, binary oppositions are not merely permeable; they are annihilated. Sarduy's Orient is the moment when difference disappears, when opposites convert themselves into one another, when distinctions between Occident/Orient, man/woman, self/other, sacred/profane collapse.

Let us examine Cobra's transsexual surgery through the lens of Maria Lugones's configuration of the "postcultural" gaze. According to the author, the dominant individual in a given society is he who believes that he is outside history, outside culture, he who is not marked in any way as different or cultural. His eye looks for purity, to fragment or to break down into its supposedly pure parts that which is composite (such as Lugones's example of an egg), rather than seeing that a composite nature can in itself be pure in its multiplicity (such as Lugones's example of mayonnaise). As transsexual, Cobra is both multiple, to the lover of impurity, and fragmented, to the lover of purity. When Cobra has his male genitalia surgically removed, he is submitting to the logic of purity, which now is able to comprehend her as a woman, albeit a cultured entity. Sarduy's novels in general may also be seen through this lens of purity and impurity. He presents aspects of all levels of culture and people in society, rather than the lives of only certain social strata. He purposely revels in multiplicity, with which he is able to open the interstices of the traditional archive and insert himself.

Latin American writing has always been plagued by an ontological anxiety, a vestige of a struggle to define itself as a product of a formerly colonized culture, the admixture of which is held together, in the main, by a common and borrowed language—Spanish. The language with which the Spanish named their new "American" reality arrived pregnant with European signifiers that frequently displaced the indigenous nomenclature, despite substantive errors, in geographical orientation, for instance.[88] The first encounters among the Spaniards and the various indigenous tribes of today's Americas established a precarious relationship between the Hispanic and Oriental worlds. The Spaniards never did reach the site of the Japanese Emperor's court while on their voyage to India/the East, yet they were eager and ready to believe they had. Consequently, the identity of a group that was to become an integral part of the Hispanic mixture (the "Indians") has, as its origin, a false denomination. Hence, when a "Latin American" consciousness is later born, it is always already displaced.

The spurious birth of Latin American letters is further complicated by the loss of the original of its first written text in the New World, Christopher Columbus's diaries. In the wake of this missing Latin American ur-text, a black hole in literary history is left, the gravitational pull of which is so intense that Latin American writers have found it almost impossible to escape the search for the origins of Latin American writing through a return to Columbus's foundational text.

Sarduy's treatment of the Orient, like his treatment of nations and genders, rejects the binary opposition as an organizing and constraining principle. However, Sarduy's representation of national identity is unstable and negotiable, with reference to the representation of India, for example, in *Cobra*. In the "Diario Indio" section of *Cobra*, India functions as a surrogate Cuba, the Other—recognition of which enables the Self (Cuba) to know itself. However, India offers no guarantees, neither of the cohesion of the self nor of its own cohesion as the object searched for. From the mundane answers given by the maharishi to the parodic funeral rites of Cobra's death, India frustrates expectations that it will be the mystic site of the answer, the authentic, the traditional, and the timeless.[89]

Sarduy's embrace of superficiality, *pacotilla,* and visual excess suggests that representations of the Other can escape replications of ethnocentric fantasy to the extent that they reject the notion that desire for the Other can be satisfied by knowledge of the Other. Edward Said's statement that "Orientals were rarely seen or looked at: they were seen through" points to an ethic of transparency common to Western Orientalist gazes upon the Orient.[90] While rendering the Orient as a site of excess, fantastic wealth, and pansexual promise, nameless multitudes can and have been incorporated into a Western Orientalist mythology of a despotic, decadent Orient. Excess can also be read as a strategic rejection of the Orientalist vision. Excess can frustrate the transparency to which the visual pretends by refocusing the eye on the interplay of surface and texture, thereby detracting from the insistent wish to see "underneath" the image, "behind" that veil, or "inside" that burkha, so synecdochical of the fantasized Orient. Sarduy's formulation of *pacotilla* theatricalizes the veil rather than lifting it, just as his theatricalization of the transvestite body privileges the incessant questions posed by a cross-coded body over the answers that would result from knowing if Cobra were "really" a woman or not.

If both men and women can perform "woman," then why would men not be able to perform "man"? These questions and issues may seem rarefied or even pointless, so let us discuss them in terms of idealizations. By saying that there are idealized versions of manliness and womanliness, we are less likely to fall into an essentialist trap. Back to the original question: How do men perform "man"? We may specify that the ideal "man" that may be performed, certainly in Cuban and Argentine cultures, is the *macho,* an exaggerated performance, as much rhetorical and discursive as physical: after all, as Sarduy maintains, reality is conveyed through language. Although *machismo* is not a uniquely Latin American cultural trait, it has been associated with a longstanding tradition of male dominance and patriarchy in the Hispanic world, and especially with the avatar of this tradition—the dictator: "The historical and linguistic associations of the figure [of the dictator embodying authority] with Hispanic *machismo* are too obvious. . . . Reaching all the way back to Arabigo-Germanic Spain, through the *caudillos, comandantes en jefe,* and *generales* of today's Latin America, the dictator figure clearly embodies paternal authority."[91]

Cobra, a male who simulates "woman," replaces the traditional protagonist of the Latin American novel. Cobra's body is made up of discourse—generally a collection of Eastern images that delimit her physicality and consciousness. Cobra is still male, and thus this privilege still frames the marginal discourses he presents, even when donning the identity of "woman"—a marginal discourse—herself. The marginal Eastern discourses *Cobra* gives us are not only the Other to Western culture, but also fetishized images that do not even pretend to capture the "true" Eastern Other. But the rapidly changing cast of "Orientalized" Cuban drag queens, Tibetan motorcycle gangs, and Indian mystics, and the equally radical plot devices of sex-change operations, global wanderings, and religious transmogrifications, emphasize the scattered over the centered and the partial over the whole, thereby contradicting the metonymic logic of the fetish. The fetish is at stake in two senses in *Cobra,* first as an epistemological mechanism by which we can know the East, and secondly as a stereotype into which the East dissolves. And this is the problem; *Cobra*'s parade of partial identities leaves intact a series of highly fetishistic images of the East.

Sarduy writes from the interstice separating East and West when he addresses national and cultural identities. He says that the only way to get at *lo cubano* is indirectly, "alluding to something else": whether that other thing be the transvestite body, Asian countries, or Baroque language, a certain bricolage-like idea of *lo cubano* redounds.[92] The conversion of *lo cubano* into a state in which it cannot be seen frontally, but only tangentially, posits a framework in which national identity can only come into being when it displaces itself. This displacement is both literal, as in Sarduy's emigration to Paris in order to ask the question "¿Qué es Cuba?" [What is Cuba?], and thematic, as in Sarduy's use of the transvestite Other and the cultural Other in order to unravel the Cuban self.

In making use of gender terminology, discourse on the nation seeks to cover the constructedness of the nation with the borrowed clothes of gender, which is assumed to be at once original, natural, indisputable. But what if gender is revealed to be none of the above—what if gender is just as constructed, as performative, as "invented" as the nation? This question is implicit in Severo Sarduy's use of the transvestite and transsexual/transgendered characters in novels such as *De donde* and *Cobra*, which undertake the search for national identity even as they disavow it. Sarduy deconstructs or, better, dismembers nationality and gender with his use of the transvestite body as a locus in which questions of identity proliferate turbulently, and with the presence and presentation in *Cobra* of that "Other" so much at stake in cultural theory in the late twentieth century.

Sarduy mapped his search for national identity in a 1966 interview with Emir Rodríguez Monegal: [Upon distancing myself from Cuba I understood what Cuba was, or at least I asked myself the question with all clarity: What is Cuba? When it was at a distance, I could begin asking myself that question, which is the one that, little by little, has centered my work].[93] Though writing from Paris, Sarduy associated his imperatives with those of other Cubans writing in the wake of the Revolution, in response to what he calls [an inquisitive order about what we Cubans are. About what "*Cubanness*" is].[94] Ultimately, Sarduy's writing of *la cubanidad* does not answer the question of identity any more than his emigration evaded those questions. In Paris, Sarduy asked himself about Cuba and *la cubanidad*. Just as migration displaces the nation even as it rewrites it, so too does metamorphosis both displace and narrate identity. We are led to believe in gender and nationality as masterful classificatory modes that will name and fix as indubitably "something"—man or woman, Cuban or French. When, in *De donde*, Sarduy writes *lo cubano* as a collage of Cuban, African, and Chinese cultures and peoples, and when, in *Cobra*, he scatters the text with transvestites and transsexuals, he demonstrates the precariousness of nationality and gender. At the same moment, Sarduy reveals the definitional force with which nationality and gender interpellate human subjects into the fabric of cultural ideology. As gender and nationality self-destruct in Sarduy's work, his texts become (or so it seems to many of us) unreadable, difficult, confusing; Jorge Aguilar Mora has found *Cobra* "a consciousness of the destruction of a novelistic form."[95] Readers' frustration with Sarduy's text confirms the status of gender, nation, and identity as constructs made real to the extent that subjects invest them with fetishistic belief in a coherence and wholeness that is not there.[96] If culture is, as Sarduy once suggested, a form of curiosity, then what the subject ends up "knowing" is not culture per se, but a series of substitute objects, fragments, or fetishes of culture and identity.[97]

A cultural fetish through which the nation has been translated, especially in Boom novels, is the family. We need only think of three major instances: *La muerte de Artemio Cruz, Paradiso,* and *Cien años de soledad.* In *Cobra,* however, there is no family, either traditional or nontraditional. In *Cobra,* the Lyric Theater of the Dolls is the closest thing to a home for any of the characters: "fonda, teatro ritual y/o fábrica de muñecas, quilombo lírico . . . [la Señora] [s]urgía en la cocina, en el humo anaranjado de una salsa de camarones . . . iba y venía pues la buscona . . . por corredores de aquel caracol de cocinas, cámaras de vapor y camerinos, atravesando en puntillas las celdas oscuras donde dormían todo el día . . . las mutantes" [boardinghouse, ritual theater and/or doll factory, lyric brothel. . . . (Madam) would rise in the kitchen, in the orange smoke of a shrimp sauce . . . she would come and go after the *buscona* [swindler] . . . through hallways in that seashell of a kitchen, steam chambers and dressing rooms, crossing the dark cells on tiptoes, where . . . the mutants slept all day].[98] This is the interior space in which, if any familial alliances exist, they are weak. Sarduy offers an alternative family, without a significant genealogy. In *Cobra*'s Lyric Theater, it is not important to have physical progeny. What is valued instead is that one be able to reproduce oneself, according to the wishes of the bordello's clientele, "cumplimentando las peticiones de los más insistentes y manisueltos, . . . para corregir una vez más las leyes naturales y salvar el siempre incierto equilibrio entre la oferta y la demanda . . . sabían las malhadadas quién era foot adorer y ante quién había que bailar una javanesa en traje de Mata Hari y poniéndose un lavado" [carrying out the requests of the more insistent and grabby ones, . . . in order to correct once more the natural laws and to save the always uncertain balance between the offer and the demand . . . the ill-fated ones knew who was a foot adorer and before whom they would have to dance a Javanese in a Mata Hari costume while taking an enema] (14–15). Part of the reproduction of the self, in *Cobra,* is equated with the reproduction of a gender with which one's anatomy is not traditionally associated. Whoever is best able to perform "woman," while also performing the client's request, is the most successful within the Theater. The relationships are more that of rivals competing for roles than that of relatives. The Lyric Theater of the Dolls sets the stage for an anxiety of replacement. It is a home for characters who do not live in real time (they sleep all day), but in performance time instead.

The Lyric Theater of the Dolls is also a corporeal archive, housing all sorts of repertoires of performances, as we see above. It is a nontraditional library, unlike the one in which Cobra "indagaba en los ficheros de la Biblioteca Nacional" [was investigating in the National Library's card catalogue] (29) looking for "la solución en la *'Méthode de réduction de têtes des sauvages d'Amérique selon l'a veue Messire de Champignole serviteur du roy'*" [the solution in the 'Method of shrinking heads of savages from America according to how Mister Champignole, the king's servant, saw it'] (29). Cobra's collection is odd and stands out—her feet are too big for the "woman" she is supposed to simulate. Ironically, she must seek knowledge from a canonical institution—the national library—in order to fit within the Theater's nontraditional one.

As a figure of the Escorial, the Theater houses iconic dolls—"las mutantes[,] presas en aparatos y gasas, inmovilizadas" [the mutants, imprisoned in apparatuses and gauzes, immobilized] (13)—and body parts described as saintly relics—"eran momias, niños de medallones florentinos" [they were mummies, children in Florentine medallions] (29). This latter reference is to Cobra's feet. They are never named until long after they are first referred to, however. Instead, her feet are first alluded to through the direct object pronoun "Los." This is also the first word of the novel. Her feet are more directly referred to through the use of the adjective "ortopédico" [orthopedic] (11). Neither of these references directly names the objects, but alludes to them obliquely, and through a reference to something else—"*determinismo* ortopédico" [orthopedic *determinism*] (11).[99] Moreover, as "niños," Cobra's feet are her relatives. This family alliance is created through metonymy. Cobra's feet (a part) represents the whole (her un-elidible original anatomy, which defines her entire being). Her feet are her children. They are children that result from a self-reproduction. Like the Escorial, the Theater is both a museum for the exhibition of these items and a mausoleum for the dead and the dying: "las sufrientes" [the suffering ones] (13); "celdas oscuras" [dark cells] (13); "dormían todo el día" [they slept all day] (13); "inmovilizadas por hilos" [immobilized by threads] (13); "emplastadas de cremas blancas" [plastered with white creams] (13).

The Lyric Theater of *Cobra* is also described as a house of worship, an antichurch, if you will, within which an unholy alliance or family lives. The sick and ailing are healed here, but with "un algodón empapado en éter . . . , un gin tonic . . . , compresas de terebentina ardiendo y emplastes de hojas machacadas" [a cotton ball drenched in ether . . . , a gin and tonic . . . , flaming turpentine compresses and dressings made of crushed leaves] (13). Here, they dedicate their lives "al mismo dios" [to the same god] (16), whoever or whatever that may be. They act "con la devoción de quien flagela un penitente blandiendo una disciplina" [with the devotion of he who whips a penitent who is brandishing a discipline] (22). Some of the Theather's members are described as Christ figures on the road to Calvary to be crucified: "Sintió en la boca un esponjazo de vinagre. Con una mano abierta se golpeó la frente. Iba / descalza, arrastrando incensarios, . . . con cruces de aceite negro, / en hábitos carmelitas, de saco, un cordón amarillo a la cintura . . . / desnuda y llagada, bajo un capirote" [She felt a sponge full of vinegar in her mouth. She beat her forehead with an open hand. She walked/barefoot, dragging censers around, . . . with crosses of black oil, / in a brown habit, made of gunny, with a yellow cord around her waist . . . / naked and bruised, under a penitent's hood] (22). There are priestlike figures and references to the Inquisition: "*La Señora*—encerrada en paño crudo, autosacramental, torquemadesca—: ¡Mal convertidos! . . .— se persignó tres veces" [*Madame*—enveloped in a crude cloth, self-sacrificing, Torquemadaesque—: False converts! . . .—crossed herself three times] (24). Cobra, at one point early on, is described through hagiographic discourse: "Mientras más se pudrían los cimientos de Cobra, más bello era el resto de su cuerpo. La palidez la transformaba. Sus crespos rubísimos, de cáñamo, caían—espirales prerrafaelistas—descubriendo sólo una mitad de la cara, un ojo que agrandaban líneas azules, moradas, diminutas perlas" [The more Cobra's foundation rotted away, the more beautiful her body became. Her paleness transformed her. Her most blond hemp frizz, fell—Pre-Raphaelite spirals—exposing only one half of her face, an eye made large by blue, purple, and tiny pearl lines]. In order to live within the Theater and be a member, one must abide by its rituals. When Cobra is on the verge of dying, its members conjure the gods to whom they make a promise:

> En una tableta de bambú, que luego dividieron en dos, redactaron un contrato con los dioses: prometían respetar la gimnasia, la higiene sexual y la dialéctica; exigían en cambio la cura y reducción inmediatas. Con esa escritura como talismán, la Señora subiría a la montaña; parado sobre una tortuga y surgiendo entre jinjoleros, un Inmortal le entregaría en un cofre de laca el producto de la novena sublimación; éste, debidamente aplicado, operaría el milagro.

[On a bamboo tablet, which they later split in two, they drafted a contract with the gods: they promised to keep fit, to practice sexual hygiene and dialectics; they demanded in exchange the cure and immediate reductions. With that writing as a talisman, the Madame would climb the mountain; standing on a tortoise and rising above Jujube trees, an Immortal would hand her in a lacquer coffin the product of the ninth sublimation; properly applied, this would work the miracle] (37).

Both the hagiographic discourse and this last ritual, no doubt, prefigure the Tantric rituals and hagiographic discourse of Cobra's body in *Cobra II,* the novel's second part, especially beginning with *La Iniciación* [*The Initiation*].

The Lyric Theater of Dolls is therefore an anti-image of the church, cultural institution/repository, and the patriarchal family. In *Cobra,* the body is the central object of worship and exchange. In the worlds of Cobra, love and pleasure are the goals of relationships. She is not in the business of matchmaking for issue (courtship and marriage), but of recreating pristine bodies on which to signify. The bodies that are part of the economies of pleasure in this work are palimpsests that get written on over and over again, but which try to hide their prior use from the next customer.

Sarduy's *Cobra* seeks to articulate the body as the central locus of signification; not of any one particular type of meaning, however, but the locus of all signification, from which language derives and beyond which language cannot go. The signs of identity could be either deciphered on the body or hidden in it. As a locus of dissimulation, the body may be reconstructed or veiled, as is the case in piercings, scarification, transsexual operations, and circumcision. The body's use, or history, may also be read as in the loss of a maidenhead as proof of a loss of virginity. In this case we are talking about the female body as a text to be read by a heterosexual gaze. The woman's body can be "repaired," however, to simulate a pristine condition. This is precisely the business of the old bawd in *La Celestina* (1499)—re-virginizing women whose services she sells. Ultimately, *Cobra* orchestrates a world of characters trying to simulate the "other," themselves, and each other, all within the frame of traditional and canonical discourses such as religion, the heterosexual gaze on the female body, and Latin America as the aura of the original East. The characters in Sarduy's novel, however, function within their own versions of these canonical discourses: the brothel, the motorcycle gang's initiation ritual, the simulation of gender and sexual identities, and the voyage to/the search for the idealized version of the East for which Latin America was originally mistaken.[100] *Cobra* does not seek to eradicate the former canonical discourses as much as it seeks to uncover their originating myths and constructions. In this way, Sarduy sheds light on the origins of cultural productions and their national enfranchisement—a process that might just as easily enfranchise the alternatives *Cobra* presents to the figures of the archival.

6

Severo Sarduy:
Raiding Archives and Reformulating
Narrative Traditions: *Maitreya* and *Colibrí*

SARDUY PUBLISHED *MAITREYA* (1978) AND *COLIBRÍ* (1982) DURING the Boom's reverberations. These two novels engage archival traditions in Latin America, but through radial portrayals—the former focuses on Eastern cultures mostly, while the latter examines literary traditions within the Latin American canon. We saw in the last chapter that Sarduy's *Cobra* fashions a corporeal museum out of the protagonist's multivalent and protean body. In *Maitreya*, he makes archives out of his characters' bodies—archives that are dispersed or violated, "para demostrar la impermanencia y vacuidad de todo"[1] [to prove the impermanence and the emptiness of everything].[2] *Colibrí*, the main character has a penchant for setting manuscripts on fire, and ultimately burns down the brothel-archive on whose stage he once performed culture in agonic rituals.

Maitreya begins with the death of the Lama, or patriarchal leader, who presides over the Tibetan culture's religious and historical archive and ends in the Muslim world after "violar los anales del imperio" (161) [violating the annals of the empire] (133). There certainly are numerous significant themes and issues in this novel, such as doubles, the postcolonial condition, and so forth, but in this chapter I will focus on the most relevant topics of the archive and the "Orient."

There is clearly a historicopolitical backdrop to this novel. The Lama's death in the Himalayan monastery is accompanied by gunfire from invading Chinese forces in the distance, which impels the remaining monks to flee to India. Despite their haste, they make sure to take with them the archive of sorts that they and the Lama have been guarding. We see two types of archives here: the first is hidden within the monastery, and the second turns out to be the Lama's body itself.

Tibetan religious and cultural possessions, or patrimony, are the first things to be gathered and ferreted away when the monks realize they must go into exile. They look for "los tankas más valiosos, abandonando al invasor . . . , las imitaciones" (18) [the most valuable tankas, leaving only imitations to the invader] (4), "en hilachas y descoloridas . . . , herencia de antiguos monasterios, que los monjes habían conservado de guía a discípulo a lo largo del tiempo" (19) [faded shreds inherited from ancient monasteries, which the monks passed down from guide to disciple for many generations] (6). Their speedy escape forces them to abscond with their collections in improvised vessels: "En canastos de mimbre amoritonaron a la carrera los objetos que desde hacía tiempo envolvían en periódicos y esparadrapos, o disimulaban entre dos esteras" (26) [In wicker baskets they hurriedly piled the objects which for a long time they had kept in newspapers or bandages, or hidden between two rush mats] (12). We see order restored once the new Lama, whose identity is opaquely revealed by the dying Lama, is found and made to occupy in exile "un trono con tres cojines recubiertos por bandas de brocade, ante una colección de cuños y documentos oficiales" (36) [a throne of three cushions covered with stripes of brocade, before a collection of official seals and documents] (20).

We readers are given the sense that, while the monastery, and the Lama himself, are guardians of this culturoreligious patrimony, the archived objects are metonyms of a decaying and fragmented world. The objects are faded, in tatters, wrapped in newspaper, and hidden between rush mats, after all. We are also told that among the authentic objects are imitations designed to be "burla final y acertijo" (18) [a final mockery and riddle] (4) to the plundering Chinese forces. This archive contains dangers such as the ones I look at in chapter 2. Borges's library contains false copies, imitations, ersatz documents as well: "the vast, contradictory Library, whose vertical wilderness of books run the incessant risk of changing into others that affirm, deny, and confuse everything like a delirious god."[3] Derrida defines this danger within the archive, in his work *Archive Fever*, as analogues of Freud's death drive. Storage, whether in memory or in the archive, makes the items being housed susceptible to being lost, forgotten, or confused with false versions. In the case of storage in memory in *Maitreya*, the latter proves advantageous.

The Lama's body is itself an archive, susceptible to loss through his death and the corruption of his flesh, as well as through his body's dismemberment or fragmentation into relics. After the first Lama dies, his body is subjected to a ritual of decay before it is burned. As his corpse is being worked on, "brotaba abultada la piel, entre ideogramas verdosos" (30) [the skin swelled, spotted with greenish ideograms] (14). His body becomes the text on which culture is recorded and stored. The second Lama, the boy who grows into adolescence, also dies. We are told that the narrative we are reading about his corpse's fate is "contradictorio y deshilvanado . . . , reconstituido a partir de algunas tabletas que, dada su escasez, pronto se erigieron en canon" (65) [choppy and contradictory . . . , reconstructed from tablets which given their scarcity soon became canons] (46). This novel (and Sarduy generally) [disdains writing].[4] These canonical sources cannot and do not reveal legitimate or reliable information to the reader.

Truth in this novel is as scattered as the Lama's body. His corpse is dismembered, and the fragments are dispersed as relics among his ecstatic followers. Some of the pieces are stored away in a reliquary, or what the original Spanish calls an "ark," while the English translation refers to it as a "chest": "Vaciaron la cabeza: meticulosamente salada y envuelta en paños de seda que separaban finos estratos de cal viva, fue encerrada en un arca de sándalo" (74) [They emptied out the head: salted meticulously and wrapped in silk cloths separated by fine layers of quicklime, it was locked away in a sandalwood chest] (54). The mob of followers fights over the corpse's pieces, splintering "cofres y fémures" (75) [caskets and femurs] (55) and runs off with stolen parts. Eventually, these dispersed artifacts are held in "El Museum of Fine Arts, de Boston, conserva en su sección oriental. . . . En Sotheby hay otra" (76) [The oriental collection at the Boston Museum of Fine Arts. . . . In Sotheby there's another] (56).

Once the relic fever seems to subside, the faithful disciples set about complying with posthumous instructions. They build sepulchral mounds, "túmulos funerarios imponentes y blancos, que encerraron para siempre las reliquias" (77) [imposing white tumuli to enshrine the relics forever] (57), in which to bring together the scattered relics and archive them. In scenes that echo the building of the Escorial—the mausoleum-archive par excellence (and an ossuary for Spanish royalty), the faithful parlay "algún huesecillo desmoronado, pulverizable al menor soplo" (78) [some dilapidated little bone that would crumble at the slightest puff] (58) into "los andamios circulares del primer mausoleo" (78) [the circular scaffolding of the first mausoleum] (58). These "osarios" [ossuaries] eventually become numerous, such that "la isla . . . quedó ceñida de estupas encaladas, que atesoraban cada una un resto legítimo, aunque a veces—un diente, un pelo" (80) [the island . . . was encircled by whitewashed stupas, each one enshrining a legitimate remnant, though sometimes a tooth, a hair] (60).

Archival adumbrations are made clearer in these last few scenes. What at first may seem like the creation of houses of worship or several interrelated sects, each one drawing in parishioners or worshipers through the relic it displays, ends up being an effort on the part of the faithful to bring the relics—the bones, the cadaver, and, by extension, the Lama—together again. The figure of the archive in this novel is emblematic of the antidote to exile. The archive, the site of reunion of the scattered relics, symbolizes a restored homeland. It is the final resting place of the dispersed.

As we saw earlier, both in this chapter and in chapter 2, the archive is also a place of obfuscation, forgetting, and loss. In fact, even in this culminating scene in which the relics are reunited, we are told that their archives enshrine "un resto legítimo,. . . a veces . . . indistinguible del cemento y nimio" (80) [a legitimate remnant,. . . sometimes . . . it was so small it could not be seen against the cement] (60) of the building itself. We will remember Derrida's warning, let us call it, against the possibility of loss and death of that which is archived. Access to the archive's contents, for their own protection, is also in question in this culminating scene. The one relic that always proves to be most problematic in the novel, because it is the most coveted one, is the Lama's head, or skull at this point. The head's donor manages to use sleight of hand, or sleight of head, as it were, by obscuring the contents of the new cupola dome destined to house the skull, to keep the precious relic from falling into the wrong hands: The archive in this novel is one in which its author is all too aware of the dangers of storage. Archival dangers are also present in more intimate corporeal annals.

Maitreya explores the "violation" of the "anales del imperio" [annals of the empire], as the possibility that the archive could be raided and its rules subverted. The sexual act of anal fisting becomes an archival scene in this novel, where the fister is the archon who has control over access to the archive, and the partner's anus is the repository. Some literary critics label anal fisting in Sarduy's work "sodomy," which, in its less moralistic sense, is a legal term for rape, and therefore a strange marker for describing most of the scenes in *Maitreya;* "sterility," an irrelevant association given that sexual encounters are not just for procreation—and this happens to be the case in all of Sarduy's works, probably without exception; and "perversion and sado-masochism" and "*fist fucking* y otras prácticas sadomasoquistas" [fist fucking and other sadomasochistic practices]— moralizing and not always accurate terms, respectively, whose connections with Sarduy's work are patently alien to anyone who reads it.[5] Sexuality experts, on the other hand, refer to the same act as "spoken of in almost spiritual terms by its practitioners;" report that "people who engage in anal fisting . . . experience it as almost a meditative union of mind and body, involving total relaxation and receptivity"; and inform us that "fisting is an esoteric sexual discipline that has been practiced around the world throughout history."[6] Now, this is certainly what Sarduy had in mind, even down to the Zenlike atmosphere and discourse through which these sexuality experts describe anal fisting. Moreover, "in many cultures or religions the hand has deep spiritual significance."[7] Sexual practices that might seem recondite, taboo, or even perverse to some in the West—such as in Tantra, which "embrace[s] both the sacred and the profane"[8]— are considered by others "a means of spiritual enlightenment."[9] The one scene in *Maitreya* that depicts violence involving fisting is the sheik's violation, an image of archival raiding.

We certainly are given the sense that anal fisting in *Maitreya* is portraying esoteric disciplines, describing spiritual practices, and achieving meditative unions of mind and body. In fact, that is, generally speaking, the entire background and foreground of the novel. Specifically, fisting becomes intimately tied to a few characters in the second part of the novel, when Lady Tremendous, Lady Divine, Luis Leng, and the mural-painting dwarf called Pedacito (Little Piece) arrive in Miami and join the sect known as the "f.f.a," or Fist-Fuckers of America. Once in New York, Lady Divine disappears and the Iranian chauffeur—with whom Lady Tremendous falls in love— appears. The two lovers and the dwarf end up in the Middle East, where they continue practicing their sect's rigid rules by opening a "fist-fucking" massage emporium. They are expelled from Iran by an irate potentate and end up in the *Gran Hotel de Francia*. There, they continue their avocation, which results in the birth of Lady Tremendous's monstrous anal baby.

From the very first description of anal fisting, we see an archival suggestion: "En ano metía primero las yemas unidas de los dedos, como para cerrar una flor o acariciar el hocico de un tapir; luego, ya entrada la mano hasta la muñeca, la giraba lentamente, con precaución, de un lado a otro, como si esperara el ruido leve que abre una caja fuerte" (156) [First he put his joined fingertips into the anus, as if to close a flower or caress the snout of a tapir; then, the hand already inside up to the wrist, he turned it slowly, with precaution, from one side to the other, as if waiting for the slight sound that opens a strong box] (128). "Strong box" in the translation refers to a safe. The fist that is entering the anus above is unlocking a safe or an archive. This description is a tender one—"caress," "slowly," "with precaution," "slight"—and not rape or sadomasochism, as critics have alleged reflexively.

I contend that the anus is an archive in Sarduy's *Maitreya:* so let us look at some other convincing passages. In another nearby description, the hand is depicted as "dedillos enguantados y brillantes de bálsamo en los aflojados esfínteres" (158) [gloved and shiny embalmed fingers (deepening) into the loosened sphincters] (130). I have already considered the Escorial as a mausoleum-archive, containing relics, among other items, as well as an ossuary for Spanish royalty. Here, the fingers are similar to the embalmed and sheathed corpses one would find in a mausoleum. The sphincters are obvious allusions to gateways, or controls to entrance and egress. In a different scene shortly after this one, the dwarf painter, while performing the act of fisting in the Iranian massage parlor, "seguía catalogando eses y emes para la próxima sesión" (159) [continued cataloguing S's and M's for the next session] (130). To catalogue and to arrange letters are obvious archival activities and, in this case, also a reference to sadomasochism (S & M); but the reference is not violent. Fisting connotes special access to a hidden archive—to the West's most taboo orifice. The end of access to the anal archive in the massage parlor comes when a drunken potentate from Oman enters the emporium, too inebriated to be able to consent to being, or to realize that he is about to be, fisted. The mischievous dwarf realizes that this is his opportunity to enter this verboten archive and penetrates the unsuspecting sheik abruptly. Amidst shock, pain, and anger, the sheik expels the dwarf and his cohort from the region, pronouncing the sentence, "Has abusado de la tolerancia califal para liberarte a un manejo de trastienda y violar los anales del imperio" (161) [You have abused Caliphal tolerance, allowing yourself backroom backhanded handlings, violating the annals of the Empire] (133).

What is this association of annals and anus? Clearly it is an easy pun, on which Sarduy capitalizes. "Annals," however, means historical records or chronicles—an obvious reference to the archive. The concepts of empire and annals together, as in the Omanian potentate's quotation above, are then an apparent allusion to the historical Spanish archives and their direct relation to the Habsburg Empire—the worlds of Charles V and, especially, Philip II. As I say in chapter 2, the institution of the archive and the consolidation of the Spanish Empire in the fifteenth and sixteenth centuries go hand-in-hand; Philip II's obsession with death and its memorializing are legendary. The annals of the Empire are, therefore, also the anuses of the Empire.

And we know what anuses often contain, what they archive—feces. In fact, Sarduy makes mention of excrement several times throughout *Maitreya;* and tellingly, right before he describes the first anal-fisting scene, he writes: "Jugaban con excrementos y monedas" (156) [They played with excrement and coins] (128). The violated sheik has his archive raided against his wishes. Anal fisting, an unusual and even taboo practice for many, in this novel stands in for the violation of the state archive, for the entrance into a sanctum sanctorum.

Let us not forget also that, as I say above, the anus sometimes contains excrement. We must read this association of Sarduy's as an analogy between feces and books, or the typical contents of the archive. Sarduy, as Puig also does, subverts the traditional archive. Rather than a repository for master-narratives and hegemonic culture, the annals of Sarduy's Empire contain shit, as it were. These archives (the anus/annals) are a site of pleasure and not just a storehouse of cultural knowledge. The archon here (the active or inserting partner, the "fister") controls pleasure and not just knowledge; or perhaps the archon controls pleasure en route to, or as a predicate of, knowledge.[10] Foucault says that a productive aspect of power "induces pleasure and forms knowledge," rather than just being "a law that says no."[11] The models contained within Sarduy's archives, those models he holds out for the future writers of the Latin American novel, do not hew closely to the molds creates by Boom novelists. Sarduy's novelistic models seem to derive more closely from *the pleasure of the text.*[12]

In *Maitreya,* there is also a clear allusion to García Márquez's *Cien años de soledad* (*One Hundred Years of Solitude*), the most recognizable of Boom novels as a sendup of the Boom novel. In addition, there is a confirmation of Sarduy's archive-cum-pleasure at the end of his novel. Once the trio of the dwarf, the Iranian chauffeur, and Lady Tremendous resurfaces in the novel's last section—"El Puño II" ["The Fist II"]—in the Grand Hotel de France, their room in the hotel takes on the atmosphere of an archive. It has a "mihrab," or archival niche in the wall of a mosque. We are told that our trio is "reunidos bajo la bóveda" (172) [gathered under the vault] (144); and the room is described as a "museo de cera" (172) [wax museum] (144). The dwarf sets the mood for the driver to have sexual relations with Lady Tremendous. He penetrates her anally with his fist, as per their sect's rigid rules, and she becomes pregnant. The obese one gives birth anally to a "engendro tramado por el enano" (181) [runt hatched by the dwarf] (153). The monstrous baby in *Maitreya* suffers from what seem to be severe birth defects:

Su cráneo presentaba una protuberancia. El pelo, trenzado a la derecha, era azulado. El lóbulo de la oreja tres veces más largo que lo normal. Cuarenta dientes sólidos y parejos protegían una lengua larga y afilada: excelente sentido del gusto. Mandíbula fuerte, como tallo de yaro; amplio de torso, pecho de toro, hombros redondos, muslos llenos, piernas de gacela. una fina membrana le unía los dedos de las manos y pies. (181)

[His skull displayed a protuberance. His hair, braided on the right, was bluish. His earlobes, three times longer than normal. Forty solid, even teeth protected a long, pointy tongue: excellent sense of taste. Strong jaw. Delicate, golden skin. A body both flexible and firm like an arum stalk; wide torso, the chest of a bull, rounded shoulders, full thighs, the legs of a gazelle. A thick membrane joined his toes and fingers] (153).

The birth of the monstrous baby in *Maitreya* is an obvious allusion to the inbred birth of "el caudal," as he is called, which occurs at the end of García Márquez's *Cien años de soledad*.[13] This birth is the fulfillment of Ursula's much-feared prediction: "La comadrona se puso a quitarle con un trapo el ungüento azul que le cubría el cuerpo" [The midwife began wiping off the blue unguent that covered his body with a rag] (552); "Sólo cuando lo voltearon boca abajo se dieron cuenta de que tenía . . . una cola de cerdo" [It was only when they turned him face down that they realized that he had . . . a pig's tail] (552–53).[14] The child, who is associated with the color blue in both novels, is described in *Cien años* as "el animal mitológico que había de poner término a la estirpe" [the mythological animal who would put an end to the bloodline] (558), while his corpse is described as a parchment:

Y entonces vio al niño. Era un pellejo hinchado y reseco, que todas las hormigas del mundo iban arrastrando trabajosamente hacia sus madrigueras por el sendero de piedras del jardín. Aureliano no pudo moverse. No porque lo hubiera paralizado el estupor, sino porque en aquel instante prodigioso se le revelaron las claves definitivas de Melquíades, y vio el epígrafe de los pergaminos perfectamente ordenado en el tiempo y el espacio de los hombres. *El primero de la estirpe está amarrado en un árbol y al último se lo están comiendo las hormigas.*

[And then he saw the boy. He was a bloated and dried-out hide, which all of the world's ants were dragging laboriously toward their ant hole through the garden's rock path. Aureliano was frozen. Not because the amazement would have paralyzed him, but because in that fabulous instant Melquiades's definitive codes had revealed themselves to him, and because he saw the parchments' epigraph ordered in man's time and space. *The first of the lineage is tide to a tree and the last one is being eaten by ants*] (556, emphasis in the original).

In *Cien años de soledad,* the deformed baby's corpse, his body, reveals itself to be a parchment that holds the key to understanding the treasures of knowledge of Mequiades's room—the symbol of the archive throughout the novel. García Márquez's work, arguably the quintessential and best known of the Boom novels, therefore also reinforces the connection between the baby's deformed body and the archive.

Sarduy is obviously sending up the Boom novel's archival obsessions and connections, and he is doing so through the antics of "la secta naciente del templete a mano: 'f.f.a.' Fist Fucking of America" (110) [the up-and-coming sex sect "F.F.A.": Fist Fuckers of America] (86) in Miami, whose "propósito. . . : el caos total" (113) [goal is . . . total chaos] (89).[15] Sarduy establishes a connection here between "the generative power of the hand and the Nexus between this extremity and the phallus."[16] The fisting hand, the hand of the archon or of the archive's user has procreative powers—it can also write novels as a consequence of its having delved into the archive, just as the penis has the ability to germinate life after delving into another archive. If the Boom novels are phallogocentric, foregrounding male privilege and the 'voice of the master'—and I have been suggesting just that throughout this book, as have some of the sources from whom I quote about the Boom—then Sarduy is providing an alternative to that privilege. According to Alan West, Foucault states in an interview that "physical practices, like fist-fucking, are practices that one can call devirilizing, or desexualizing. They are in fact *extraordinary falsifications of pleasure,* which one achieves with the aid of a certain number of instruments, of signs, of symbols, or of drugs such as poppers or MDA . . ." to make one's body a place for the production of extraordinarily polymorphic pleasures, while simultaneously detaching it from a valorization of the genitalia, and particularly of the male genitalia" [*sic*] (West, "Inscribing the Body of Perfection," 122). Consequently, in *Maitreya,* fisting allows the novel to obviate the centrality of or even the need for the penis, as a symbol of phallic dominance of both plot and discourse. The anus-archive is, therefore, entered by the hand and its metonymic power to write literature, and not by the penis and its own germinative associations. Sarduy's archive is, in view of this perspective, an archive of profound pleasure, and not an archive that is meant to produce the phallogocentric models of the Boom.

West adds to the understanding of the physical sensations linked to anal fisting, as he explains:

> The intensity of the act is so great that it shatters the self's notion of itself in sexuality. If one is on the receiving end it is an act of total abandon-

ment, of releasing any control of your body and your pleasure. (Many testimonies clearly state, for men at least, that during fisting they get neither hard nor aroused in any usual way.) It is as feminized as a man can get; the rectum is the only "canal" or source of men's fantasies of child birth. In the case of Lady Tremendous, fisted by the Iranian chauffeur, it is a devirilizing gesture that is also germinative, since she gives anal birth to a creature, albeit somewhat deformed. . . . After the miraculous birth, the Iranian disappears, his paternity vanishing with him. . . . Is it a trick [in Sarduy's novel] to turn the void into a mirror . . . ? ("Inscribing the Body of Perfection," 122)

Despite the essentialized, bipolar, heterosexist roles West invokes ("It is as feminized as a man can get; the rectum is the only "canal" or source of men's fantasies of child birth"), his observations do highlight the source of sex-as-pleasure, which fisting represents over sex-for-reproduction. Lady Tremendous's abortive issue is a result of a "devirilizing gesture" and therefore represents a parody of the Boom novel, especially as the "paternity" of this novel, to use West's term, is left in doubt. The runaway Iranian chauffeur leaves an absence of paternity, a mockery of the Boom's search for authority, or even of paternity, for Latin American literary history. I will answer the final question West poses in the passage I quote above: Sarduy does make of the void (the *horror vacui,* the anus, the annals, and, finally, the archive) a mirror. Sarduy's use of this theme in *Maitreya* is not the first time he employs it. We will recall the early scene in his *De donde son los cantantes,* when Socorro is in the Domus Dei. Upon her arrival, a maid opens the door wide and, Sarduy says, "como si abriera las piernas, su cajita hialina" [as if she were opening her legs, her little hyaline box] (94). Here too, the void, the *horror vacui,* the vagina, is depicted as a miniature mirrored box, or a series of reflections. As González Echevarría comments in his editor's note to this passage in the Cátedra edition of the novel, [(T)hat is to say, being, essence itself, is a series of reflections].[17] In the end, Sarduy shows the pleasure of the void, the Baroque answer to the *horror vacui.* Boom novelists searched for essence, origins, and being in the void of the archive, while Sarduy, dispensing with the phallus as solely a germinator of life, locates pleasure and simulacra in the void.

The final scene in *Maitreya* reinforces the archival connection when the dwarf and the short-lived freak of nature are buried. They are described as "embalsamados" (186) [embalmed] (158) twins whose "pies [están] cifrados de letras de oro" (186) [feet (are) ciphered in gold letters] (158). The mummylike burial, "bajo minaretas" (186) [beneath minarets] (158), and the feet ciphered in letters, remind us of the archival nature of the Escorial, both a mausoleum-ossuary and a more traditional archive. Furthermore, Lady Tremendous's baby is referred to as her "hijo caudal" (186) [anal son] (158). The Spanish "caudal" is exactly the same word in English—"caudal," which means "of or near the tail"—crystal-clear references to the monstrous baby of the same appellation and to his porcine appendage in García Márquez's 1967 novel. The sense of the phrase "hijo caudal" is imaginatively captured by Suzanne Jill Levine, however, when she translates it as "anal son." This phrase is, therefore, referring to the baby as a son of Lady Tremendous's anus. In keeping with the association I established earlier between "anal" and "annal," the phrase therefore refers to an "annal" son, or to a son of the "annals." For Sarduy, the traditional archival convention of Latin American literature is miscarried. It is an abomination which, rather than proving the legitimate origins of a Latin American literary history, "[demuestra] la impermanencia y vacuidad de todo" (187) [it prove[s] the impermanence and the emptiness of everything] (158).

The novel's title, *Maitreya,* at first primes the reader versed in Eastern cultures to expect a novel about enlightenment, or at least about Eastern philosophy. Maitreya is the name of the future Buddha, who will appear on Earth, achieve and teach enlightenment, and embody the end of the chain of reincarnation. In an archival sense, he will have all knowledge, and every being will unfold into him. Maitreya therefore is a meta-narrative and the universal archive. He is to the East the vessel of ultimate enlightenment—what the archive is to the West. Sarduy's novel does not achieve, or even really strive for, this final illumination, as evidenced by the novel's final line, which I quote at the end of the previous paragraph. From the opening of *Maitreya* until the end, the novel takes us readers on a syncretic world excursion, from the Far East, through Cuba and the United States, to the Middle East and beyond. However, we are no more enlightened at the end of the novel than we were at its beginning.

Sarduy's excursion through the "Orient," the concept Edward Said deconstructs so remarkably in his well-known study published in the same year as *Maitreya,* explodes the notion of a single and monolithic Orient that can be known generically. As Asian, Middle Eastern, and African countries or regions were conquered in the nineteenth century, their European colonizers promoted projects of cultural knowledge as an effective way to know and, therefore, to own the lands and to control their peoples. These early Orientalist scholars paved the way for more direct forms of colonial control. Their projects, however, are based on the notion of knowledge as power. As Said says, "Orientalism is the discipline by which the Orient was (and is) approached systematically, as a topic of learning, discovery, and practice."[18] The East is thereby essentialized and reduced to a set of predictable and knowable surface signs and stereotypes that allow the West to see itself by contrast as more advanced and civilized.

In *Maitreya*, the West cannot know itself without knowing the East. We see a West "through Buddhism."[19] Historicopolitical events are parallel in both parts of the world. Culture in this novel is syncretic—it is a world culture that is shared and consumed by its inhabitants; yet we often see the signs of colonialism (or neocolonialism in some cases). Archival knowledge, and the West's self-knowledge, also depends on knowing the East. Eastern knowledge begins in the East, unlike the Orientalist enterprises, and informs the West—Cuba, for example. In Sarduy's presentation of Cuban culture, the East must be known as well. His archive is not content to leave it out.

Many of the scenes in *Maitreya* are either narrated from a Western perspective or conflate Western and Eastern events. The earliest example of a syncretic description takes place in the second chapter of part I, during the Lama's funerary rites, when "[s]e oían a lo lejos . . . , unas flautillas: la orquesta Aragón" (30) [little flutes could be heard from afar: the Aragón Cha-Cha Band] (15). The theme of Cuban culture, which will be woven into the main story line (or into the characters' picaresque wanderings, to be more accurate) in the novel's second part, makes an appearance early on. One of the effects of this premature peek at Cuba is to link the Chinese invasion of Tibet and the resulting exile of its people to the Cuban Revolution and the Cubans' subsequent exile.[20]

A Western point of view is clear in other parts of the novel. A very early depiction of the monks describes one of them as having "dos ojos almendrados" (19) [two slanting eyes] (5), which is clearly an observation through the Western gaze, as is the description of "las amarillas" (120) [the yellow girls] (96) with whom Luis Leng has relations. There is mention of symbols of Western culture, such as Billie Holiday (41) and English hotels (42). Western curiosity is often suggested: "como quien desgarra el velo de una mahometana" (66) [as if tearing the veil off a Muslim woman] (47) and "chinoiseries" (56). Finally, there is a pervasive sense of colonialism throughout the novel: "Todo iba muy bien—recitó puños cerrados, rígido como un salvaje ante una cámara—hasta que llegaron los hombres con pelo en el cuerpo" (31) ["Everything was going very well here" he recited, stiff like a savage before a camera, "until the men with hair on their body arrived"] (15); "Vivían en un palacio colonial de madera" (89) [They lived in a colonial wooden palace] (67); and "último reducto de la servidumbre indígena; mimando las exigencias del esplendor colonial" (169) [the last strong-hold of native servitude; catering to the requirements of colonial splendor] (141).

The West and the East are tied together in *Maitreya*. Actually, they flow into one another as in a Möbius strip. One of the leitmotifs that runs throughout this novel is the double. The West and the East are each other's double. After all, the Columbian voyagers thought they were heading toward the East and believed they encountered it. The earliest identity of Latin America in the fifteenth century is conflated with the identity of the East. A description of Miami upon Lady Tremendous's arrival mentions "dormilón y arcaico, un manatí" (101) [a sleepy, archaic manatee] (79)—the "archaic" descriptor clinches this as a clear allusion to the manatees Columbus describes as mermaids in his diaries when he arrives in the Caribbean. Sarduy, therefore, reverses the Orientalist gaze, such that the West is the subject of a powerful perspective. The East approaches the West in this novel, mixes with it, and returns to the East.

Maitreya reworks the archival paradigm. The body, writing, sexuality, and archiving are tied together in this work. The archive here is not located in one essential and immutable location. It is, of political and historical necessity, an itinerant archive: originating in the East, traveling to the West, and returning to the East. The East in which the archive originates, however, has always already been shaped by the West, Sarduy shows.

Colibrí

In *Colibrí* (1982), Sarduy raids the archive of the Latin American *novela de la tierra* and its variant, *la novela de la selva*—traditions that he treats as the origins of Latin American narrative.[21] As he makes incursions into this archive, Sarduy at times infuses it with new characters and new twists, while at other times attempts to burn it altogether. At the end of this, Sarduy's fifth novel, the main character, Colibrí, burns down the brothel in which he used to work—*la Casona*, becoming now its new owner in a repetitive cycle whose theme has been equated with Latin American fiction's penchant for dictator novels.[22] It can be said by analogy, therefore, that Sarduy, the author, is trying to burn down the Latin American archive and to insert his own works as the new archival fiction. He exploits undeveloped tensions in some of these canonical novels, such as the homoeroticism present in José Eustasio Rivera's *La vorágine* (1924), for example, and the racial tensions and anxiety over modernity inherent in other novels of autochthony.

The first words in *Colibrí*, "CABEZA COLOSAL OLMECA" [COLOSSAL OLMEC HEAD] set the stage for a voyage, not in or through the Caribbean, but on the mainland of the Americas, and within a strongly inflected indigenous culture.[23] A literal touchstone of sorts, the Olmec head is not just a starting point in Colibrí's early flight from la Casona, when we readers first see it along with the protagonist, but also a place of refuge evocative of home when he returns to the brothel. This non-Caribbean beginning marks an exotic and elusive origin. It represents the cultures that Europeans thought they were encountering when they arrived in today's Americas in the fifteenth and sixteenth centuries.

This novel conflates Eastern cultures with indigenous American cultures, not unlike what the early Europeans in the Americas did. We are told on the very second page of the novel that "los espejos simétricos multiplicaban, al este y al oeste, el ondulante cuerpo central" [the symmetric mirrors multiplied, from the East and from the West, the central undulating body] (14). Bodies and cultures will be multiplied and viewed from both Eastern and Western perspectives. This is a text about desire for the unattainable and about the delusion of having attained something whose identity is mistaken. Again, we are reminded of the early European explorers' search for the elusive fountain of youth or cities of gold and about the proliferation of European misnomers for indigenous reality—often the superimposition of an Asian identity on indigenous reality in the Americas.

One of the clearest examples of the elusive, misunderstood, and misnamed East is *el Japonesón*—Colibrí's friend and love interest in the novel. The inversion of desire works in the following way: our eponymous character represents the elusive desires of la Casona's clientele. Colibrí is the golden one, but this is only an illusion. After all, he is not a natural blond—his eyebrows are "negras de azabache, como si pertenecieran a otro cuerpo" [jet-black, as if they belonged to another body] (14) and his hair is "engrifado" [kinky] (13)—a sign that he is of color and not purely white.[24] Nonetheless, when he is on stage and performing, he is pure art, mimetic, and desired. Colibrí, or his sobriquet, "el Dorado" [the golden one] (42), representa the myth of El Dorado—the legendary city of gold that motivated the disastrous Spanish expedition in the sixteenth century, originally inspired by the South American tribal chief who covered his body in gold dust and dived into a mountain lake. He is the imperfect simulacrum of what is desired. Rather than desiring the Japonesón—the Japanese young man—the clientele of la Casona desire what is not the East and what is not truly golden—Colibrí. The twist is that the novel's protagonist does desire the true East—el Japonesón. The desire of the whalelike (cetaceous) clientele represents the Spanish conquistador's desire for the East, which they mistakenly project onto the indigenous people and cultures of America. In this novel, their desire for the exotic—for the golden one—is, unbeknownst to them, really a desire for a local boy from the muddy towns of the estuary (13).

What the cetaceous ones do not know, however, is that within Colibrí there has always been—or at least there is from the very beginning of the novel—a link to the East: the grain of jade he brings with him. Jade is a greenish ornamental stone, mineral, and rock, which has been very important for over five thousand years (even giving rise to jade cults) in both Chinese and Mesoamerican cultures in utensil-making, adornments, or amulets, and even as a substrate for inscriptions and writing. It is therefore a link between the East and the indigenous cultures of Latin America, those which the early European colonizers confused with the East. Another clue as to the meaning of jade in this novel lies in the origin of the term. "Jade" comes from the Spanish term, *piedra de ijada,* or "loin stone," from its alleged power to cure ailments of the loins.[25] Jade is therefore also a talisman meant to cure sensitive and vital areas of the bodies of Colibrí and the Japoncsón. Jade is furthermore a link to archival storage in this novel.

We will remember from chapter 2 that the term "archive" also means a storage vessel for a culture's sacred objects, such as the Hebrew Ark of the Covenant. In Sarduy's novel, Colibrí himself is the storage vessel for the piece of jade. He arrives with it in his pocket when the novel opens: "Traía en los bolsillos un grano de jade y varias monedas remotas y cuarteadas" [He brought in his pockets a grain of jade and several remote and quartered coins] (13). These are obviously his valuables, which he carries with him. Once he is on the run with the Japonesón, Colibrí lovingly stores the jade inside his lover's mouth: "Se sacó de la boca un grano de jade. Le abrió los labios al durmiente y se lo puso en la lengua" [He removed a grain of jade from his mouth. He opened the sleeping man's lips and put it on his tongue] (36). At this point, the jade is archived within the real East—represented by the Japanese man—and no longer in the covered-over East, the local, which is mistaken for the true East. Further along in the novel, once Colibrí is naked and being chased by the Regente's men, having no pockets, he stores the jade in an intimate place again: "Colibrí sacó de la boca el grano de jade" [Colibrí removed the grain of jade from his mouth] (69). In a scene toward the end of the work, after having sexual relations with the Japonesón, Colibrí once more "se sacó, y volvió a colocárselo debajo de la lengua, el grano de jade" [removed and, once again, inserted the grain of jade under his tongue] (148–49). Jade represents the conflation of the search and desire for the East and for the treasures of the Americas. Colibrí stores this desire within himself, where he keeps it until he is ready to assume the position of the new head of la Casona. At this point, "abrió un cofrecillo de plata en forma de corazón. Allí escupió el grano de jade" [he opened a small silver, heart-shaped chest. There he spat the grain of jade] (178). He is both the archon and the archive, just two of many doubles throughout this work.

The themes of doubles and multiplicity dot the entire novel. Usually they are conveyed by Sarduy through the figure of the mirror—a Baroque trope. The first time we see Colibrí in the novel, he is dancing nude between two mirrors, "entre dos espejos" (13). We instantly get an image of the infinite reproduction of his likeness within the facing mirrors. Other characters are similarly reproduced: the dwarf "bailaba entre los espejos . . . , fascinada por la progresión al infinito" [danced between two mirrors . . . , fascinated by the infinite progression] (54); and the Japonesón positioned himself "para . . . contemplarse entre dos espejos . . . " [to regard himself between two mirrors] (176). Mirrors also are jarring and sobering. Colibrí is frightened by reflections, "como atemorizado por un espejismo" [like frightened by a mirage] (102), while he is trekking through the jungle, but, more significantly, he sees a grotesque image in a mirror of what he has become at the very end of the novel: "En ese espejo, él que desde hacía tanto tiempo no se miraba en uno, corrió a mirarse Colibrí. En el primer instante: como si detrás del mercurio apareciera otro. Fue su gesto de asombro lo que a sus propios ojos lo identificó. Diós mío—se dijo—, cuánto pelo perdido. . . . Y estas cejas, que no encajan con el resto. Olió todo los frascos. Con agua oxigenada, que encontró en uno, y un hisopo, se tiñó las cejas" (178) [In that mirror, he who had not looked at himself in one for a long time now, Colibrí ran to look at himself. At first glance: as if someone else appeared behind the mercury. His expression of shock is what identified him to his own eyes. My God—he said to himself—, how much hair is gone. . . . And these eyebrows, they do not fit with the rest. He smelled all of the bottles. With hydrogen peroxide, which he found in one of them, and a brush, he dyed his eyebrows]. Colibrí seems to enter a postlapsarian world through the looking glass. He is first aware of his jet-black eyebrows—as though he were first becoming aware of his nakedness or mortality, as in the Judeo-Christian story of the expulsion of Eve and Adam from the Garden of Eden— as an incongruity with the rest of his appearance.

This is a significant anagnorisis in Colibrí. He becomes aware of his aging—his mortality—and his ineluctable path toward becoming the new *Regente*. In part, this is what spurs him on to take over la Casona and to become its next madam. What is significant, however, is how he reacts upon seeing his reflection. Rather than choosing to leave or to dye his hair black, he dyes his eyebrows blond. It is as though, precisely at the moment when he comes into his own, he starts believing his own myth. He is now *el dorado* itself, and not just a desire—a legend—that is mistakenly projected onto something or someone else. We see that Colibrí's body is the locus for many things: desire, art, multiplicity, and the archive (for the grain of jade).

The archive in general is an important theme in this work. We see it in several adumbrations: the museum and funerary objects (reliquaries, ossuaries, sarcophagi, mausoleums, and tombs), newspaper collections, the flea circus, metal storage boxes, and the pharmacopoeia. The novel's atmosphere is saturated with archival imagery or references. This abundance of archival references reinforces the notion that *Colibrí* is itself an archive of a Latin American literary tradition and of what that tradition leaves unsaid.

The wax museum is one of the earliest references to an archive in this novel. La Casona and its clientele are described early on as "derretido museo de cera" [a melted wax museum] (39). The description of the cetaceous ones as preserved in vanishing wax connotes death and mummification. Further along, in another section, "Diós es simulación," Colibrí comes upon a room where he finds the lid of a trunk—read, the remains of the archive—which he describes as "sarcófago" [sarcophagus] (89) and "tapa funeraria" [funerary lid] (89). Near this lid is a taxidermic eagle whose "pico parecía lanzar un último grito, sanguinario, o agónico" [beak seemed to shout a final scream, bloodthirsty or moribund] (89). The room in which these items are stored appears as if it were an old and abandoned museum. Toward the end of the novel, Colibrí is said to leave a hovel, "abandona un museo de cera" [abandons a wax museum] (108) that is also described as a deteriorating museum. I would add that the focus on the flea circus in the novel is also another symbol of the museum of death—"osarios para enanas" [ossuaries for dwarfs] (63) in little tin boxes. The concept of the museum in this novel is, therefore, also a link to the funerary archives throughout the novel.

The various funerary archival references in *Colibrí* immediately make the reader think of Philip II's Escorial—both an archive and a tomb. As Colibrí is being tracked by La Regente's henchmen in the jungle, the latter wear some of his belongings as "reliquias para auspiciar un sacrificio" [relics to favor a sacrifice] (44) and keep them in "relicarios" [reliquaries] (44). The reliquary is an archive of religious significance. It is often an element of hagiographic discourse. In the jungle, to which Colibrí has escaped, we see "las ruinas de un mausoleo devastado por lo vándalos" [the ruins of a mausoleum devastated by the Vandals] (101). Back at la Casona, toward the end of the novel, some of its denizens are described as "penitentes de una tumba" [a tomb's penitents] (134).

Another archive of sorts is symbolized through collections of old newspapers that are kept by elderly men on the outskirts of the jungle. As Colibrí travels away from la Casona, he comes upon an old store. Described as a stereotypical South American tourist trap, where food and second-rate handicrafts are sold to tourists, the store is run by old men with powdered faces who refuse to discard the daily newspaper, which they keep in "pilas inestables aunque regulares" [unstable, but regular piles] (61). What they are collecting—the venerable Mexican newspaper the *Excelsior* [*sic*]—is another indication of the non-Caribbean setting of this novel.[26] They accumulate these papers like packrats so they might have some "'instructivos artículos' de la sección cultural" ["instructive articles" from the arts section] (61) if they should ever become bored. The old store is a veritable archival labyrinth: "Así, durante años habían acumulado, primero en gavetas y mesitas de noche, o bajo los orinales de loza, luego por el suelo, en ordenadas pilas junto a la consola, y finalmente sobre sillones, balances, un radio de galena, una bañera en desuso, la mitad de la cama camera, un lavadero y el fogón, la remesa diaria, que ni siquiera desplegaban, ajenos al barullo estridente y reiterativo de la actualidad, del espeso informativo matinal" (61–62) [That is how they had accumulated for years, first in drawers and nightstands, or underneath earthenware chamber pots, later on the floor, in ordered piles near the console, and finally on armchairs, rockers, a crystal radio, an obsolete bathtub, half of the double bed, a sink and the stove, the daily shipment, which they did not even unfold, outside present time's strident and repetitive hubbub, of the dense morning information]. There is one more, if not directly related, reference to newspapers when a henchman transmuted into a nun arrives in search of Colibrí. She is said to levitate in the air and to land on "una tonga de periódicos" [a pile of newspapers] (74).

The newspaper here represents a type of homemade archival collection—the personal and intimately proximate one—that Sarduy's characters, and Sarduy's novels for that matter, collect. It is not an archive of official chronicles and histories, as those of the Habsburg Empire were in the sixteenth century. There are certainly echoes of those types of archives at other moments in *Colibrí*—"como un traje de cronista oficial del Imperio" [like the uniform of the official Imperial chronicler] (84) and "la archivera de la Casona" [la Casona's archivist] (102)—but this novel collects what is valuable to the subaltern, and not what is valuable to power. Newspapers are the only source of history that some subaltern groups have, and archiving and preserving them is not done easily or well, because of their ephemeral nature. As the aging archons (the old men with powdered faces) of this improvised archive say, they might need to refer to these papers on cultural matters some day. Their sense of culture comes from a popular medium—the newspaper, which they trust over history. Similarly, the recurring image of the pharmacopoeia peppered throughout the novel is an archive of home remedies and potions, in contradistinction to Western medicine. Toward the end of the novel, we hear the chant, "¡Viva el que escapa del Códex!" [Long live he who escapes the Codex!] (158). This could very well read, Long live he who escapes from the archive.

The ultimate escape from the archive involves its destruction. The character of the author—Sarduy himself—threatens to burn the manuscript he is writing (the novel we are reading) or the parts of it he feels are getting away from him, under momentum and undue influence of his characters or the literary tradition. Sarduy's novel seems ineluctably drawn to the vortex of the *novela de la tierra* and its subgenre la *novela de la selva*, the Latin American literary traditions I noted above. The obvious corollary to Sarduy's book burning is the burning down of la Casona itself by Colibrí at the end of the novel. He does this so that he can then rise from its ashes as the new Regente. Is this Sarduy's Trojan horse within his version of the archive? Is there a mechanism in the archive that counters attempts to destroy it? Is he trying to tell us that all destruction of the archive is doomed to end in a cyclical repetition of its precepts, just as Colibrí is doomed to replace la Regente and become the new dictator of both the brothel and the Latin American dictator novel? Is there no true escape from the power and allure of the archive?

Colibrí ultimately burns down la Casona, the place where various cultural scenes are put on stage as *tableaux vivants*, wrestling matches, or agons between local ephebes. His actions destroy that living archive of traditional cultural possibilities; yet he finds that he cannot escape the institution, becoming its next head. Similarly, Sarduy, the author-character called "Yo" [I] at times, threatens to burn the manuscript of *Colibrí* the novel when its "coreógrafas" [choreographers]— the novel's other narrators—try to set a scene or portray characters in a way that gets confused with reality. Sarduy's "yo" threatens to destroy his archive of subaltern culture when it seems to be achieving mimetic authenticity. He explicitly tells the reader several times such things as "¿Cómo ha podido creer que . . . era la realidad?" [How could he have believed that . . . it was reality?] (111), given that this work is full of "arcaísmos . . . de novelas pastorales, adjetivos inútiles,. . . complicaciones gratuitas" [archaisms . . . of pastoral novels, useless adjectives,. . . gratuitous complications] (112).

The author wrestles with his text and tries to get it to conform to his "authentic" vision of plot and character development. The novel goes in its own directions, however, and the characters develop a life of their own, whether because of the multiple narrators at work or because of the reader's ability to form his or her own interpretations. At the end of the section called "Regreso al país natal," the section about a return to the origins—*un viaje a la semilla,* or a journey back to recover the disapproving father—Sarduy is once again burning his manuscript: "¡Otra vez quemando papeles!" [Burning papers again!] (129). The only power the author has over his own text after he writes it is to destroy it before others read it, that is, before he publishes it. The "Yo"'s insistence on the primacy of his variant of the story illustrates ironically what Rivero-Potter identifies as the existence of [*an original,* a notion discarded by Sarduy and the post-Structuralists].[27] This notion of an original that is more authentic than another interpretation or reading is something I will explore further at the very end of this chapter, when I discuss the *novelas de la tierra* and *de la selva.* Sarduy, the real person, knows that once he publishes a novel, his intentions and vision for the work are only nominally important. Each reader will decide for himself or herself where the novel is going, and will interpret the characters accordingly.

Sarduy knows that his only ability to intervene is not to allow the work to see the light of day to begin with. That is why his father's homophobia-inspired command in the second-to-last sentence of this section, "Así es que ahora mismo vas a quemar también esas cuatro mierdas" [So you are going to burn those four pieces of shit also right now] (129) rings hollow. The four works his father denigrates presumably correspond to Sarduy's first four novels, leading up to *Colibrí: Gestos, De donde son los cantantes, Cobra,* and *Maitreya.* His father wants them destroyed in order to preserve the family's so-called honor in not having had any gay members, something those four novels obviously belie. Clearly, even the destruction of these works would arrive too late because they have already been disseminated and read. Destroying the texts, Sarduy's corpus, would not destroy the subaltern identities within them—the archive of marginalized cultures and peoples—and it would not destroy Sarduy's homosexuality.

The force that could infiltrate and contaminate the archive must come from within. The dominant, hegemonic master-stories must be reworked or complemented from inside the archive, just as the only one who can destroy la Casona is Colibrí. He is "el único que puede introducirse en la Casona y tomar el poder sin resistencia alguna . . . para quemar. Para destruir" [the only one who could enter la Casona and grab the power with no resistance whatsoever . . . in order to burn. To destroy] (158). Similarly, in order to subvert or reformulate the hegemonic notion of the archive, Sarduy must use its conceits and work as a Trojan horse from within, sabotaging its iconic traditions.

Colibrí is a collage of scenes and characters of the *novela de la tierra* and *novela de la selva*. Sarduy treats these traditions as origins of the modern Latin American literary tradition. These traditions are in the archive that Sarduy raids, and from which he gets the origins of his own fiction. He returns to the literary forms at the origin and finds that there is already a formed origin. There is no pristine origin or tabula rasa with which to start—even at the presumptive heart of Latin America and its culture, the land and the jungle; just as there was always already a presumed origin to Latin America itself: the Far East as well as the legal contracts entered into between Columbus and the Spanish monarchs prior to his first voyage in 1492. Sarduy, in *Colibrí*, infuses these telluric texts with new characters and new twists.

If, as González Echevarría asserts, [the novel of the jungle constitutes the epic stratum of Latin American literature, that which narrates the origin and evolution of the founding characters and their values],[28] then Sarduy's *Colibrí* tries to rewrite that origin and to include variants that could be eventually deemed as models for writing about subaltern cultures and characters. We see a number of scenes, themes, characters, and direct allusions via quotations that share a limpid correspondence with some of the best known *novelas de la tierra* and *de la selva:* la Regente herself reminds us of Rómulo Gallegos's character Doña Bárbara; la Casona reminds us of Mario Vargas Llosa's *La casa verde;* the Venezuelan words—"catire" (48) for blonde and "zaperoco" (17) for free-for-all—remind us of José Eustasion Rivera's *La vorágine;* as does the quoting twice, but with slight variations, of Rivera's novel's last words: "se las tragó la selva" [the jungle swallowed them] (48) and "¿No se lo había tragado la vorágine?" [Had the vortex not swallowed him up?] (176). A direct reference to "la vorágine" [the vortex] (150); the rubber workers (15); smugglers; and the illegal hunting of monkeys (46) reminds us of the cruel exposé we read in *La vorágine* about the latex industry; travel in a boat on a river covered with jungle growth reminds us of

Los pasos perdidos (42); we find scenic similarity to *Los pasos perdidos:* "Había emprendido el camino de regreso. Volvía sin saberlo, y por sus propios pasos, a la Casona. . . . El sendero se perdía entre los peñascos de la ribera opuesta" [He had undertaken the path of return. He returned without knowing it, and by his own steps, to la Casona. . . . The path became lost among the large rocks of the opposing river bank] (100–101); and a lost jungle city similar to *Santa Mónica de los Venados* in *Los pasos perdidos* is seen at one point and then alluded to in a reference to la Casona: "En medio del paisaje descubrió una covacha desvencijada, y luego otra, y otra. Los restos de un caserío despamarado . . . una improbable ciudad" [In the midst of the landscape he discovered a dilapidated hut, and then another, and another. The remains of an abandoned small village . . . an improbable city] (107, 116).

The most obvious plot similarity to a jungle novel is the escape of Colibrí and the Japonesón from la Casona into the jungle, paralleling the escape of Alicia and Arturo Cova into the jungle in Rivera's *La vorágine* (1924). The most obvious setting similarity to a jungle novel is la Casona itself, paralleling la casa verde—the bar and bordello at the edge of the Peruvian city of Piura in Mario Vargas Llosa's *La casa verde* (1966). And the most obvious character similarity to a telluric novel is la Regente, paralleling Doña Bárbara in Rómulo Gallegos's novel by the same name (1929). We have looked at many detailed similarities between these and other *novelas de la tierra* and *de la selva* above, but now I will examine two of these works in particular. Analyses of Gallegos's *Doña Bárbara* and of Rivera's *La vorágine* will reveal some of the sub-versions of these traditions that Sarduy uses to reformulate the Latin American archive.

Doña Bárbara is the living embodiment of the "barbarism" pole of the "civilization and barbarism" dichotomy that has defined the Latin American literary tradition since the nineteenth century. In Gallegos's novel, we are told that she is an ugly woman who is cunning and violent. She is a caudillo figure who behaves arbitrarily toward people until she falls in love with Santos Luzardo, whom she cannot have ultimately, and because of whom she is finally destroyed. Significantly, she is also *mestiza*.

Sarduy's la Regente is also described as an ugly, cunning, and violent woman. Actually, in all probability, she is a man who dresses like a woman. Her name is an obvious satirical grammatical (hyper)-correction of the Spanish novelist Clarín's *La regenta*. The invariable ending "e" on regente is in fact correct when applied to a woman. Nowadays, the word tends to be spelled with an "a" when it refers to a woman (as do words such as *presidenta*) because of hypercorrection, analogy, and a tradition of mistaken spelling—not helped by Clarín's title. Sarduy takes advantage of this invariable ending for a person of variable gender. He uncovers one of the uncomfortable subtexts in Gallegos's novel: that Doña Bárbara's behavior and characterization are manly—not just unladylike, but unwomanly. Sarduy brings this to the fore by having his version of Doña Bárbara be a gay transvestite. La Regente falls in love with Colibrí—an obsession that leads to her doom, just as Doña Bárbara's obsession with Santos Luzardo leads to her end. La Regente, too, is the caudillo figure, ruling a local area.

Let us also not forget that I have already analyzed Colibrí's racial characteristics in this chapter. La Regente's obsession with him is for him as the golden one—as a brunette who has kinky hair, but is disguised, dyed, covered over. La Regente herself is described as having indigenous features and wearing white powder on her face: "el rostro . . . , como el de un indonesio travesti senecto" [her face . . . , like that of an old, Indonesian transvestite] (168) and "cubierta de polvo blanco" [covered with white powder] (52). In *Colibrí*, Sarduy highlights racial and ethnic issues in Latin America. Doña Bárbara, the character, is symbolic of barbarism, in some measure because she is mestiza—not unlike Sarmiento's Facundo Quiroga, who is also mestizo, a caudillo, and the archetypical symbol of barbarism in Latin America. We will remember that Cobra's fatal flaw was her oversized feet, because they did not fit the composite of her as woman. Colibrí's fatal flaw is his black eyebrows, because they do not fit his composite as the golden one. Nonetheless, he is able to dye these incongruous corporeal signifiers and to assume his rightful place at the end of the novel as the new Regente. Sarduy is also able to cover over his characters, plots, and themes and to take his rightful place within the archive of Latin American literature.

Tensions in Rivera's *La vorágine* are also examined in *Colibrí*. Racial others, such as Indians and mestizos, seem to be treated sympathetically, while women and ethnic others (*la turca Zoraida*) are marginalized in *La vorágine*. Also, homoerotic tensions explode in Rivera's novel, but are ultimately sublimated into heterosexual love. This novel from 1924 serves as a model of sorts for other telluric and jungle novels that are written later. It is also significant because of its muckraking exposé of the rubber or latex industry's exploitation of marginalized people.

There are numerous obvious parallels between *Colibrí* and *La vorágine*, among which are the two sets of lovers' respective escapes into the jungle and the burning down of la Casona (in Sarduy's novel) and of La Maporita (in Rivera's). Ethnic issues are front and center in *La vorágine*. We see a diverse group of characters: criollos, mestizos, mulattos, blacks, Indians, foreign non-Hispanic Europeans, and Middle Easterners. The cruel treatment of the Indians and mestizos who are practically enslaved to the rubber industry is criticized through intercalated stories: "Esta nueva especie de esclavitud vence la vida de los hombres y es transmisible a sus herederos" [This new type of slavery conquers men's lives and is transferable to their heirs].[29] Other groups, such as Middle Easterners (represented by *la turca*) are depicted as conniving, greedy, and socially monstrous. Zoraida Ayram is a forty-something, hard, unmarried woman, owner of a local watering hole—"una pulpería de renombre" (178). She steals rubber at night, exploits people, and is sexually free. As a general matter, women are depicted as traitorous and wild—la niña Griselda runs off on Franco with Barrera, as does Alicia.

There is an intense homosociality and eventually a homoeroticism, on the other hand, between men and between women in *La vorágine*. Cova recounts a homoerotic scene between Alicia and Griselda in the novel's second part:

> Cierta vez la niña Griselda, ausente yo, le daba clases de tiro al blanco. Sorprendílas [*sic*] con el revólver humeante, y permanecieron impasibles, como si estuvieran con la costura.
> —¿Qué es esto, Alicia? ¿A tal punto has perdido la timidez?
> —¡Es que las mujeres debemos saber de todo! Ya no hay garantía ni con los maríos.
>
> [Once Griselda, in my absence, was teaching her target practice. I surprised them with the smoking revolver, and they remained impassive, as though they were sewing.
> —What is this, Alicia? Have you lost your shyness to such a degree?
> . . .
> —Well, we women must know about everyting! There is no longer any guarantee, not even with husbans] (169).

The erotic nature of the encounter is so obvious—smoking revolver, loss of shyness, knowing about everything, no guarantee even with husbands—that even Cova is taken aback as he feels his masculinity threatened with replacement by Griselda and/or Alicia's sexual self-sufficiency.

Male homoeroticism is even more explosive. Feeling jilted and abandoned, both Franco and Arturo Cova share a strong bond over their wayward female companions and the women's escape with Barrera. Tensions mount, generally, until Arturo and Barrera fight at the very end of the novel:

> No sé quién me dijo que Barrera estaba en el baño. . . . Hallábase desnudo sobre una tabla . . . desprendiéndose los vendajes de las heridas,

ante un espejo. Al verme, abalanzóse [sic] sobre la ropa, a coger el arma. Yo me interpuse. Y empezó entre los dos la lucha tremenda. . . .
 Aquel hombre era fuerte, y aunque mi estatura lo aventajaba, me derribó. Pataleando, convulsos, arábamos la maleza y el arenal en nudo apretado, trocándonos el aliento de boca a boca, él debajo unas veces, otras encima. Trenzábamos los cueros como sierpes . . . , y volvíamos sobre la ropa, y rodábamos otra vez, hasta que yo, le agrandé con mis dientes las sajaduras, lo ensagrenté, y . . . lo submergí . . . para asfixiarlo como a un pichón.

[I do not know who told me that Barrera was in the bathroom. . . . There he was naked on a table . . . removing the bandages from his wounds, in front of a mirror. Upon seeing me, he rushed toward his clothes, to get his weapon. I interposed myself. And the tremendous struggle between the two of us began. . . .
 That man was strong, and, although my height gave me an advantage, he knocked me down. Kicking, convulsing, we ploughed through the undergrowth and the quicksand in a tight knot, exchanging breaths from mouth to mouth, he on the bottom some times, and on top at others. We braided our skins like serpents . . . , and we returned onto the clothes, and we rolled again, until I enlarged his open cuts with my teeth, bloodied him, and . . . submerged him . . . to asphyxiate him like a dove] (312).

The homoeroticism in this scene—bathroom, naked, interposed myself between him and his weapon, convulsing, tight knot, exchanging breaths from mouth to mouth, he on bottom and on top, we braided our skins—is patently obvious. In fact, if one does not read it carefully or within its full context, one could easily confuse this for a scene right out of *Colibrí*. Sarduy writes wrestling scenes, jungle escape scenes, and lovemaking scenes that are almost identical to this. He therefore indirectly reveals a homoerotic tension that builds up in *La vorágine* under the guise of homosociality. In Rivera's novel, this homoerotic fight ends in Barrera's death and in the coming together again of Cova and Alicia (even the enemy's name, "barrier," was an obvious impediment to heterosexual consummation). In Sarduy's version, the impediment is to the consummation of East and West and to the desire for "el Dorado" and its attainment.
 If these telluric and jungle novels represent the origins of modern Latin American literature, as both Roberto González Echevarría and Carlos Alonso assert, then Sarduy is deliberately subverting that tradition, while using its frame to enfranchise his own brand of modern literature and his own marginalized characters.[30] His actions do not come out of left field, however, because their seeds are already embedded within these telluric and jungle novels' subtexts. Sarduy merely identifies and exploits these inherent tensions. The warning

with which he leaves his readers is contained within the final scene in *Colibrí*. The novel's eponymous hero does indeed destroy and supplant la Regente and la Casona, but he ends up replacing them in what we are led to believe is a vicious cycle. This theme has been identified with the Latin American literary tradition of the dictator novel, as I mention above.[31] Sarduy shows how easily what is marginal one day can become hegemonic the next. The marginal and the pursued can become the dominant and the pursuer. We will remember the closing words of *Colibrí*, both the novel and the character: "A ver si traen dos o tres muchachos del estuario, que bailen un poco, para que animen esto" [See about bringing two or three guys from the mouth of the river and have them dance a bit, so they can liven this up] (179). The victim has become the victimizer, and at this point, Sarduy has become canonical and ensconced within the archive of Latin American literature, just as his characters and stories have.

I end this book with a discussion of *Colibrí*, without examining Sarduy's subsequent novels, because, as I explain in my introduction, the four works I analyze here represent the various types of archival notions Sarduy explores. As Jacobo Machover observes, [*Colibrí* signified the end of a cycle, that of oriental fantasies and of telquelist experiments. It is the first attempt at recuperating the American contexts of narrative].[32] *Colibrí* does close Sarduy's "orientalist" cycle and his most significant venture into the archive. Sarduy manages to create a place for misfits in the archive and not just to create an archive of misfits.

Notes

CHAPTER 1. INTRODUCTION

1. Roberto González Echevarría's *Myth and Archive* promotes the archival origins of Latin American literature and of Latin America itself. I will delve into these notions further in this book.

2. Another aspect of the theory focuses on the practical use of the archive, if not its birth, during the consolidation of Spain under the Catholic Monarchs and the Habsburgs at the same time as the birth of the modern novel.

3. Maria Lugones, the philosopher, uses the terms "cultural" and "post-cultural" in her article, "Purity, Impurity, and Separation" to configure the basic framework of hegemonic forces and the concept of the subaltern in her exploration of dominance. I will analyze her work directly further along in this chapter as well as in chapters 3 and 4. The term "subaltern" here and in my work refers generally to a person holding a subordinate position or being inferior in respect to some characteristic. More specifically, "subaltern" may be anchored in Antonio Gramsci's discussion of hegemony and dominance, and especially within the question of the 'structure of discourses in dominance': "The different areas of social life appear to be mapped out into discursive domains, hierarchically organized into *dominants* or *preferred meanings*" (Hall, "Encoding, Decoding," 98). In contrast, hegemony refers to a situation in which a temporary alliance of social groups can exert authority over other "subaltern" groups, not by direct domination, but by creating and harnessing consent so that the power of the dominant classes appears natural and legitimate.

4. I would not want to fall into the trap of "transferring the formalist program of dehabituation of perception from the sphere of high culture to the form of mass culture, now seen as more aesthetically dynamic and effective," as John Beverly warns is all too possible, even if done unwittingly (*Subalternity and Representation*, 111).

5. Ángel Rama's *La ciudad letrada* (*The Lettered City*) is a significant, if tendentious, study of this tradition in Latin America. I will consider his ideas in this book.

6. I would like to acknowledge the discussions I have had with Maria Lugones for this configuration of and approach to the philosophical concepts of homogeneity and heterogeneity.

7. This living diversity in Latin America is one of the main elements of what Alejo Carpentier called *lo Real Maravilloso de América* (the Marvelous Real of America), in contradistinction to Europe's Surrealism.

8. Moreiras, "Mentoring Past the Ruins," 7.

9. Ibid.

10. Ibid.

11. Ibid.
12. Ibid.
13. Ochoa, "Uses of Literary History," 297.
14. Ibid., 300.
15. Ibid.
16. Moreiras, "Mentoring Past the Ruins," 7.
17. Ibid.
18. Ochoa, "Uses of Literary History," 301.
19. Ibid. (emphasis mine).
20. Ibid., 306.
21. Quoted in Ochoa, "Uses of Literary History," 298–99.
22. Jusdanis, *Belated Modernity*, 49.
23. Ibid., 50.
24. Smith, *Contingencies of Value*, 30 (emphasis in the original).
25. Jusdanis, *Belated Modernity*, 51. Texts may or may not endure the test of time (accidental destruction notwithstanding), for specific reasons; some lend themselves more easily than others to certain ends.
26. Ibid., 59.
27. Read, "Althusser," 762.
28. Foucault, *Archaeology of Knowledge*, 129.
29. Alonso, *Burden of Modernity*, 38.
30. The relationship between writing and power/fame is also represented in a potent way during the Boom years. Latin American writers became celebrities and wielded the kind of cultural capital that neither they nor Latin Americans in general were used to wielding around the world, until then. Puig, who was always on the margins of the Boom and its successes (in great measure because of homophobia—see Herrero-Olaizola's *The Censorship Files* for an excellent and well-documented account of this), often parodied the Boom's *Pléiade* by reading the "Boom as a Hollywood affair, where stars compete for fame and awards (Levine 200–201), thus 'playing up' the Bourdieu model of jockeying for position that is characteristic of cultural production" (Herrero-Olaizola, *Censorship Files*, 165).
31. Lugones, "Purity, Impurity, and Separation," 458.
32. González Echevarría, *Voice of the Masters*, 14.
33. Ibid., 15.
34. Ibid.
35. Ibid., 8.
36. Lugones, "Purity, Impurity, and Separation," 458.
37. Alonso, *Burden of Modernity*, 187n49.
38. See Emir Rodríguez-Monegal's "The New Latin American Novel"; Roberto González Echevarría's *La Ruta de Severo Sarduy* and *The Voice of the Masters;* Alberto Moreiras's "Despatriación y política en la novela de Severo Sarduy"; and Roland Barthes in "Sarduy: La Faz Barroca," inter alia. Roberto Echavarren thinks these novels are downright revolutionary, for, as he says, "They shook the literary consciousness of the time" ("Manuel Puig: Beyond Identity," 81).
39. The possessors of the phallus (a symbol of the penis or of power conceived in its stereotypically male forms, or, for Jacques Lacan, a signifier that evokes that which would overcome the 'lack' felt by human subjects) and the logos (identity *qua* discourse, language, and logical argument) privilege phallogocentrism. This latter term, coined by Jacques Derrida, denotes the privilege accorded to the phallus as a mark of presence; phallogocentrism "indicates a certain sexual scene behind

or before—but always within—the scene of philosophy" (Kamuf, *Derrida Reader,* 313).

40. The implications of this suggestion go beyond literary studies to the realm of identity politics, where two often-debated strategies for enfranchisement are assimilation versus the celebration of differences.

41. Franco, *Plotting Women,* xxiii. Jean Franco notes that "women have long recognized the imaginary nature of the master narrative," but "without the power to change the story or to enter into dialogue, they have resorted to subterfuge, digression, disguise, or deathly interruption."

42. Prometheus-like, Manuel Puig and Severo Sarduy provide marginalized entities the access to the rhetorical touchstones of truth of various social strata, to patriarchal rhetoric, and thus to power, which they may enjoy. Roberto González Echevarría's *The Voice of the Masters* concerns Latin American literature's questioning of the relationship between language and authority. His description of the coetaneous and dependent nature of power and rhetoric in Latin America serves as a backdrop to my examination of Puig and Sarduy's texts.

43. Echavarren, "Manuel Puig: Beyond Identity," 581.

44. González Echevarría, *Voice of the Masters,* 96.

45. Franco, *Plotting Women,* 186.

46. Pellón, "Juan Goytisolo y Severo Sarduy," 486–87.

47. Ibid., 487.

48. Alonso, *Spanish American Regional Novel,* 14.

49. Although there are different opinions regarding the phenomenon known as the "Boom," many have described it as a period of unprecedented productivity in and worldwide recognition of the Latin American narrative, from about the decade of the 1960s. Two particularly interesting works are *The Boom in Retrospect: A Reconsideration,* edited by Yvette E. Miller and Raymond Leslie Williams, and *The Boom in Spanish American Literature: A Personal History,* by José Donoso.

50. González Echevarría, *Voice of the Masters,* 36.

51. Roberto Echavarren contrasts the use of popular culture in Puig's novels with Borges's sense of literary decorum: "Borges's fiction consists of a web of allusions to other books, to a universal living library [what I am calling "archive" here], a solitary adventure in reading and researching and rewriting. Even when Borges wrote on film in the thirties, he never integrated it into his literature. Neither did he incorporate other aspects of contemporary popular culture" ("Manuel Puig: Beyond Identity," 581).

52. "The great Boom novels rewrite, or un-write, foundational fiction as the failure of romance, the misguided political erotics that could never really bind national fathers and mothers, much less the *gente decente* to emerging middle and popular sectors" (Sommer, *Foundational Fictions,* 28). So, whether refashioning or programmatically disintegrating a national imaginary, Boom novels lent currency to the discourse of grand national traditions.

53. Some examples of the Neobaroque are Carlos Fuentes's *La muerte de Artemio Cruz* (1962) and Lezama Lima's *Paradiso* (1966); and of the self-conscious, all-encompassing novel are Cortázar's *Rayuela* (1963), Vargas Llosa's *La casa verde* (1966), and García Márquez's *Cien años de soledad* (1967).

54. In *The Voice of The Masters,* González Echevarría goes as far as to say that "the established novelists who rose to fame during the Boom have become the *epigones* of a younger group whose most important figures are Severo Sarduy and Manuel Puig" (96; emphasis mine). The author further lists Fuentes in *Terra Nostra,* Mario Vargas

Llosa in *Capitán Pantoja and the Special Service* and *Aunt Julia and the Scriptwriter*, and Juan Goytisolo in *Count Julian* as having abandoned the novel of cultural knowledge.

In addition, Jean Franco explains that in the late sixties, the interpretive power of the nation and religion was vitiated: "The mass media, particularly radio, television, and comic book literature, 'internationalized' culture in ways that were seen as subversive to national ideals and at the same time liberating, in that they often introduced elements in contradiction to the dominant national ideology" (*Plotting Women*, 175).

55. "Although the avowed aim of their policies may differ, authoritarian leaders in Latin America vary little, regardless of the political doctrines they profess: they are male . . . and wield almost absolute personal power" (González Echevarría, *Voice of the Masters*, 1).

56. Franco, *Plotting Women*, 175.

57. Jusdanis, *Belated Modernity and Aesthetic Culture*, xi.

58. Ibid., 1.

59. Ibid.

60. González Echevarría, *Voice of the Masters*, 4. As the author notes in that work, there was a Latin American literature even before the romantics, but only because "it was conceived retrospectively by romantic thought" (4).

61. In *The Spanish American Regional Novel*, Carlos Alonso asserts that a rhetorical dialectics of crisis has both characterized and structured Latin American discursive space from the outset, if one takes into consideration that the demand for an autochthonous cultural expression has been the dominant concern in Latin American intellectual history. See especially chapter 1.

62. Alonso, *Spanish American Regional Novel*, 22.

63. Ibid.

64. Santos, *Kitsch tropical*, 11–12.

65. Ibid., 12.

66. Kerr, *Suspended Fictions*, 4.

67. Ibid., 10.

68. Alter, "An Argentine Tour de Force."

69. In his first novel, *Gestos* (1963), Sarduy exhibits a technique somewhat different from that in his next two novels: this early technique is "a combination of the objectivist technique of the *nouveau roman* and of the committed novel" (Pellón, "Juan Goytisolo y Severo Sarduy," 486–87).

70. González Echevarría, *La ruta de Severo Sarduy*, 252.

71. González Echevarría, *Relecturas*, 121.

72. "Al alba empezaron de nuevo, hasta que en el horizonte las deidades apacibles y detentoras del crepúsculo muestran sus dedillos anaranjados. Entonces contemplaremos en silencio la lentitud con que el sol se hunde entre los valles nevados, del otro lado de las montañas, junto a las grandes estupas ya vacías y los borrados sobre las torres del país natal" [At dawn, they began again, until on the horizon the gentle and holding deities of the dusk show their fingertips. Then we will contemplate in silence the slowness with which the sun sinks between the snowy valleys, on the other side of the mountains, near the already-empty, large stupas and the erasures on the towers of the native country] (262–63).

Dawn's personification here evokes imagery similar to that in the Homeric epics: "Dawn showed again with her rosy fingers" (*Iliad*, 72), "Dawn of the rosy fingers" (*Iliad*, 457), "Dawn showed again with her rosy fingers" (*Odyssey*, 64), "Dawn of the rosy fingers" (*Odyssey*, 341), and so forth. The juxtapositioning of this clear allusion to classical culture—the quintessence of the "West"—with snowy valleys and stupas—clear Eastern imagery—is a gesture toward an exhibition of a universal culture. The cyclical beginning at dawn is reminiscent of the frame narrative's master trope.

73. In one of the oldest and best known collections of frame tales, *The Thousand and One Nights* (also, *Tales from the Arabian Nights*), Scheherazade's storytelling must resume each day, in an entertaining narration, lest she be executed. While not always so literal, this metaphor of literature as a living, changing texture with inherent contradictions is common to frame narratives. The open-ended nature of this type of narrative invites a proliferation of tales that do not necessarily contribute to a centralized, unifying meaning.

74. I will unfold the sources of these ideas later in my book's corresponding chapters.

75. González Echevarría, *Myth and Archive*, 8 (emphasis mine).

76. Ibid., 8.

77. Spivak, "The Politics of Translation," 188.

CHAPTER 2. RAIDING THE ARCHIVE

1. Featherstone, "Archive: Problematizing Global Knowledge," 596.

2. This list is obviously an abridged series of highlights. It is known that, as early as the third millennium B.C.E, scribes in Mesopotamia adopted systematic shelving of their clay tablets, which they catalogued with content descriptions appended to their edges.

3. The archive has been studied in the last forty years by very many people (see Marlene Manoff's 2004 article, "Theories of the Archive from Across the Disciplines," and its excellent bibliography, which lists many of these formulations), but these thinkers I am engaging are the most relevant to Latin American literature and culture.

4. Guillory's main focus is the canon and canonicity, as is obvious from his book's title. His work, however, has some points of contact with my own in that much of his study of the canon, and of the archive for that matter, is predicated on the ideas of Pierre Bourdieu regarding cultural/symbolic capital.

5. Bolstered by Derrida's assertion that "nothing is less clear today" than the meaning of the term "archive" ("Theories of the archive," 10), Marlene Manoff considers the ambiguity of the concept: "Even librarians and archivists have become somewhat careless in their use of the term" (10). She also points to experts who "[argue] that the distinctions between libraries, archives, and museums have always been ambiguous" (10). Ultimately, she decides that "for purposes of [her] essay [she] will use the term archive in its broadest sense, because that is how the majority of writers [she] will be discussing use it" (10). I too offer a broad semantic field for the concept of the archive, girded by the familiar, necessary points of reference for Hispanists and specifically for Latin Americanists, because Puig and Sarduy work with the complexities of the archive and across its multidisciplinary nexus.

6. Borges, *Selected Non-Fiction*, 214. While modern in the aspect that is suggestive of digital media, Borges's Total Library has precedents in universal library cataloguing systems such as the Library of Congress Classification, Dewey, and the Universal Decimal Classification. David Greetham has criticized as "archival hubris" these attempts to "achieve an *anatomy* of the archive that will somehow derive from an empirical analysis of the full body of extant writings and yet try to stand outside of the

time and place of its making" ("Who's In, Who's Out: The Cultural Politics of Archival Exclusion," 18 [emphasis in the original]).

7. Borges, *Selected Non-Fiction*, 216.
8. Ibid., 214.
9. Ibid., 216.
10. The infinite monkey theorem "states that a monkey hitting keys at random on a typewriter keyboard for an infinite amount of time will almost surely type a particular chosen text, such as the complete works of William Shakespeare" (Wikipedia, s.v. "Infinite monkey theorem," accessed January 22, 2008).
11. Borges, *Selected Non-Fiction*, 216.
12. Ibid.
13. Borges, *Obras Completas*, 499.
14. Ibid., 500.
15. Ibid., 499.
16. Ibid., 503.
17. Ibid.
18. Purging of items by archivists—museum curators and librarians, for example (deaccession, as it is called in polite company) happens relatively often. Manoff cites "the intensity of the debates over the stewardship of library collections sparked by Nicholson Baker's allegations that libraries have betrayed a public trust by disposing of material that should have been preserved for present and future generations" ("Theories of the Archive," 12). Political ideologies could also be a motivation for deaccessioning, as those involved in the polemic over whether Cuba's National Library is currently purging its collection would argue. See http://www.penultimosdias.com/2009/12/03/una-polemica-sobre-la-destruccion-de-los-fondos-de-las-bibliotecas-cubanas/ for a (tendentious) discussion of the problem.
19. Alejandro Herrero-Olaizola exemplifies this for us by way of an anecdote, the likes of which with which we who have done archival research are all too familiar, in his *The Censorship Files*. When he started his research in Spain's *Archivo de la censura*, or "Censorship Archive", he would be shepherded by the staff to a dingy area where he was allowed very little time to examine files and to gather several requisite codes with which to request boxes that did not always contain what they were suppose to: "the researcher has the illusion of having mastered the system, and, as it were, 'broken the code.' S/he may now request the boxes, assuming that they contain the reports. . . . This, however, is not always the case. Many reports are missing or misplaced. There is an average wait of thirty to forty-five minutes before the coveted boxes arrive in the reading room. . . . Researchers can request only ten boxes at once, and a total of twenty-five per day. . . . For my strategy to bypass some of these restrictions . . . I spent my first few weeks . . . befriending the reading room supervisor and her assistants, always acknowledging that they had the authority to 'censor' me if they pleased. . . . I gradually became their confidant. . . . As a result, I soon figured out that I could actually see thirty-five boxes in a given day, since there is an unwritten rule" (xv–xvi). This cathartically amusing account illustrates the archon and the "sub-archon's" arbitrary powers as well as how false is the illusion that an archive actually contains everything it advertises or that it makes everything it should have easily accessible.
20. Foucault, *Order of Things*, xv (emphasis in the original).
21. Borges, *Obras completas*, 2:91.
22. Lakoff, *Women, Fire, and Dangerous Things*, 92.
23. Foucault, *Archaeology of Knowledge*, 38.

24. Foucault does not try to bring together unifying concepts as a structural description of historiography. Instead, he clarifies his idea that discontinuity is typical of discursive statements. Furthermore, it is important to contextualize Foucault's *Archaeology of Knowledge* of 1969 "against the background of a very public intellectual confrontation between Foucault and Sartre," in direct opposition to Sartre's *Search for a Method* (*Question de méthode*) of 1967, and not just in the wake of the structuralist fashion (Paras, *Foucault 2.0*, 9).
25. Foucault, *Archaeology of Knowledge*, 129.
26. Ibid.
27. "Archive: Problematizing Global Knowledge," 591.
28. Foucault, *Archaeology of Knowledge*, 98.
29. Higgins, *Constructing the Criollo Archive*, 9.
30. Foucault, *Archaeology of Knowledge*, 117.
31. Ibid., 130, 129.
32. Foucault, *The Order of Things*, xxi-xxii.
33. "Archive: Problematizing Global Knowledge," 596.
34. Paras, *Foucault 2.0*, 35.
35. Foucault, *The Archaeology of Knowledge*, 129.
36. Dopico Black, "Canons Afire," 96.
37. Van Zyl, "Psychoanalysis and the Archive," 39.
38. Ibid.
39. Derrida, *Archive Fever*, 34. This work was published in French in 1995, and subsequently published in English in 1996 in *Diacritics* as well as in a separate monograph that year.
40. Ibid., 1.
41. Ibid., 3.
42. Derrida, "Archive Fever," 42.
43. Ibid., 11.
44. Ibid., 26.
45. The literary result of this trope is to create a *mise-en-abyme* effect for the reader. Freud, it would seem, prefigures Yerushalmi, who, in turn, prefigures Derrida. I wish to invoke Erich Auerbach's notion of *figura*, as well as Harold Bloom's notion of the anxiety of influence. Derrida is not just positioning himself as the inheritor or recipient of this theoretical and ethno-religious legacy, which he interprets through inverse diachrony—in the present through the linking of signifiers and signifides back through time, but also as the modern victor in the causal teleology of ideas. Derrida also feels anxiety of influence, which Yerushalmi, previously, feels in regard to Freud.
46. "Archive: Problematizing Global Knowledge," 596.
47. Derrida, *Archive Fever*, 4–5.
48. Harris, "Shaft of Darkness," 65.
49. Ibid.
50. Ibid.
51. White, "Archive Power," 167.
52. Derrida, *Archive Fever*, 11–12.
53. Ibid., 11.
54. Harris, "Shaft of Darkness," 69.
55. Rapaport, *Later Derrida*, 77.
56. Derrida, *Archive Fever*, 68.
57. Derrida, "Archive Fever," 44.

58. Derrida, *Archive Fever,* 11.
59. Ibid., 17.
60. Harris, "Shaft of Darkness," 65.
61. Derrida, *Archive Fever,* 68.
62. Ibid., 100.
63. Ibid.
64. Harris, "Shaft of Darkness," 75.
65. Derrida, *Memoirs of the Blind,* 19–20. The French edition of the text (*Mémoires d'aveugle: L'autoportrait et autres ruines*) was first published on the occasion of an exhibition of the same name held in the Napoleon Hall at the Louvre Museum, from October 26, 1990 to January 21, 1991. Derrida himself organized the exhibition as the first in a new series entitled *Parti Pris*—or "Taking Sides." The exhibition became a book, first published in English in 1993, with a fuller text and a wider selection of drawings.
66. *The Compact Oxford English Dictionary, Second Edition,* s.v. "Ignore."
67. Unruh, "Review of *Myth and Archive,*" 77.
68. The three major Spanish archives are El Archivo General de Simancas, in Valladolid; the Escorial, just outside of Madrid; and El Archivo General de Indias, in Seville. The archives at Simancas were begun by Charles V, but finished by Philip II. They are considered the first and vastest European storehouses. A more detailed discussion of these will be given further along in this chapter.
69. The kingdoms of Castile and Aragon (Christian kingdoms of "reconquered" Spain) were united in 1479 after the marriage of Ferdinand II of Aragon and Isabella I of Castile in 1469.
70. It should be noted, however, that Corominas's entry for *archivo* in his 1980 edition of *Diccionario crítico etimológico castellano e hispánico* dates the earliest documented entry of the word to 1560 and not to 1490, the date given for the first appearance of the word in the Spanish language by González Echevarría, who refers to Corominas's 1961 edition of *Breve diccionario etimológico de la lengua castellana* in a footnote to document his reference to the 1490 date. The 1980 text says, "ARCHIVO, tomado del lat. tardío *archīvum* y éste del gr. ἀρχεῖμον 'residencia de los magistrados'. . . .*1.ª doc.:* h. 1560 (P. Las Casas)" (Corominas, *Diccionario crítico,* 317).
71. González Echevarría's *Myth and Archive* describes the *relación,* a type of legal deposition, which provides the formulaic basis for addressing power in colonial Spanish America.
72. As quoted in González Echevarría, *Myth and Archive,* 30.
73. See Elliott, *Imperial Spain, 1469–1716* and *Spain and its World, 1500–1700.*
74. El Archivo General de la Corona de Aragón traces its origins to 1318, but both the edifice that housed it and its "national" pretensions were much less grand and transcendental than those of the Habsburg archives.
75. González Echevarría, *Myth and Archive,* 29.
76. As quoted in González Echevarría, *Myth and Archive,* 30.
77. González Echevarría, *Myth and Archive,* 191.
78. Arrom, *Esquema generacional,* 31.
79. Ibid., 233.
80. González Echevarría, *Myth and Archive,* ix.
81. The term "Latin" America, as opposed to "Spanish" America, is obviously a nineteenth-century coinage, which owes much to a Napoleonic desire to mark the American hemisphere. I use it here (especially when referring to *Myth and Archive*),

however, anachronistically to mean the colonies and possessions of Spain since 1492. In González Echevarría's text, the term Latin America also encompasses Brazil.

82. González Echevarría, *Voice of the Masters*, 10.
83. It also reminds us of Felipe Montero's true professional passion in Carlos Fuentes's *Aura*—to write the text that would bridge transatlantic Hispanisms and encompass all of history.
84. González Echevarría, *Myth and Archive*, 186.
85. Ibid.
86. Higgins, *Constructing the Criollo Archive*, 10.
87. Foucault, *Order of Things*, 308–10 (emphasis in the original).
88. Paras, *Foucault 2.0*, 25 (emphasis in the original).
89. Guillory, *Cultural Capital*, ix.
90. Ibid. (emphasis in the original).
91. Ibid., ix.
92. Ibid., 30.
93. Grafton, "Future Reading," 50.
94. Kelly, "Scan This Book!", 4.
95. Grafton, "Future Reading," 54.
96. Ibid.
97. Manoff, "Theories of the Archive," 12.
98. Adorno, "The Archive and the Internet," 1.
99. Manoff, "Theories of the Archive," 15.
100. Sarduy uses this image to "envision the blending of oppositions in Latin American Orientalism" (Kushigian, "Ríos en la noche," 776).

Chapter 3. El "doble irrisorio"

1. Foucault, *Archaeology of Knowledge*, 129.
2. Higgins, *Constructing the Criollo Archive*, 10.
3. González Echevarría, *Myth and Archive*, 44.
4. Gerard Genette refers to the paratext as the thresholds we must cross before we encounter the text itself. Edward Bishop, like Genette, says these mediating thresholds—"dust jackets . . . bookstores, and . . . page design"—mediate our experience of the text (Bishop, "Archives and Readers," 52).
5. Higgins, *Constructing the Criollo Archive*, 10.
6. García Canclini, *Culturas híbridas*, 187.
7. Ibid.
8. Ibid., 185.
9. Ibid., 184.
10. Triviños, "La destrucción del verosímil folletinesco," 125.
11. Zamora, "Language and Authority," 229.
12. Ibid., 228.
13. Tittler, *Manuel Puig*, 67–68.
14. Featherstone, "Archive: Problematizing Global Knowledge," 594.
15. Bishop, "Archives and Readers," 52.
16. Ibid.
17. Bishop, "Archives and Readers," 53.
18. Ibid.

19. Quoted in Bishop, "Archives and Readers," 53.
20. Derrida, *Archive Fever*, 7.
21. Santos, *Kitsch Tropical*, 36.
22. Ibid., 34n3.
23. Ibid., 39.
24. Tittler, "Order, Chaos, and Re-order," 188.
25. In the main, the two types of rereadings of the serial novel have been the feminist one and the sociological one; see, for example, Catherine Jagoe and Brigitte Magnien. Both of these positions hold that novels, as opposed to serials, were not always the appropriate or desired vehicle, given certain specific political or social contexts, for a given readership. These schools of thought, as it were, differentiate between the exterior form and marketing of the novel, and its rhetorical and discursive resources, showing these latter two to hew closely to Bakhtinian stylistic definitions of the genre of the novel—heteroglossia, dialogization, and so forth. As a result, serial fiction, these schools of thought hold, stood in for the novel in certain situations and times, and for certain readers.
26. See Herrero-Olaizola's *The Censorship Files*, especially chapter 5, "Betrayed by Censorship: Manuel Puig Declassified," for a well-documented yet concise analysis of Puig and the Boom. Literary Critics such as Carlos Barral posed exceptional impediments to Puig's success during those years.
27. Among the Boom writers who embed the trope of the archive at the heart of their novels are Gabriel García Márquez, Alejo Carpentier, Carlos Fuentes, and Augusto Roa Bastos. In *Cien años de soledad*, for example, Melquíades's room holds the parchment in which he has encoded the history of Macondo from its beginnings. Fuentes's *Terra Nostra* harkens back to Charles V, Phillip II, and their creation of the Archive at Simancas and the Escorial. In *Los pasos perdidos*, Carpentier returns to the heart of the Latin American jungle, only to find the foundational colonial city of Santa Mónica de los Venados, the archival city, deserted and empty of its manuscripts. Carpentier's protagonist must write his own documents there, in the jungle, in a gesture that inaugurates Latin American narrative once more. Finally, Roa Bastos's *Yo, el supremo* is full of postindependence archives.
28. González Echevarría, *Myth and Archive*, 8.
29. Ibid., 4.
30. González Echevarría, *Myth and Archive*, 22. See footnote 10 in Chapter 2 for the definition of the *relación*.
31. Lindstrom, *Twentieth-Century Spanish American Fiction*, 197.
32. Ibid.
33. González Echevarría, *Myth and Archive*, ix.
34. Ibid., jacket cover.
35. Unruh, "Review of *Myth and Archive*," 76.
36. González Echevarría, "Archival Fictions," 185.
37. Ibid., 184.
38. Kerr, *Suspended Fictions*, 4.
39. Ibid., 10.
40. Alicia Borinsky's *Ver/ser visto* concerns this issue of control.
41. Sarduy, "Notas a las Notas a la Notas," 556.
42. Puig takes his title, "Boquitas pintadas," from an Alfredo Le Pera song, although not from one of his tangos, a fox-trot sung by Carlos Gardel in the movie *El tango en Broadway*.
43. McCracken, "Manuel Puig's *Heartbreak Tango*," 28.
44. Bacarisse, *Impossible Choices*, 2.

45. Sarduy, "Notas a las Notas a las Notas," 555.
46. Tittler, "Order, Chaos, and Re-order," 27.
47. Puig, *Boquitas pintadas: Folletín*, 9 (hereafter cited in text).
48. Well, obviously Puig is ironic here, for it is he, a man in real life, who is simulating the voices of women.
49. Colmeiro, "Lenguajes propios y lenguajes apropiados," 165.
50. Frost, "From Screen to Page."
51. Rodríguez Monegal, "El folletín rescatado," 29.
52. Puig, *Buenos Aires Affair*, 106 (hereafter cited in text).
53. Santos, *Kitsch Tropical*, 105. The author looks at the influences of French philosopher Edmond Goblot (1858–1935) and his study of distinction as the key component of middle-class mentality on Bourdieu's work. Santos's study is anchored to the concept of kitsch and is not applied to *The Buenos Aires Affair*.
54. Bourdieu, *Distinction*, 95–96.
55. Ibid., 41.
56. Santos, *Kitsch Tropical*, 105.
57. Alter, "Argentine Tour de Force."
58. Tittler, *Manuel Puig*, 41.
59. Ibid., 41.
60. "Argentine Tour de Force."
61. Colmeiro, "Lenguajes propios y lenguajes apropiados," 181.
62. Ibid., 170–71.
63. Todorov points to three basic paradigms of detective novel in "Typologie du roman policier": the "roman à énigme" (whodunit), the "roman noir" (thriller), and a third, historically intermediary and of the same period as the thriller, which "combines the properties" of the two previous forms (55–64). Puig's *Buenos Aires Affair* does not adhere to any of these plot conventions, although he does employ some of their recognizable elements.
64. Colmeiro, "Lenguajes propios y lenguajes apropiados," 186.

Chapter 4. The Patriarch Betrayed

1. Foster, *Alternative Voices*, xv. Manuel Puig is certainly not the first Latin American author to pay attention to subordinate groups. After all, two major subgenres of the Latin American novel are the Caribbean slave narrative of the nineteenth century and works of the Mexican Revolution in the early twentieth century.
2. Richard, "Postmodernism and Periphery," 6.
3. Bourdieu, *Distinction*, 69.
4. Ibid., 231.
5. Swartz, *Culture and Power*, 122.
6. Santos, *Kitsch Tropical*, 12.
7. Sapir, *Culture, Language, and Personality*, 90.
8. See Josefina Ludmer's *El género gauchesco: Un tratado sobre la patria* for the landmark study of this tradition. A translation by Molly Weigel, *Gaucho Genre: A Treatise on the Motherland*, was published in 2002 by Duke University Press.
9. This tradition of the captive in Argentine literature dates back to the sixteenth century, but is especially rich in the nineteenth century. See my "Cuerpos y voces de cautivos: Los espacios discursivos en un *corpus* argentino" for a study of the latter period.

10. Lindstrom, *Twentieth-Century Spanish American Fiction*, 143.
11. González Echevarría, *Celestina's Brood*, 221–22.
12. Ibid., 222.
13. Some critics have argued that the post-Boom is a periodization that satisfies our desire for symmetry. Just as there is "postmodernism" to "modernism," there might be a post-Boom to a Boom. González Echevarría makes this point in his *La ruta de Severo Sarduy* when he warns that the post-Boom does not necessarily correspond to the postmodern nor the Boom to the modern. Nonetheless, this concept of the post-Boom gained traction in the 1970s and 80s, when the writers themselves, such as Sarduy in his *Escrito sobre un cuerpo*, defined their own works that way.
14. Gilligan noticed that researchers were drawing conclusions about girls from studies of boys. In 1975 she published a paper, "In a Different Voice," that grew into the landmark book.
15. Gilligan's work leads to greater emphasis on context and on relationships and to less emphasis on individual independence and autonomy, as women would provide an alternative morality that would emphasize long-term relationships and mediation over disputes.
16. Gilligan, *In a Different Voice*, 33.
17. Ibid., 173–74.
18. Foster, *Alternative Voices in the Contemporary Latin American Narrative*, 82.
19. Puig, *La traición de Rita Hayworth*, 9 (hereafter cited in text).
20. Tittler, *Manuel Puig*, 22.
21. Santos, *Kitsch Tropical*, 15.
22. Ibid., 15n11.
23. Anderson, *Imagined Communities*, 14.
24. I rely on Sir Richard Burton's 1978 variant and translation of this collection of stories.
25. Foucault's notion of heterotopia first appears in a lecture he gave in March 1967, which was then published by the French journal *Architecture-Mouvement-Continuité* in 1984 under the title "Des Espaces Autres," and translated into English in *Diacritics* in 1986.
26. Foucault, "Of Other Spaces," 24.
27. Ibid.
28. Ibid., 25.
29. Ibid., 26.
30. Ibid.
31. Dopico Black, "Canons Afire," 106.
32. Ibid., 103.
33. Ibid., 108.
34. Ibid., 105.
35. As quoted in Dopico Black, "Canons Afire," 105.
36. Ibid.
37. Ibid., 109.
38. Cervantes, *Don Quijote de la Mancha*, I.129.
39. Speranza, *Manuel Puig: Después del fin de la literatura*, 105; emphasis in the original.
40. Ibid., 105.
41. Bacarisse, *Impossible Choices*, 149.
42. González Echevarría, *Love and the Law in Cervantes*, 231.
43. Ibid.
44. Thiebaut, "*El beso de la mujer araña*: Novela comprometida."

45. Puig, *El beso de la mujer araña*, 22 (hereafter cited in text).
46. Cervantes, *Novelas ejemplares II*, 563.
47. Thiebaut, "*El beso de la mujer araña:* Novela comprometida."
48. There are nine unnumbered footnotes, which are connected to the rest of the text in chapters III–XI via asterisks.
49. Kerr, *Suspended Fictions*, 186.
50. Ibid.
51. We will remember a similar authorial voice coming through in Borges's footnotes in his "La biblioteca de Babel."
52. Thiebaut, "*El beso de la mujer araña:* Novela comprometida" (emphasis, boldface in the original).
53. Kerr, *Suspended Fictions*, 192.
54. Lidia Santos studies the substantive genesis of popular culture in Latin American art in her *Kitsch Tropical*. She states that popular culture entered it through political art, but that Puig used literature to supplant art's role as the denouncer of national truths.
55. Santos, *Kitsch Tropical*, 201.

Chapter 5. *Monstrorum Artifex*

1. González Echevarría, *Myth and Archive*, 8 (emphasis mine).
2. The possessors of the phallus (a symbol of the penis or of power conceived in its stereotypically male forms, or, for Jacques Lacan, a signifier that evokes that which would overcome the "lack" felt by human subjects) and the logos (identity *qua* discourse, language, and logical argument) privilege phallogocentrism. This latter term, coined by Jacques Derrida, denotes the privilege accorded to the phallus as a mark of presence; phallogocentrism "indicates a certain sexual scene behind or before—but always within—the scene of philosophy" (Kamuf, *Derrida Reader*, 313).
3. The implications of this suggestion go beyond literary studies to the realm of identity politics, where two often-debated strategies for enfranchisement are assimilation versus the celebration of differences.
4. Franco, *Plotting Women*, xxiii.
5. In his first novel, *Gestos* (1963), Sarduy exhibits a technique somewhat different from that in his next two novels: this early technique is [a combination of the objectivist technique of the *nouveau roman* and of the committed novel] (Pellón, "Juan Goytisolo y Severo Sarduy," 486–87).
6. González Echevarría, *La ruta de Severo Sarduy*, 252 (emphasis in the original).
7. González Echevarría, *Relecturas*, 121.
8. González Echevarría relates Lezama and Vitier to Sarduy in his *La ruta de Severo Sarduy*.
9. Montero, "Modernismo and Homophobia," 114. In this essay, Montero discusses the various portrayals of homosexuality, especially in Modernismo but also throughout the twentieth century. Montero asserts that the parceling of the homosexual body was "incorporated into the legacy of *modernismo*, whose aesthetic sublime is at once erotic and homophobic."
10. Ibid.
11. Balderston, *Sex and Sexuality in Latin America*, 1.
12. Mañach, *Indagación del choteo*, 32.
13. Sarduy, *La simulación*, 11.

14. José Lezama Lima, cofounder of *Orígenes* in 1944, shares with Cintio Vitier a desire to examine Cuban culture through its literature while simultaneously making that literature and literary history the Cuban culture itself. It was Vitier who proclaimed Lezama as heralding the "beginning of a new poetic discourse," with a sense of impulse (González Echevarría and Pupo Walker, *Cambridge History of Lain American Literature*, 342). A distillation of Lezama's critical method is found in his essays *La expresión americana* (1957) and *Las eras imaginarias* (1971), while the apotheosis of this same method is his magnum opus, *Paradiso* (1966).

15. The opening of a gnostic space is itself an image that Lezama uses that is akin to the analogy or metaphor. We see Lezama's illustration of the gnostic space when José Cemí in *Paradiso* ponders two proximate objects. He realizes that their interstice can be perceived as a third object. The apparition of the third object is dependent on contact between the first two, for the silhouette of the third object manifests itself only then. Lezama's idea of the gnostic space provides an implicit ontological comment. In its search for the answer to the question of "being," Western philosophy (Western metaphysics, that is) has determined "being" as "presence." Lezama's gnostic space is just that—a space, or nonbeing that, however, manifests an object. Or, at least the gnostic space manifests the perception of an object. Lezama seems to say that the manifestation of this third object is as significant as the manifestation of the first two. The perception of the first two objects, Lezama might concur, is always already a representation, and no more "being" than the third object. In Lezama's poetic theory, the first two objects may represent one type of linguistic sign, but the third object, although an "image," only represents a different type of linguistic sign. The two types, however, are each still signs, and therefore fungible, in his poetic economy. Lezama's poetic elaborations in *Paradiso* manifest a gnostic space, or a missing center, in the traditional family unit if not in genealogy itself.

16. Sarduy, "*Boquitas pintadas*," 63.
17. Ibid., 68.
18. Ibid.
19. Cabanillas, *Escrito sobre Severo*, 11.
20. Sarduy, "*Boquitas pintadas*," 69.
21. Ibid.
22. Ibid. In *Escrito sobre un cuerpo,* Sarduy diagrams an example of this process of achieving Cuban reality as:

[immediate reality]		[cultural reference]	
	[AS]		
[Cuban character]	→	[Assyrian hunger king, Chinese emperor, Etruscan liver, etc.].	= [Cubanness as super-position]

23. Sarduy, "*Boquitas pintadas*," 69.
24. Ibid.
25. Ibid., 70 (emphasis in the original).
26. Ibid.
27. Ibid.
28. Ibid., 77.
29. Ibid., 103.
30. Sarduy, *La simulación*, 13.

31. Ibid.
32. Ibid.
33. Ibid.
34. For landmark works in these areas of inquiry see Judith Butler's *Gender Trouble* and *Bodies that Matter;* Marjorie Garber's *Vested Interests;* Eve Kosofsky Sedgwick's *Epistemology of the Closet* and *Between Men; The Cultural Studies Reader* edited by Simon During; and *The Lesbian and Gay Studies Reader,* edited by Abelove, Barrale, and Halperin.
35. See Doris Sommer's *Foundational Fictions* and Roberto González Echevarría's *The Voice of the Masters* on the transposition of the family romance to the national romance and on patriarchal discourse, respectively.
36. Ortega, "De donde son los cantantes," 193. For other major critics, *De donde son los cantantes* establishes Sarduy's mature work: Roberto González Echevarría considers it a mock epic of the search for origins; Ana María Barrenechea sees it as a depiction of the constant death and rebirth of language, a combat between the linguistic sign and its referent that results in the ultimate destruction of the latter; Enrico Mario Santí questions the novel's radicalism and suggests that the very act of denying Cuban specificity through parody may be the most peculiarly Cuban gesture of all.
37. Sarduy, *De donde son los cantantes,* 235 (hereafter cited in text).
38. Sarduy, "Página para Lezama," 467. This fragment of the quotation comes from a very short letter from 1973 that Sarduy wrote to Lezama, whose presence was being solicited in Paris for the debut of the French translation of *Paradiso.* The rest of the line reads "Inscribo, en esta patria que es la página, en minúsculas y sobre una cifra, mi paso por la Era Lezama" [I inscribe, on this homeland that is the page, in lower-case letters and through code, my passage through the Lezama Era].
39. Ana María Barrenechea comments in her "Severo Sarduy o la aventura textual" that language is the main protagonist of *De donde son los cantantes.*
40. Sarduy's essay *Barroco* (1974) contains entries, "Big Bang," and "Steady State," which detail these two opposing cosmological theories, on which he bases his writing.
41. Cabanillas, *Escrito sobre Severo,* 45.
42. Ibid., 36.
43. González Echevarría takes the approach that *De donde* is "underwritten" as a reply to Vitier and Lezama in his *La ruta de Severo Sarduy.*
44. Menéndez Rodena expands the notion of "unstable identities" and of Cuba as cultural amalgam in her *Severo Sarduy: El neobarroco de la transgresión.*
45. Several critics have questioned Sarduy's representation of Chinese Cubans, but a recent and apposite source on the "coolie narrative" in Cuba, in general, is Lisa Yun's *The Coolie Speaks.*
46. See Gustavo Pérez Firmat's *The Cuban Condition: Translation and Identity in Modern Cuba,* 24–28, for the term *ajiaco:* a combination of "the African name of an Amerindian condiment, the *ají* or green pepper, with a Spanish suffix *-aco.*"
47. This idea of projecting an "Other" is further elaborated in Edward Said's seminal *Orientalism.*
48. Cabanillas discusses the notion of performance in his *Escrito sobre Severo.*
49. Justo C. Ulloa's important essay, "Contenido y forma yoruba en 'La Dolores Rondón' de Severo Sarduy," discusses the use of dialogue as a specifically African cultural form.
50. In the editor's note to his Cátedra edition of *De donde son los cantantes,* Roberto González Echevarría traces Dolores Rondón's cultural ancestry to the antislavery

sentiments of nineteenth-century Cuba, as concentrated in Cirilo Villaverde's 1880 *Cecilia Valdés* and other works by members of the so-called *círculo delmontino*.

51. The author González Echevarría, *De donde son los cantantes*, ed. nt. 13, 57–58, also refers his reader to William Luis's "La novela antiesclavista: Texto, contexto y escritura," 103–16, for the relationship between the antislavery novel and the origins of Cuban literature. See also Salvador Bueno's *Las ideas literarias de Domingo Del Monte* and Jill Netchinsky's "Engendering a Cuban Literature."

52. Kutzinski, *Sugar's Secrets*, 19. Along with Vera Kutzinski, William Luis argues that neither the short story "Cecilia Valdés" nor the first part of the novel by the same name (both published in 1839) can be called antislavery, in his *Literary Bondage: Slavery in Cuban Narrative;* and Jill Netchinsky argues that Villaverde's text lacks "the immediacy of . . . poetic identification," in her study, "Engendering a Cuban Literature," 17.

53. The term is obviously derived from González Echevarría's *The Voice of the Masters*.

54. See Riobó's "The Medieval Inheritance of Manuel Puig and Severo Sarduy."

55. An interesting way of referring to Sarduy's use of religion is contained in the title of Rolando Pérez's book, *Severo Sarduy and the Religion of the Text*.

56. The newly consolidated Christian Spanish kingdom officially expelled Jews in 1492 and Spaniards of Arab origins by the early seventeenth century in an effort to "cleanse" itself of any Semitic, non-Christian "stain." This obsession with *limpieza de sangre* ultimately proves academic, since the Arabs and Jews had become inseparable components of the Spanish culture after many hundreds of years of living on the Peninsula. See Riobó's "The Medieval Inheritance."

57. We will recall that in Calderón's *La vida es sueño*, Rosaura is depicted as a monster primarily because she is simultaneously man and woman—masculine in her attire as the play opens, and in her thirst for revenge, which she plans to carry out herself. She describes herself as "monstruo de una especie y otra, / entre galas de mujer / armas de varón me adornan [monster of both genders, / in women's garb / man's arms adorn me]" (III, 2725–27).

58. According to González Echevarría, "The Latin Americans were able to focus on the bizarre elements of baroque aesthetics and discover in them a source as well as a tradition. . . . Monstrosity appears in the baroque . . . as the image of the self . . . that includes the sense of belatedness inherent in Latin American literature" (*Celestina's Brood*, 5). See this work for an in-depth study of *La Celestina* and the continuities of the Baroque, as well as a consideration of these subjects in Sarduy.

59. Lezama does not believe that the origin of that which is American can be found in the indigenous cultures or in simple forms from Renaissance Spain.

60. Carpentier, "El barroco y lo real maravilloso," 207.

61. Borges, *Historia universal de la infamia*, 9.

62. Olalquiaga, "Dark Side of Modernity's Moon," 25.

63. Fossey, "Severo Sarduy," 16.

64. Sarduy, *Barroco*, 19.

65. Kushigian, *Orientalism in the Hispanic Literary Tradition*, 73.

66. Fernández Moreno, *América Latina en su Literatura*, 168.

67. Ibid.

68. Sarduy, *El barroco y el neobarroco*, 1385.

69. Chartier, *The Order of Books*, vii.

70. Molloy, *Signs of Borges*, 121.

71. As quoted in Smith, *The Body Hispanic*, 105.

72. Ibid.

73. Molloy, *Signs of Borges*, 85.
74. González Echevarría, *Myth and Archive*, 165.
75. Molloy, *Signs of Borges*, 124.
76. García Canclini, *Hybrid Cultures*, 15.
77. Ibid., 15–16.
78. Dwivedi, *Museums and Museology*, 4.
79. Ibid., 7.
80. See also "Rewriting the Museum's Fictions" by Sharon MacDonald and Roger Silverstone, "Telling, Showing Off" by Mieke Bal, "The Space of the Museum" by Eileen Hooper-Greenhill, and "On the Museum's Ruins" by Douglas Crimp.
81. Giambattista Vico's sense of the *corso e ricorso* of history is present here. Vico's *New Science* (1725) rejects eighteenth-century scientific empiricism and locates historical significance in the process of history as a whole without privileging a progressive dialectic such as Hegel's. Vico's metaphoric expression of history as a spiral encompasses the linear time of Western thought and the circular time of indigenous mythology.
82. It is not my interest here to focus in depth on transvestism, other than as a problematic metaphor for the mediation of reality. Varied studies have been done on transvestism, to which I might refer the otherwise interested reader. Among these are a few that are particularly curious: Marjorie Garber's *Vested Interests;* Benigno Sifuentes Jáuregui's "Scars of Decision"; Oscar Montero's "Lipstick Vogue: The Politics of Drag," 35–42; and Judith Butler's "Performative Acts and Gender Construction," 270–82.
83. Sarduy, *Written on a Body*, 37.
84. Butler, "Imitation and Gender Insubordination," 13–31, 21.
85. Garber, *Vested Interests*, 336.
86. Ibid., 19.
87. Sarduy, *La Simulación*, 65. This simplistic discussion, of course, obviates the all-important mind-body divide and does not consider that, in someone's mind, there is no "leaping," but a feeling of having been trapped in the wrong body.
88. As Gerald Gravette tells us, "Having spent eight weeks in search of the 'Indies' and briefly encountering . . . natives . . . , the Spanish mariners called Cuba's friendly inhabitants, 'Indians.' The first proper Indian settlement the sailors were to see after leaving the Spanish port of Palos was known locally as 'Cubanacan.' The adventurers believed this to be the site of the Japanese Emperor's court (*el gran can*) [the Great Khan], but found, to their dismay, that it was the native name for a primitive colony established at the center of the island" (*Cuba: Official Guide*, viii).
89. In an interview with Emir Rodríguez Monegal, Sarduy spoke to the force of Western fantasy about India and discussed his representation of India in *Cobra* as a strategic response to that fantasy: "*Cobra* is not about a transcendental India, profound metaphysics, but to the contrary, it is about an exaltation of the surface and I would say even of Indian kitsch. I think that the only decoding we may do as Occidentals, that the only non-neurotic reading of India that we are able to achieve stemming from our logocentrism, is the one that privileges its surface. The rest is Christianizing translation, syncretism, true superficiality."
90. Said, *Orientalism*, 207.
91. González Echevarría, *Voice of the Masters*, 14.
92. Kushigian, "La serpiente en la sinagoga" (interview with Severo Sarduy), 14–20, 20.
93. Rodríguez Monegal, "Diálogo con Severo Sarduy," 16.
94. Ibid.

95. Aguilar Mora, "Cobra, Cobra la Boca Obra, Recobra, Barroco," 26.
96. I use "fetish" here in a Freudian sense, to refer to a particular mode of psychic disavowal of what the subject knows to be true (that anatomical sexual difference exists and that men may be defined as those people who have penises and women as those who do not) by means of redirecting the gaze and the libido toward a substitute object whose function is to cover over the knowledge of "lack."
97. Aguilar Mora, "Cobra, Cobra la Boca Obra, Recobra, Barroco," 9.
98. Sarduy, *Cobra*, 12–13 (hereafter cited in text).
99. Adriana Méndez Rodenas also notes a similar tendency, in general: "*Cobra* is based on a juaxtapositioning and proliferation of meanings, which requires a 'radial reading' in order to decipher the different levels of meaning" (*Severo Sarduy*, 37). She further conveys Sarduy's explanation that "the mechanism of [the 'radial reading'] consists of 'suppressing' the signified through a series of signifiers that 'surround' it and that conjugate different-and simultaneous-levels of meaning] (*Severo Sarduy*, 37).
100. As Carole-Anne Tyler notes in "Boys Will Be Girls" (32), "Once masculinity is seen as a put-on, mere style, its phallic imposture is exposed as such and so delegitimated, according to proponents of drag."

Chapter 6. Raiding Archives

1. Sarduy, *Maitreya*, 187 (hereafter cited in text).
2. Sarduy, *Maitreya*, Eng. trans. Suzanne Jill Levine, 158 (hereafter cited in text).
3. Borges, *Selected Non-Fiction*, 216.
4. Rivero-Potter, *Autor/Lector*, 108.
5. The first three quotations in English are from Prieto, "The Ambiviolent Fiction of Severo Sarduy," 57, and the last one, quoted in the original Spanish first, is from González Echevarría, *La ruta de Severo Sarduy*, 182.
6. Winks, *Good Vibrations Guide to Sex*, 174.
7. West, "Inscribing the Body of Perfection," 115.
8. Ibid.
9. Ibid.
10. Eastern traditions, such as those of the Kamasutra and Tantrism, are known to combine pleasure in the pursuit of knowledge of the divine.
11. Foucault, "Truth and Power," 120.
12. Dipping into Sarduy's archive facilitates a more *scriptible* (writerly) text, promising Barthesian bliss.
13. García Márquez, *Cien años de soledad*, 553 (hereafter cited in text).
14. In his article, "The Ambiviolent Fiction of Severo Sarduy," René Prieto sees the birth of Lady Tremendous's son in *Maitreya* as symbolic of the birth of the last historical Buddha, who also did not have a conventional birth. Prieto offers little in the way of textual or other evidence, however, except that Maitreya is said to have been born from someone's flank. Prieto equates this birth with the caudal son's unusual birth. The parallel is obviously interesting, despite the thin and stretched textual evidence for it.
15. Peter Hallward also quotes these parts of Sarduy's *Maitreya* in his plot summary of this part of the novel (*Absolutely Postcolonial*, 295).
16. Prieto, "The Ambiviolent Fiction of Severo Sarduy," 58.

17. Sarduy, *De donde son los cantantes*, 94n11.
18. Said, *Orientalism*, 73.
19. Machover, *La memoria frente al poder*, 83.
20. The obvious difference, of course, is that the former is the result of an exogenous force—an invasion—while the Cuban revolution is from within.
21. Several scholars, González Echevarría first among them, have identified the *novela de la selva* as the source of Sarduy's sendup in *Colibrí*. However, it will be patently obvious, that this is the case—as Sarduy intended it to be, to anyone familiar with the Latin American literary tradition who gives *Colibrí* even the most cursory reading. Similarly, the accession of Colibrí as the new caudillo at the end of the eponymous novel, also identified by several scholars, including González Echevarría, is a transparent twist of Sarduy's at the end of the novel.
22. Roberto Echavarren asserts, "*Colibrí* is a dictator novel," in general, like *Tirano Banderas, Otoño del patriarca,* and *Yo el supremo* (*Margen de ficción*, 132).
23. Sarduy, *Colibrí*, 13 (hereafter cited in text).
24. "Engrifarse," the reflexive form of Sarduy's verb here, means in Spanish to drug oneself or to take drugs. Sarduy takes advantage of this pun, as many of the characters in la Casona will often be in a drug-induced stupor.
25. See Easby's work on Costa Rican jade for a more detailed explanation of the etymology and historicocultural significance of the term "jade."
26. The *Excélsior* is Mexico's second oldest newspaper (after *El Universal*) and was first published in 1917. In 1938, the paper's ownership was turned over to its staff of reporters and employees, who formed a cooperative, until it was sold in 2005 to a private concern.
27. Rivero-Potter, *Autor, Narrador y Lector en Severo Sarduy*, 236.
28. González Echevarría, *La ruta de Severo Sarduy*, 227.
29. Rivera, *La vorágine*, 181 (hereafter cited in text).
30. As I describe at the beginning of this chapter, González Echevarría asserts this in his discussion of *Colibrí* in his *La ruta de Severo Sarduy*. This notion of the modern aspect of the telluric novel, *la novela de la tierra*, is Alonso's central idea—his thesis—in his *Spanish American Regional Novel: Modernity and Autochthony*.
31. See footnote 22, above.
32. Machover, *La memoria frente al poder*, 97.

Bibliography

Abelove, Henry, Michele Aina Barale, and David M. Halperin, eds. *The Lesbian and Gay Studies Reader.* New York: Routledge, 1993.

Adorno, Rolena. "The Archive and the Internet." *The Americas* 61, no.1 (2004): 1–18.

Agamben, Giorgio. *Stanzas: Word and Phantasm in Western Culture.* Translated by Ronald L. Martinez. Minneapolis: University of Minnesota Press, 1993.

Aguilar Mora, Jorge. "Cobra, Cobra la Boca Obra, Recobra, Barroco." In *Severo Sarduy*, edited by Jorge Aguilar Mora, 25–33. Madrid: Editorial Fundamentos, 1976.

Alonso, Carlos J. *The Burden of Modernity: The Rhetoric of Cultural Discourse in Spanish America.* New York: Oxford University Press, 1998.

———. *The Spanish American Regional Novel: Modernity and Autochthony.* New York: Cambridge University Press, 1990.

Alonso, Dámaso. "Poesía arábigoandaluza y poesía gongorina." In *Estudios y ensayos gongorinos*. 1955. Reprint, Madrid: Editorial Gredos, 1960, 31–65.

Alpízar, Luis. "La clasificación y catalogación en el Archivo Nacional." In *Revista de la Biblioteca Nacional José Martí* 23, no. 1 (1981): 35–43.

Alter, Daniel Stuart. "Confronting the Queer and Present Danger: How to Use the First Amendment when Dealing with Issues of Sexual Orientation Speech and Military Service." *Human Rights* 22, no. 3 (1995): 22–27, 32.

Alter, Robert. "An Argentine Tour de Force." *New York Times on the Web* September 5, 1976. <http://www.nytimes.com/books/00/08/13/specials/puig-buenos.html>.

Althusser, Louis. "Ideology and Ideological State Apparatuses." In *Lenin and Philosophy and Other Essays.* Translated by Ben Brewster. New York: Monthly Review Press, 1971, 127–86.

Anderson, Benedict. *Imagined Communities: Reflections on the Origins and Spread of Nationalism.* New York: Verso, 1991.

Anderson, Perry. "Nation-States and National Identity." *London Review of Books.* May 9, 1991.

Andreu, Alicia G. "El folletín: De Galdós a Manuel Puig." *Revista Iberoamericana*, 49, nos. 123–24 (1983): 541–46.

Arac, Jonathan, ed. and intro. *Postmodernism and Politics: Theory and History of Literature*, vol. 28. Minneapolis: University of Minnesota Press, 1986.

Aristotle. *On Poetry and Style.* Translated by G. M. A. Grube. Indianapolis, IN: Bobbs-Merrill, 1958.

Arjona, Marta. *Patrimonio cultural e identidad*. Havana: Editorial Letras Cubanas, 1986.

Arnold, Matthew. *Culture and Anarchy*. 1869. Reprint. New Haven, CT: Yale University Press, 1994.

Arrom, José Juan. *Esquema generacional de las letras hispanoamericanas: Ensayo de un método*, 2nd ed. Bogotá: Instituto Caro y Cuervo, 1977.

———. *Imaginación del Nuevo Mundo: Diez estudios sobre los inicios de la narrativa hispanoamericana*. Mexico City: Siglo Veintiuno Editores, 1991.

Auerbach, Erich. *Mimesis: The Representation of Reality in Western Literature*. Translated by Willard R. Trask. Princeton, NJ: Princeton University Press, 1953.

Bacarisse, Pamela. *Impossible Choices*. Calgary, CA: University of Calgary Press, 1993.

Bakhtin, Mikhail. *The Dialogic Imagination: Four Essays*. Translated by Caryl Emerson and Michael Holquist. Edited by Michael Holquist. Austin: University of Texas Press, 1981.

———. *Rabelais and His World*. Translated by Hélène Isowolsky. Bloomington: Indiana University Press, 1984.

Bal, Mieke. "Telling, Showing, Showing Off." *Critical Inquiry* 18 (1992): 556–94.

Balderston, Daniel, and Donna J. Guy, eds. *Sex and Sexuality in Latin America*. New York: New York University Press, 1997.

Bareiro Saguier, Rubén. *Literatura guaraní del Paraguay*, no. 70. Caracas, Ven.: Biblioteca Ayacucho, 1980.

Barrenechea, Ana María. "Severo Sarduy o la aventura textual." In *Textos hispanoamericanos: de Sarmiento a Sarduy*, 221–34. Caracas, Ven: Editorial Monte Ávila, 1978.

Barrett, Michele. *Women's Oppression Today: Problems in Marxist Feminist Analysis*. London: Verso, 1980.

Barthes, Roland. "An Introduction to the Structural Analysis of Narrative." Translated by Lionel Duisit. *New Literary History*, 6 (1975): 242–43.

———. *The Pleasure of the Text*. Translated by Richard Miller. New York: Farrar, Straus and Giroux, 1975.

———. "Sarduy: La Faz Barroca." In *Mundo Nuevo* (Paris) no. 14 (1967): 70–71. Caracas, Ven.: Editorial Fundamentos, Colección Espiral, 1976.

Bazin, German. *The Museum Age*. New York: Universe Books, 1967.

Beauvoir, Simone de. *Le Deuxième Sexe*. New York: Random House, 1952.

Bejel, Emilio. *Escribir en Cuba: Entrevistas con escritores cubanos, 1979–1989*. Río Piedras: Editorial de la Universidad de Puerto Rico, 1991.

Benda, Julien. *The Treason of the Intellectuals*. Translated by Richard Aldington. New York: W. Morrow, 1928.

Benjamin, Walter. *Illuminations*. Translated by Harry Zohn. Edited by Hannah Arendt. New York: Schocken Books, 1968.

Bennett, Tony. "The Exhibitionary Complex." *New Formations* 4, no. 2 (1990): 176–91.

———. "The Political Rationality of the Museum." *Continuum* 3, no.1 (1990): 35–55.

Benveniste, Emile. *Problems in General Linguistics*. Translated by Mary Elizabeth Meek. Miami, FL: University of Miami Press, 1971.

Berelowitz, JoAnne. "From the Body of the Prince to Mickey Mouse." In *Oxford Art Journal* 13, no. 2 (1990): 70–84.

Beverley, John. *Subalternity and Representation: Arguments in Cultural Theory.* Durham, NC: Duke University Press, 1999.

Bhabha, Homi K., ed. *Nation and Narration.* New York: Routledge, 1990.

———. "The Other Question . . . Homi K. Bhabha Reconsiders the Stereotype and Colonial Discourse." *Screen* (1982): 18–36.

Bishop, Edward L. "Archives and Readers: From Frass to Foucault: Mediations of the Archive." In *Virginia Woolf Out of Bounds: Selected Papers from the Tenth Annual Conference on Virginia Woolf,* edited by Jessica Berman and Jane Goldman, 52–88. New York, NY: Pace University Press, 2001.

Bloom, Harold. *The Anxiety of Influence: A Theory of Poetry.* New York: Oxford University Press, 1973.

Boorman, Joan Rea. *La estructura del Narrador en la Novela Hispanoamericana Contemporánea.* New York: Hispanova de Ediciones, 1976.

Borges, Jorge Luis. "La biblioteca total." In *Literatura Argentina Contemporanea,* edited by María Kodama. Buenos Aires: Emecé, 2000.

———. "El cautivo." In *Cuentos: Antología.* Buenos Aires: Capítulo. Biblioteca argentina fundamental, 1981.

———. "Emma Zunz." In *El Aleph.* Buenos Aires: Emecé, 1990.

———. "Historia del guerrero y de la cautiva." In *El Aleph.* Buenos Aires: Emecé, 1990.

———. *Historia universal de la infamia.* Buenos Aires: Emecé, 1935.

———. "El idioma analítico de John Wilkins," 1952. In *Otras inquisiciones.* Madrid: Alianza Editorial, 1997, 154–61.

———. *Obras Completas,* edited by Sara Luisa del Carril. Vols. 1–4. 2nd ed. Buenos Aires: Emecé, 2005.

———. *Selected Non-Fiction.* Edited by Eliot Weinberger. New York: Viking Penguin, 1999.

Borinsky, Alicia. *Ver/ser visto: Notas para una analítica poética.* Barcelona: Bosch, 1978.

Bourdieu, Pierre. *Distinction: A Social Critique of the Judgement of Taste.* Translated by Richard Nice. Cambridge, MA: Harvard University Press, 1984.

Brenner, Philip, et al., eds. *The Cuba Reader: The Making of a Revolutionary Society.* New York: Grove Press, 1989.

Brooks, Peter. *Body Work: Objects of Desire in Modern Narrative.* Cambridge, MA: Harvard University Press, 1993.

Brundage, James A. *Law, Sex, and Christian Society in Medieval Europe.* Chicago, IL: University of Chicago Press, 1987.

Bueno, Salvador. *Las ideas literarias de Domingo Del Monte.* Havana: Editorial Hércules, 1954.

Burton, Sir Richard, ed. *Tales from the Arabian Nights.* New York: Crown Publishers, 1978.

Butler, Judith. *Bodies that Matter: On the Discursive Limits of "Sex."* New York: Routledge, 1993.

———. *Gender Trouble: Feminism and the Subversion of Identity.* New York: Routledge, 1990.

———. "Imitations and Gender Insubordination." In *Inside/Out:Lesbian Theories/Gay Theories,* edited by Diana Fuss, 13–31. New York: Routledge, 1991.

———. "Performative Acts and Gender Construction: An Essay in Phenomenology and Feminist Theory." In *Performing Feminisms: Feminist Critical Theory and Theater,* edited by Sue-Ellen Case, 270–82. Baltimore, MD: The Johns Hopkins University Press, 1990.

Caballero, Ronald, and José Manuel. *Narrativa cubana de la revolución.* 2nd ed. Madrid: Alianza Editorial, 1969.

Cabanillas, Francisco. *Escrito sobre Severo: Una relectura de Sarduy.* Miami, FL: Ediciones Universal, 1995.

Cabrera Infante, Guillermo. *Mea Cuba.* Translated by G. Cabrera Infante and K. Hall. New York: Farrar, Straus and Giroux, 1994.

Campos, René Alberto. *Espejos: La literatura cinemática en "La traición de Rita Hayworth."* Madrid: Editorial Pliegos, 1985.

Canepa, Gina. "Representatividad y marginalidad literarias y la historiografía de la literatura latinoamericana." In *Literaturas más allá de la marginalidad: Hacia una historia social de la literatura latinoamericana* vol. 3, edited by Thomas Bremer and Julio Peñate Rivero. Giessen and Neuchâtel: AELSAL, 1988.

Carpentier, Alejo. *El arpa y la sombra.* México: Siglo Veintiuno Editores, 1979.

———. "El barroco y lo real maravilloso." In *Tientos y diferencias,* 205–15. Montevideo: Arca, 1967.

———. *Concierto barroco.* México: Siglo Veintiuno Editores, 1974.

———. *Los pasos perdidos.* Santiago, Chile: Editorial Andrés Bello, 1953.

Carrera Pedroza, Liduvina. *Reflexiones de Lezama: Cinco ensayos de crítica literaria.* Venezuela: Fondo Editorial Toromaina, 1995.

Cedola, Estela. "La crónica de viaje y su recuperación paródica." In *Alba de América: Revista Literaria* 13, no. 24–25 (1995): 283–95.

Cervantes, Miguel de. *El ingenioso hidalgo Don Quijote de la Mancha,* I and II, 10th ed. Edited by John Jay Allen. Madrid: Ediciones Cátedra, S.A., 1988.

———. *Novelas ejemplares II,* edited by Florencio Sevilla Arroyo and Antonio Rey Hazas. Madrid: Espase Calpe, 1991.

Chartier, Roger. *The Order of Books: Readers, Authors, and Libraries in Europe between the Fourteenth and Eighteenth Centuries.* Translated by Lydia G. Cochrane. Oxford: Polity Press, 1994.

Christ, Ronald. "Fact and Fiction." *Review 73,* no. 9 (1973): 49–54.

Cixous, Hélène. "O,C,O,B,R,A,B,A,R,O,C,O,: A Text-Twister." *Review* 74 (1974): 26–31.

Colmeiro, José F. "Lenguajes propios y lenguajes apropiados en *The Buenos Aires Affair* de Manuel Puig." *Hispanic Review* 57 (1989): 165–88.

Colón, Cristóbal. *Los cuatro viajes del almirante y su testamento.* Edited by Ignacio B. Anzoátegui. Madrid: Espasa-Calpe, 1946.

Corbatta, Jorgelina. *Mito personal y mitos colectivos en las novelas de Manuel Puig.* Madrid: Editorial Orígenes, 1988.

Corominas, Joan. *Diccionario crítico etimológico castellano e hispánico,* vol. 1. Col. José A. Pascual. Madrid: Editorial Gredos, 1980.

Cortázar, Julio. *Rayuela.* Caracas: Biblioteca Ayacucho, 1980.

———. *Realidad y literatura en America Latina/Reality and Literature in Latin America.* Edited and translated by Gabriella de Beer and Raquel Chang-Rodríguez. The Jacob C. Saposnekow Memorial Lectures. The City College Papers. No. 19. April 1980.

Crimp, Douglas. "On the Museum's Ruins." In *The Anti-Aesthetic*, edited by Hal Foster, 44–64. Port Townsend, WA: Bay Press, 1983.

Curtius, Ernst Robert. *European Literature and the Latin Middle Ages*. 1948. Translated by Willard R Trask. Princeton, NJ.: Princeton University Press, 1990.

Danto, Arthur. *After the End of Art: Contemporary Art and the Pale of History*. Princeton, NJ: Princeton University Press, 1997.

Debicki, Andrew, and Enrique Pupo-Walker, eds. *Estudios de literatura Hispanoamericana en honor a José J. Arrom*. Valencia: Artes Gráficas Soler, 1974.

Deleuze, Gilles. *Nietzsche and Philosophy*. Translated by Hugh Tomlinson. New York: Columbia University Press, 1983.

Deleuze, Gilles, and Félix Guattari. *Anti-Oedipe/Anti-Oedipus: Capitalism and Schizophrenia*. Translated by Robert Hurley et al. Minneapolis: University of Minnesota Press, 1983.

de Man, Paul. *Blindness and Insight: Essay in the Rhetoric of Contemporary Criticism*. Minneapolis: University of Minnesota Press, 1983.

Derrida, Jacques. *Archive Fever: A Freudian Impression*. Translated by Eric Prenowitz. Chicago, IL: University of Chicago Press, 1996.

———. "Archive Fever: A Seminar by Jacques Derrida, University of the Witwatersrand, August 1998." Transcribed by Verne Harris. In *Refiguring the Archive*, edited by Carolyn Hamilton, et al., 38–80. Boston, MA: Kluwer Academic Publishers, 2002.

———. *Dissemination*. Translated by Barbara Johnson. Chicago, IL: University of Chicago Press, 1981.

———. *Of Grammatology*. Translated by Gayatri Chakravorty Spivak. Baltimore, MD: The Johns Hopkins University Press, 1976.

———. *Memoirs of the Blind: The Self-Portrait and Other Ruins*. Translated by Pascale-Anne Brault, and Michael Naas. Chicago, IL: University of Chicago Press, 1993.

Donoso, José. *The Boom in Spanish American Literature: A Personal History*. New York: Columbia University Press in association with the Center for Inter-American Relations, 1977.

Dopico Black, Georgina. "Canons Afire: Libraries, Books, and Bodies in *Don Quixote*'s Spain." In *Cervantes' "Don Quixote": A Casebook*, edited by Roberto González Echevarría, 95–123. New York: Oxford University Press, 2005.

Dowling, William C. *Jameson, Althusser, Marx: An Introduction to the Political Unconscious*. Ithaca, NY: Cornell University Press, 1984.

During, Simon, ed. *The Cultural Studies Reader*. New York: Routledge, 1993.

Dwivedi, V. P., ed. *Museums and Museology: New Horizons*. Delhi: Agam Kala Prakashan, 1980.

Easby, Elizabeth Kennedy. *Pre-Columbian Jade from Costa Rica*. New York: André Emmerich, Inc., 1968.

Echavarren, Roberto. "Manuel Puig: Beyond Identity." *World Literature Today* 65 (1991): 581–85.

———. *Margen de ficción: Poéticas de la narrative hispanoamericana*. Mexico City: Editorial Joaquín Mortiz, 1992.

———. "A partir de *Rita Hayworth:* Alteridad y heteroglosia." In *Manuel Puig: Montaje y alteridad del sujeto*. Santiago, Chile: Monografías del Maitén, Instituto Profesional del Pacífico, 1986, 26.

Echevarría, Israel. "José Antonio Ramos y la Biblioteca Nacional." In *Revista de la Biblioteca Nacional José Martí* 20, no. 2 (1978): 117–48.

Echevarría, Israel, y Siomara Sánchez. "Cronología histórica de la Biblioteca Nacional." In *Revista de la Biblioteca Nacional José Martí* 23, no. 2 (1981): 65–90.

Elliott, J. H. *Imperial Spain: 1469–1716.* 1963. Reprint. New York: Penguin Books, 1990.

———. *Spain and its World, 1500–1700.* New Haven, CT: Yale University Press, 1989.

El Saffar, Ruth Anthony. *Rapture Encaged: The Suppression of the Feminine in Western Culture.* New York: Routledge, 1994.

Entralgo, Pedro Laín. *El cuerpo humano: Teoría actual.* Madrid: Espasa Calpe, 1989.

Epple, Juan Armando. "Bibliografía de Manuel Puig y sobre él." *Latin American Literary Review* 14 (1979): 73–74.

———. "*The Buenos Aires Affair* y la estructura de la novela policíaca." *La palabra y el hombre* 18 (1975): 50.

Estrada, Isabel M. "*Casas Viejas: el grito del sur* (1995) de Basilio Martín Patino: memoria, televisión y documental." In *Historias de la pequeña pantalla. Representaciones históricas en la televisión de la España democrática,* edited by George Cueto López, 197–216. Madrid: Iberoamericana/Vervuert, 2009.

———. "Catalan Television Documentaries and the Negotiation of Memory in Democratic Spain: The Works of Dolors Genovès." *Catalan Review* vol. 20, nos. 1 and 2 (2006): 117–30.

———. "Transitional Masculinities in a *Labyrinth of Solitude:* Replacing Patriarchy in Spanish Film (1977–1987)." *Bulletin of Spanish Studies.* LXXXIII, no. 2 (2006): 265–80.

Featherstone, Mike. "Archive: Problematizing Global Knowledge—Library/Archive/Museum." *Theory, Culture & Society* 23, no. 2–3 (2006): 591–96.

Felman, Shoshana. *Jacques Lacan and the Adventure of Insight: Psychoanalysis in Contemporary Culture.* Cambridge, MA: Harvard University Press, 1987.

———. *Literature and Psychoanalysis, The Question of Reading: Otherwise.* Edited by Shoshana Felman. Baltimore, MD: The Johns Hopkins University Press, 1977.

Felman, Shoshana, and Dori Laub, M.D. *Testimony: Crises of Witnessing in Literature, Psychoanalysis, and History.* New York: Routledge, 1992.

Fernández Moreno, César. *América Latina en su literatura.* México: Siglo Veintiuno Editores, 1972.

Fernández Retamar, Roberto. *Calibán: Apuntes sobre la cultura en nuestra América.* México: Editoriales Diógenes, 1972.

———. *Para el perfil definitivo del hombre.* Havana: Editorial Letras Cubanas, 1981.

———. "Treinta años de la Casa de las Américas." In *Revista Canadiense de Estudios Hispánicos* 14, no. 2 (1990): 370–76.

Filer, Malva E. "La historia apócrifa en las novelas postmodernistas rioplatenses." In *Alba de América: Revista Literaria* 12, no. 22–23 (1994): 193–201.

Fossey, Jean Michel. "From Boom to Big Bang." *Review* 74 (1974): 10–77.

———. "Severo Sarduy: Máquina barroca revolucionaria." *Severo Sarduy.* Caracas, Ven: Editorial Fundamentos, 1976.

Foster, David William. *Alternative Voices in the Contemporary Latin American Narrative.* Columbia: University of Missouri Press, 1985.

———. *Gay and Lesbian Themes in Latin American Writing*. Austin: University of Texas Press, 1991.

Foster, David William, and Roberto Reis, eds. *Bodies and Biases: Sexualities in Hispanic Cultures and Literatures*. Minneapolis: University of Minnesota Press, 1996.

Foucault, Michel. *L'Archéologie du savoir*. Paris: Editions Gallimard, 1969.

———. *The Archaeology of Knowledge*. Translated by M. Sheridan Smith. New York: Pantheon, 1972.

———. *Discipline and Punish: The Birth of the Prison*. Translated by Alan Sheridan. New York: Vintage Books, 1977.

———. *Language, Counter-Memory, Practice: Selected Essays and Interviews*. Edited and with an introduction by Donald F. Bouchard. Ithaca, NY: Cornell University Press, 1977.

———*Les Mots et les Choses: Une archéologie des sciences humaines*. Paris: Editions Gallimard, 1966.

———. "Of Other Spaces." Translated by Jay Miskowiec. *Diacritics* 16, no. 1 (Spring 1986): 22–27.

———. *The Order of Things: An Archaeology of the Human Sciences*. Translated by Michel Foucault. New York: Random House, 1970.

———. "Truth and Power." *Essential Works of Michel Foucault*. Edited by James Faubion. New York: New Press, 1994, 111–33.

Franco, Jean. *Plotting Women: Gender and Representation in Mexico*. New York: Columbia University Press, 1989.

Freud, Sigmund. *Civilization and its Discontents*. Translated by James Strachey. New York: W.W. Norton, 1961.

———. *The Future of an Illusion*. Translated by W. D. Robson-Scott. New York: Liveright Publishing, 1953.

Frost, Derek T. "From Screen to Page: Manuel Puig and the Rewriting of Hollywood Cinema" (January 1, 1996). *ETD Collection for University of Connecticut*. Paper AAI9708031. http://digitalcommons.uconn.edu/dissertations/AAI9708031.

Frye, Northrop. *Anatomy of Criticism: Four Essays*. Princeton, NJ: Princeton University Press, 1990.

Fuentes, Carlos. *La muerte de Artemio Cruz*. 1962. Reprint. México: Fondo de Cultura Económica, 1973.

———. *La nueva novela hispanoamericana*. Mexico: Joaquín Mortiz, 1969.

———. *Terra Nostra*. México: Joaquín Mortiz, 1975.

Fuss, Diana. *Essentially Speaking: Feminism, Nature and Difference*. New York: Routledge, 1989.

———, ed. *Inside/Out: Lesbian Theories, Gay Theories*. New York: Routledge, 1991.

Gallegos, Rómulo. *Doña Bárbara*. Caracas, Ven: Monte Ávila, 1977.

Garber, Marjorie. *Vested Interests: Cross-Dressing and Cultural Anxiety*. New York: Routledge, 1992.

García Canclini, Néstor. *Culturas híbridas: Estrategias para entrar y salir de la modernidad*. Mexico: Grijalbo, 1990.

———. *Hybrid Cultures: Strategies for Entering and Leaving Modernity*. Translated by Christopher L. Chiappari and Silvia L. López. Minneapolis: University of Minnesota Press, 1995.

García Márquez, Gabriel. *Cien años de soledad*. 1967. Madrid: Ediciones Cátedra, 1991.

García-Ramos, Juan Manuel, ed. *Manuel Puig*. Madrid: Ediciones de Cultura Hispánica, 1991.

Genosko, Gary. *Baudrillard and Signs: Signification Ablaze*. New York: Routledge, 1994.

Gilligan, Carol. *In a Different Voice: Essays on Psychlogical Theory and Women's Development*. Cambridge, MA: Harvard University Press, 1982.

González Echevarría, Roberto. *Alejo Carpentier: The Pilgrim at Home*. Ithaca, NY: Cornell University Press, 1977.

———. "Archival Fictions: García Márquez's Bolívar File." In *Critical Theory, cultural Politics, and Latin American Narrative*, edited by Steven M. Bell, et al., 183–207. Notre Dame, IN: University of Notre Dame Press, 1993.

———. *Celestina's Brood: Continuities of the Baroque in Spanish and Latin American Literature*. Durham, NC: Duke University Press, 1993.

———. "Emir and the Canon: An Obituary Note." *Latin American Literary Review* 28 (1986): 7–10.

———. *Isla a su vuelo fugitiva*. Madrid: José Porrúa Turanzas, 1983.

———. *Love and the Law in Cervantes*. New Haven, CT: Yale University Press, 2005.

———. *Myth and Archive: A Theory of Latin American Narrative*. Cambridge, UK: Cambridge University Press, 1990.

———. "Narrative and Prophecy in the Post-Modern Novel: Sarduy's *Maitreya*." *World Affairs* 150 (1987): 147–62.

———. "Plain Song: Sarduy's *Cobra*." *Contemporary Literature* 28 (1987): 437–59.

———. *Relecturas: Estudios de literatura cubana*. Caracas, Ven: Monte Avila, 1976.

———. *La ruta de Severo Sarduy*. Hanover, NH: Ediciones del Norte, 1987.

———. *The Voice of the Masters: Writing and Authority in Modern Latin American Literature*. Austin: University of Texas Press, 1985.

———, and Enrique Pupo-Walker, eds. *The Cambridge History of Latin American Literature*. Vols. 1, 2, and 3. New York: Cambridge University Press, 1997.

Gónzalez Pérez, Aníbal. *Journalism and the Development of Spanish American Narrative*. New York: Cambridge University Press, 1993.

Gordon, Samuel, ed. *La Colección Archivos: Hacia un nuevo canon: Reseñas aparecidas en la "Revista Iberoamericana."* Pittsburgh, PA: Revista Iberoamericana Colección Archivos, (1992–93): 158–59.

Goytisolo, Juan. *Furgón de cola*. Paris: Ruedo Ibérico, 1967.

———. "On the Path to Modernity." *Times Literary Supplement*, February 28, 1992: 18.

———. "Writing in an Occupied Language." *The New York Times Book Review*, March 31, 1974, 46.

Grafton, Anthony. "Future Reading: Digitization and its Discontents." *The New Yorker*, November 5, 2007: 50–54.

———. *What Was History: The Art of History in Early Modern Europe*. New York: Cambridge University Press, 2007.

Gramsci, Antonio. *Prison Notebooks*. Edited and translated by Quintin Hoare and Geoffrey Nowell Smith. New York: International Publishers, 1987.

Gravette, A. Gerald. *Cuba: Official Guide*. New York: Macmillan Education LTD, 1990.

Green, James Ray, Jr. "*El beso de la mujer araña:* Sexual Repression and Textual Repression." In *La Chispa 1981: Selected Proceedings,* edited by Gilbert Paolini, 133–39. New Orleans, LA: Tulane University, 1981.

Greetham, David. "Who's In, Who's Out: The Cultural Politics of Archival Exclusion." *Studies in the Literary Imagination* 32, no. 1 (1999): 1–28.

Guerrero, Gustavo. *La estrategia neobarroca.* Barcelona: Ediciones Del Mall, 1987.

Guillén, Nicolás. *Antología Mayor.* 2nd ed. México: Editorial Diógenes, 1974.

Guillory, John. *Cultural Capital: The Problem of Literary Canon Formation.* Chicago, IL: University of Chicago Press, 1993.

Gumbrecht, Hans Ulrich. "'Un souffle d'Allemagne ayant passé': Friedrich Diez, Gaston Paris, and the Genesis of National Philologies." *Romance Philology* 40 (1986): 1–37.

Hall, Stuart. "Encoding, Decoding." In *The Cultural Studies Reader,* edited by Simon During, 90–103. New York: Routledge, 1993.

Hallward, Peter. *Absolutely Postcolonial: Writing Between the Singular and the Specific.* New York: Manchester University Press, 2001.

Harris, Verne. "A Shaft of Darkness: Derrida in the Archive." In *Refiguring the Archive,* edited by Carolyn Hamilton et al., 61–81. Boston: Kluwer Academic Publishers, 2002.

Hart, Jonathan. *Northrop Frye: The Theoretical Imagination.* New York: Routledge, 1994.

Heath, Stephen. *The nouveau roman: A study in the Practice of Writing.* Philadelphia PA: Temple University Press, 1972.

Hellman, Elizabeth. *When the Labyrinth Is Deciphered It Will Disappear.* New York: Serious Ink Press, 2008.

Henríquez Ureña, Pedro. *Historia de la cultura en la América hispánica.* México: Fondo de Cultura Económica, 1947.

———. *Seis ensayos en busca de nuestra expresión.* Buenos Aires: Biblioteca Argentina de buenas ediciones literarias, 1928.

Hernández Lima, Dinorah. *Versiones y re-versiones históricas en la obra de Cabrera Infante.* Madrid: Editorial Pliegos, 1990.

Herrero-Olaizola, Alejandro. *The Censorship Files: Latin American Writers and Franco's Spain.* Albany: State University of New York Press, 2007.

Higgins, Antony. *Constructing the Criollo Archive: Subjects of Knowledge in the Bibliotheca Mexicana and the Rusticatio Mexicana.* West Lafayette, IN: Purdue University Press, 2000.

Homer. *The Iliad.* Translated by Richmond Lattimore. Chicago, IL: The University of Chicago Press, 1961.

———. *The Odyssey.* Translated by Richmond Lattimore. New York: Harper & Row, 1967.

Hooper-Greenhill, Eileen. "The Space of the Museum." *Continuum* 3.1 (1990): 56–69.

Ibarra, Jorge. *Nación y cultura Nacional.* La Habana: Editorial Letras Cubanas, 1981.

Illie, Paul. *Literature and Inner Exile: Authoritarian Spain, 1939–1975.* Baltimore, MD: The Johns Hopkins University Press, 1980.

Iser, Wolfgang. *The Act of Reading: A Theory of Aesthetic Response.* Baltimore, MD: The Johns Hopkins University Press, 1978.

Jagoe, Catherine. "Noncanonical Novels and the Question of Quality." *Revista de estudios hispánicos* 23 (1993): 427–36.

Jameson, Fredric. *The Political Unconscious: Narrative as a Socially Symbolic Act.* Ithaca, NY: Cornell University Press, 1981

———. *Postmodernism or, the Cultural Logic of Late Capitalism.* Durham, NC: Duke University Press, 1991.

———. *The Seeds of Time.* New York: Columbia University Press, 1994.

Jauss, Hans Robert. "The Alterity and Modernity of Medieval Literature." *New Literary History* 10 (1979): 181–27.

Jessen, Patricia B. *La realidad en la novelística de Manuel Puig.* Madrid: Editorial Pliegos, 1990.

Jusdanis, Gregory. *Belated Modernity and Aesthetic Culture: Inventing National Literature. Theory and History of Literature,* vol. 81. Minneapolis: University of Minnesota Press, 1992.

Kadir, Djelal. *Questioning Fictions: Latin America's Family Romance.* Minneapolis: University of Minnesota Press, 1986.

Kamuf, Peggy, ed. *A Derrida Reader: Between the Blinds.* New York: Columbia University Press, 1991.

Keenaghan, Eric. *Queering Cold War Poetry: Ethics of Vulnerability in Cuba and the United States.* Columbus: Ohio State University Press, 2009.

Kelly, Kevin. "Scan This Book!" *The New York Times,* May 14, 2006.

Kerr, Lucille. "The Fiction of Popular Design and Desire: Manuel Puig's *Boquitas pintadas."* *MLN Hispanic Issue* 97, no. 2 (1982): 411–21.

———. *Reclaiming the Author: Figures and Fictions from Spanish America.* Durham, NC: Duke University Press, 1992.

———. *Suspended Fictions: Reading Novels by Manuel Puig.* Chicago, IL: University of Illinois Press, 1987.

Klahn, Norma, and Wilfrido H. Corral, eds. *Los novelistas como críticos.* México: Ediciones del Norte, 1991.

Kushigian, Julia A. *Orientalism in the Hispanic Literary Tradition: In Dialogue with Borges, Paz, and Sarduy.* Albuquerque: University of New Mexico Press, 1991.

———. "*Rios en la noche: fluyen los jardines:* Orientalism in the Work of Octavio Paz." *Hispania* 70, no. 4 (1987): 776–86.

———. "La serpiente en la sinagoga." *Vuelta* 89 (1984): 14–20.

Kutzinski, Vera M. *Sugar's Secrets: Race and the Erotics of Cuban Nationalism.* Charlottesville: University of Virginia Press, 1993.

Lakoff, George. *Women, Fire, and Dangerous Things: What Categories Reveal about the Mind.* Chicago, IL: University of Chicago Press, 1987.

Lazarillo de Tormes. México: Editorial Porrúa, 1969.

Lazo, Raimundo. *La literatura cubana: Esquema histórico desde sus orígenes hasta 1964.* México: Universidad Nacional Autónoma de México, 1965.

Levin, Suzanne Jill. "Discourse as *bricolage."* *Review* 74 (1974): 123–35.

———. *Manuel Puig and the Spider Woman: His Life and Fictions.* New York: Farrar, Straus and Giroux, 2000.

Levinson, Brett. "Possibility, Ruin, Repetition: Rereading Lezama Lima's 'American Expression.'" *Revista Canadiense de Estudios Hispánicos* 18, no. 1 (1993): 49–66.

Lévi-Strauss, Claude. *Tristes Tropiques*. Translated by John and Doreen Weightman. New York: Penguin Books, 1973.

Lezama Lima, José. *Las eras imaginarias*. Madrid: Editorial Fundamentos, 1971

———. *La expresión americana*. Havana: Instituto Nacional de Cultura, Ministerio de Educación, 1957.

———. *Paradiso*. 1966. Reprint. Edited by Cintio Vitier. Madrid: UNESCO, 1988.

Lindstrom, Naomi. *Twentieth-Century Spanish American Fiction*. Austin: University of Texas Press, 1994.

Lloyd, Paul M. *From Latin to Spanish: Vol. I: Historical Phonology and Morphology of the Spanish Language*. Philadelphia: Memoirs of the American Philosophical Society, 1987.

López Segrera, Francisco. *Cuba: Cultura y sociedad*. La Habana: Editorial Letras \ Cubanas, 1989.

Lord, Albert B. *The Singer of Tales*. Cambridge, MA: Harvard University Press, 1960.

Ludmer, Josefina. "*Boquitas Pintadas:* siete recorridos." *Actual* (Jan.-Dec. 1971): 3–21.

———. *El género gauchesco: Un tratado sobre la patria*. Buenos Aires: Editorial Sudamericana, S.A., 1988.

———. *Gaucho Genre: A Treatise on the Motherland*. Translated by Molly Weigel. Durham, NC: Duke University Press, 2002.

Lugones, Maria. "Purity, Impurity, and Separation." *Signs* 19, no. 2 (1994): 458–79.

Luis, William. *Literary Bondage: Slavery in Cuban Narrative*. Austin: University of Texas Press, 1990.

———. "La novela antiesclavista: texto, contexto y escritura." *Cuadernos Americanos* 236, no. 3 (1981): 103–16.

Lukács, Georg. *The Theory of the Novel: A Historico-Philosophical Essay on the Forms of Great Epic Literature*. Translated by Anna Bostock. Cambridge, MA: The MIT Press, 1971.

Lyotard, Jean-François. *The Postmodern Condition: A Report on Knowledge*. 1979. Translated by Goeff Bennington and Brian Massumi. Minneapolis: University of Minnesota Press, 1991.

———. *The Postmodern Explained: Correspondence 1982–1985*. Translated by Don Barry, et al. Edited by Julian Pefanis and Morgan Thomas. Minneapolis: University of Minnesota Press, 1993.

Machover, Jacobo. *La memoria frente al poder: Escritores cubanos del exilio: Guillermo Cabrera Infante, Severo Sarduy, Reinaldo Arenas*. Zaragoza: Universitat de Valencia, 2001.

MacDonald, Sharon, and Roger Silverstone. "Rewriting the Museums' Fictions: Taxonomies, Stories and Readers." *Cultural Studies* 4, no. 2 (1990): 176–91.

Mafud, Julio. *Psicología de la viveza criolla*. 3rd ed. Buenos Aires: Americalee, 1968.

Magnien, Brigitte, ed. *Hacia una literatura del pueblo: del folletín a la novela*. Barcelona: Anthropos, 1995.

Maldonado, Armando. *Manuel Puig: The Aesthetics of Cinematic and Psychological Fiction*. Ann Arbor, MI: University Microfilms International, 1977.

Mañach, Jorge. *Indagación del choteo*. Edited by Rosario Rexach. Miami: Ediciones Universal, 1991.

Manoff, Marlene. "Theories of the Archive from Across the Disciplines." *Portal: Libraries and the Academy* 4, no. 1 (2004): 9–25.

Martí, José. *Nuestra América*. Caracas, Ven.: Biblioteca Ayacucho, 1977.

Masiello, Francine. *Between Civilization and Barbarism: Women, Nation, and Literary Culture in Modern Argentina*. Lincoln: University of Nebraska Press, 1992.

May, Georges. *Les Mille et une nuits d'Antoine Galland ou le chef-d'oevre invisible*. Paris: Presses Universitaires de France, 1986.

McCracken, Ellen. "Manuel Puig's *Heartbreak Tango*: Women and Mass Culture." *Latin American Literary Review* 9, no. 18 (1981): 27–35.

McGee, Michael, and Martha Martin. "Public Knowledge and Ideological Argumentation." *Communication Monographs* 50 (1983): 47–65.

McGowan, John. *Postmodernism and Its Critics*. Ithaca, NY: Cornell University Press, 1991.

Méndez Rodenas, Adriana. *Severo Sarduy: El neobarroco de la transgresión*. México: Universidad Nacional Autónoma de México, 1983.

Menéndez y Pelayo, Marcelino. *Obras completas. Orígenes de la novela*. Edición Nacional de las obras completas de Menéndez y Pelayo, vol. 3. Madrid: Consejo Superior de Investigaciones Científicas, 1961.

Menéndez y Soto, Ernesto. *Panorama de la Novela cubana de la revolución (1959–1970)*. Miami: Ediciones universal, 1977.

Merrim, Stephanie. "For a New (Psychological) Novel in the Works of Manuel Puig." *Novel: A Forum on Fiction*. 17, no. 2 (1984): 141–57.

Meulengracht Sørensen, Preben. *The Unmanly Man: Concepts of Sexual Defamation in Early Northern Society*. Translated by Joan Turville-Petre. Svendborg: Odense University Press, 1983.

Miller, James. *The Passion of Michel Foucault*. New York: Simon & Schuster, 1993.

Miller, Yvette E., and Raymond Leslie Williams, eds. *The Boom in Retrospect: A Reconsideration*. Special issue of *Latin American Literary Review* 15, no. 29 (1987).

Ministerio de Cultura. *La cultura en Cuba socialista*. La Habana: Editorial Letras Cubanas, 1982.

Molloy, Sylvia. *Signs of Borges*. Translated by Oscar Montero. Durham, NC: Duke University Press, 1994.

Montero, Oscar. "Lipstick Vogue: The politics of Drag." *Radical America* 22.1 (1988): 35–42.

———. "Modernismo and Homophobia: Darío and Rodó" in *Sex and Sexuality in Latin America*. Edited by D. Balderston and D. J. Guy. New York: New York University Press, 1997.

———. *The Name Game: Writing/Fading Writer in "De donde son los cantantes."* Chapel Hill: University of North Carolina Press, 1988.

Moreiras, Alberto. "Despatriación y Política en la Novela de Severo Sarduy." *Revista de crítica latinoamericana* 27 (1988): 167–74.

———. *Interpretación y Diferencia*. Madrid: Visor Distribuciones, 1991.

———. "Mentoring Past the Ruins." In "On the Profession." *LASA Forum* 39, no. 2 (2008): 7–8.

Morello-Frosch, Marta. "La sexualidad opresiva en las obras de Manuel Puig." *Nueva Narrativa Hispanoamericana* 5, nos. 1–2 (1975): 151–57.

Mosse, George L. *Nationalism and Sexuality: Middle-Class Morality and Sexual Norms in Modern Europe.* Madison: University of Wisconsin Press, 1985.

Netchinsky, Jill. "Engendering a Cuban Literature: Nineteenth-Century Antislavery Narrative (Manzano, Suárez y Romero, Gómez de Avellaneda, A. Zambrana)." PhD dissertation, Yale University, 1985.

The New Yorker: Cuba Issue. Jan. 26, 1998.

Ochoa, John A. "The Uses of Literary History: Some Recent Titles." *Latin American Research Review.* 42, no. 3 (2007): 297–307.

Olalquiaga, Celeste. "The Dark Side of Modernity's Moon." *Agenda: Contemporary Art Magazine* 28 (1992): 22–25.

Ortega, Julio. "De donde son los cantantes." *Severo Sarduy.* Madrid: Espiral/fundamentos, 1976.

———. "*La expresión americana:* una teoría de la cultura." *ECO* 187 (1977): 55–63.

———. *Poetics of Change: The New Spanish-American Narrative.* Translated by Galen D. Greaser and Julio Ortega. Austin: University of Texas Press, 1984.

———. *Relato de la Utopía: Notas sobre narrativa cubana de la revolución.* Barcelona: La Gaya Ciencia, 1973.

Ortiz, Fernando. *La africanía de la música folklórica de Cuba.* La Habana: Ediciones Cárdenas y cía., 1950.

———. *Contrapunteo cubano del tabaco y el azúcar.* Caracas: Biblioteca Ayacucho, 1978.

———. "La cubanidad y los negros," *Estudios Afrocubanos.* 3, nos. 1–4 (1939): 3–15.

Out There: Marginalization and Contemporary Cultures. Edited by Russell Ferguson, et al. New York: The New Museum of Contemporary Art, 1990.

Paras, Eric. *Foucault 2.0: Beyond Power and Knowledge.* New York: Other Press, 2006.

Parker, Andrew, et al., eds. *Nationalisms and Sexualities.* New York: Routledge, 1992.

Parkinson Zamora, Lois. "The Usable Past: The Idea of History in Modern U.S. and Latin American Fiction." In *Do the Americas Have a Common Literature?,* edited by Gustavo Pérez Firmat, 7–41. Durham, NC: Duke University Press, 1990.

Paterson, Lee. "On the Margin: Postmodernism, Ironic History, and Medieval Studies." *Speculum* 65 (1991): 87–108.

Pearce, Susan, ed. *Objects of Knowledge.* London: The Athlone Press, 1990.

Pellón, Gustavo. "Juan Goytisolo y Severo Sarduy: Discurso e Ideología." *Hispanic Review* 56 (1988): 483–92.

———. "Manuel Puig's Contradictory Strategy: Kitsch Paradigms versus Paradigmatic Structure in *El beso de la mujer araña* and *Pubis Angelical.*" *Symposium* 37, no. 3 (1983): 186–201.

Pérez, Rolando. *Severo Sarduy and the Religion of the Text.* New York: University Press of America, 1988.

Pérez Firmat, Gustavo. *The Cuban Condition: Translation and Identity in Modern Cuban Culture.* New York: Cambridge University Press, 1989.

———. *Literature and Liminality: Festive Readings in the Hispanic Tradition.* Durham, NC: Duke University Press, 1986.

Piglia, Ricardo. "Clase media: cuerpo y destino (Una lectura de *La traición de Rita Hayworth* de Manuel Puig)." *Nueva novela Latinoamericana* II. Edited by Jorge Lafforque. Buenos Aires: Editorial Paidós, 1972.

Pizarro, Ana. "Para ser jóvenes en cien años más." *Casa de las Américas* 33, no. 191 (1993): 5–7.

Preston, Julia. "New World's Spanish Speakers Declare Independence." *New York Times,* April 16, 1997: A8.

Prieto, René. "La ambiviolencia en la obra de Severo Sarduy." *Cuadernos Americanos* 1 (1985): 241–55.

———. "The Ambiviolent Fiction of Severo Sarduy." *Symposium* 39 (1985): 49–60.

Puig, Manuel. *El beso de la mujer araña.* Barcelona: Seix Barral, 1976.

———. *Boquitas pintadas: Folletín.* 1969. Barcelona: Seix Barral, 1972.

———. *The Buenos Aires Affair: Novela policial.* 1973. Barcelona: Seix Barral, 1986.

———. *La traición de Rita Hayworth.* 1968. Barcelona: Seix Barral, 1987.

Rama, Angel. *La ciudad letrada.* Hanover, N.H.:Ediciones del Norte, 1984.

———. "Los contestarios del poder." *Novísimos narradores hispanoamericanos en marcha (1964–1980).* México: Marcha Editores, S.A., 1981.

Rapaport, Herman. *Later Derrida: Reading the Recent Work.* New York: Routledge, 2003.

Read, Malcom K. Introduction and translator. "Althusser: Blowup (Lineaments of a Different Thought) by Juan Carlos Rodríguez." *PMLA.* New York: The Modern Language Association of America, 2008.

Readings, Bill, and Bennet Schaber, eds. *Postmodernism across the Ages: Essays for Postmodernity that Was Not Born Yesterday.* Syracuse, NY: Syracuse University Press, 1993.

Richard, Nelly. "Postmodernism and Periphery." *Third Text* 2 (1987–88): 5–12.

Riobó, Carlos. "Cuerpos y voces de cautivos: Los espacios discursivos en un *corpus* argentino." *Romance Quarterly* 46, no. 2 (1999): 112–23.

———. "Heartbreak Tango: Manuel Puig's Counter-Archive." In *Narrative Beginnings: Theories and Practices,* edited by Brian Richardson, 127–36. Frontiers of Narrative Series. University of Nebraska Press, 2008.

———. "The Medieval Inheritance of Manuel Puig and Severo Sarduy." *Medieval Encounters* 3, no. 2 (1997): 128–41.

Rivera, José Eustasio. *La vorágine.* Buenos Aires: Losada, 1998.

Rivero-Potter, Alicia. *Autor/Lector: Huidobro, Borges, Fuentes, y Sarduy.* Detroit: Wayne State University Press, 1991.

———. "Autor, Narrador y Lector en Severo Sarduy: *Cobra, Colibrí."* *Symposium* 41 (1987): 227–39.

Rivers, Elias L. *Quixotic Scriptures: Essays on the Textuality of Hispanic Literature.* Bloomington: Indiana University Press, 1983.

Roa Bastos, Augusto. *Yo, el supremo.* Madrid: Ediciones Cátedra, 1983.

Rodríguez Almodóvar, Antonio. *Lecciones de narrativa hispanoamericana, siglo XX.* Sevilla: Publicaciones de la Universidad de Sevilla, 1972.

Rodríguez Feo, José. "Breve recuento de la narrativa cubana." *Unión Havana,* 6 no. 4 (1967): 131–36.

Rodríguez Monegal, Emir. "Conversación con Severo Sarduy." *Revista del Occidente* 93 (1970): 315–43.

———. "Diálogo con Severo Sarduy: Las estructuras de la narración," *Mundo Nuevo* 2 (Agosto 1966):15–26, 16.

———. "El folletín rescatado." *Revista de la Universidad de México* 27.2 (1973): 23–35.

———. "The New Latin American Novel." *Books Abroad* 44.1 (1970): 45–50.

Roffé, Reina. "Manuel Puig: Del 'Kitsch' a Lacan." *Espejos de escritores*. Hanover. NH: Ediciones del Norte, 1985.

Ruiz Barrionuevo, Carmen. *El "Paradiso" de Lezama Lima*. Madrid: Insula, 1980.

Safir, Margery A. "Mitología: otro nivel de metalenguaje en *Boquitas pintadas*." *Revista Iberoamericana* 41.90 (1975): 47–58.

Said, Edward W. *Culture and Imperialism*. New York: Alfred A. Knopf, Inc., 1993.

———. *Edward Said: A Critical Reader.* Edited by Michael Sprinker. Cambridge, MA: Blackwell Publishers, 1992.

———. *Orientalism*. New York: Vintage Books, 1978.

———. "The Politics of Knowledge." *Raritan* 11 (1991): 17–31.

———. *Representations of the Intellectual*. New York: Pantheon Books, 1994.

———. *The World, the Text, and the Critic*. Cambridge, MA: Harvard University Press, 1983.

Saldívar, José David. *The Dialectics of Our America: Cultural Critique, and Literary History*. Durham, NC: Duke University Press, 1991.

Santí, Enrico Mario. "Textual Politics: Severo Sarduy." *Latin American Literary Review* 8, no. 16 (1980): 152–60.

Santos, Lidia. *Kitsch Tropical: Los medios en la literatura y el arte en América Latina*. Madrid: Iberoamericana, Vervuert, 2001.

———. "La narrativa del Caribe hispánico (años 70–80) como recuperación de la marginalidad." *Alba de América* 14, nos. 26–27 (1996): 313–19.

Sapir, Edward. *Culture, Language, and Personality*. Edited by David G. Mandelbaum. Los Angeles: University of California Press, 1958.

Sarduy, Severo. *Barroco*. Buenos Aires: Sudamericana, 1974.

———. *El barroco y el neobarroco*. In *Obra Completa/Severo Sarduy: Obra Crítica*, vol. 2. Edited by Gustavo Guerrero and François Wahl. Madrid: Galaxia Gutenberg, Círculo de Lectores, 1999.

———. "*Boquitas pintadas*: Parodia e injerto." *Sur* 321 (1969): 71–77.

———. *Cobra*. Barcelona: Editorial EDHASA, 1981.

———. *Colibrí*. Barcelona: Editotial Argos Vergara, 1984.

———. "Conversación con Severo Sarduy." With Emir Rodríguez Monegal. *Revista del Occidente* 93 (1970): 315–43.

———. "Diálogo con Severo Sarduy: Las estructuras de la narración." With Emir Rodríguez Monegal. *Mundo Nuevo* 2 (1966): 15–26.

———. "Dispersión: Falsas notas/Homenaje a Lezama." *Mundo Nuevo* 24 (1968): 4–17.

———. *De donde son los cantantes*. Edited by Roberto González Echevarría. Madrid: Ediciones Cátedra, 1993.

———. *Escrito sobre un cuerpo*. In *Obra Completa/Severo Sarduy: Obra Crítica*, vol. 2. Edited by Gustavo Guerrero and François Wahl. Madrid: Galaxia Gutenberg, Círculo de Lectores, 1999.

———. *Gestos*. Barcelona: Editorial Seix Barral, 1963.

———. *Maitreya*. Barcelona: Seix Barral, 1978.

———. *Maitreya*. Translated by Suzanne Jill Levine. Hanover, NH.: Ediciones del Norte, 1987.

———. "Notas a las Notas a las Notas . . . A Propósito de Manuel Puig." *Revista Iberoamericana* 31 (1971): 555–67.

———. *Obra Completa/Severo Sarduy: Obra Crítica*, Vols. 1 and 2. Edited by Gustavo Guerrero and François Wahl. Madrid: Galaxia Gutenberg, Círculo de Lectores, 1999.

———. "Página para Lezama." *Revista Iberoamericana* 92–93 (1975): 467.

———. *Pájaros de la Playa*. Barcelona: Tusquets Editores, 1993.

———. "La serpiente en la sinagoga." Interview with Julia Kushigian. *Vuelta* 89 (Apr. 1984): 14–20.

———. *La Simulación*. Caracas, Ven.: Monte Avila Editores, 1982.

———. *Written on a Body*. Translated by Carol Maier. New York: Lumen Books, 1989.

Sedgwick, Eve Kosofsky. *Between Men: English Literature and Male Homosocial Desire*. New York: Columbia University Press, 1985.

———. *Epistemology of the Closet*. Berkeley: University of California Press, 1990.

Shaw, Donald L. *Alejo Carpentier*. Boston: Twayne Publishers, 1985.

Shoo, Ernesto. "Severo Sarduy: Cuerpos y Libros." *Primera Plana*. June 3, 1969: 58–59.

Shumway, Nicolas. *The Invention of Argentina*. Berkeley: The University of California Press, 1991.

Sifuentes Jáuregui, Benigno. "'Scars of Decisions': Transvestism and Other Versions of Masculinity in Contemporary Spanish American Literature." PhD Dissertation, Department of Spanish and Portuguese, Yale University, 1993.

Smith, Barbara Herrnstein. *Contingencies of Value*. Cambridge, MA: Harvard University Press, 1990.

Smith, Paul Julian. *The Body Hispanic: Gender and Sexuality in Spanish and Spanish American Literature*. New York: Oxford University Press, 1989.

Sommer, Doris. *Foundational Fictions: The National Romances of Latin America*. Berkeley: University of California Press, 1991.

Speranza, Graciela. *Manuel Puig: Después del fin de la literatura*. Buenos Aires: Grupo Editorial Norma, 2000.

Spivak, Gayatri Chakravorty. *Outside in the Teaching Machine*. New York: Routledge, 1993.

———. "The Politics of Translation." In *Destabilizing Theory: Contemporary Feminist Debates*. Edited by M. Barrett and M. Phillips. Cambridge, UK: Polity, 1992, 177–200.

Swartz, David. *Culture and Power: The Sociology of Pierre Bourdieu*. Chicago, IL: The University of Chicago Press, 1997.

Tannen, Deborah. *Gender and Discourse*. New York: Oxford University Press, 1994.

Thiebaut, Guy. "*El beso de la mujer araña:* Novela comprometida." Talk given at the *International Colloquium on Manuel Puig and Mario Vargas Llosa*. Anfy Liard, La Sorbonne, Paris, 1982.

Tittler, Jonathan. *Manuel Puig*. Edited by David William Foster. New York: Twayne Publishers, 1993.

———. "Order, Chaos, and Re-order: The Novels of Manuel Puig." *Kentucky Romance Quarterly* 30, no. 2 (1983): 187–201.

Todorov, Tzvetan. "Les categories du récit litteraire." *Communications* 8 (1966): 125– 47.

———. *The Conquest of America*. Translated by Richard Howard. New York: Harper and Row, 1984.

———. *On Human Diversity: Nationalism, Racism, and Exoticism in French Thought*. Translated by Catherine Porter. Cambridge, MA: Harvard University Press, 1993.

———. *The Poetics of Prose*. Translated by Richard Howard. Ithaca, NY: Cornell University Press, 1977.

———. "Typologie du roman policier." *Poétique de la prose: Nouvelles recherches sur le récit*. Paris: Éditions du Seuil, 1971.

Triviños, Gilberto. "La destrucción del verosímil folletinesco en *Boquitas pintadas*." *Texto Crítico* 4, no. 9 (1978): 117–30.

Tyler, Carole-Anne. "Boys Will Be Girls." In *Inside/Out: Lesbian Theories, Gay Theories*, edited by Diana Fuss, 32–70. New York: Routledge, 1991.

Ulloa, Justo C. "Un capítulo del libro *El Espejo Enterrado*, El autor y sus ideas: Carlos Fuentes." *El diario/La Prensa*. July 7, 1992, 24.

———. "Contenido y forma yoruba en 'La Dolores Rondón' de Severo Sarduy." In *Homenaje a Lydia Cabrera*, edited by Reinaldo Sánchez, José Antonio Madrigal, and José Sánchez-Boudy, 241–50. Miami: Editorial Universal, 1978.

Unruh, Vicky. "Rev. of *Myth and Archive*, by Roberto González Echevarría." *Latin American Literary Review* 20, no. 39 (1991): 76–78.

van Zyl, Susan. "Psychoanalysis and the Archive: Derrida's *Archive Fever*." In *Refiguring the Archive*, edited by Carolyn Hamilton et al., 39–59. Boston: Kluwer Academic Publishers, 2002.

Vargas Llosa, Mario. *Captain Pantoja and the Special Service*. Translated by G. Kolovakos. New York: Harper and Row, 1978.

———. *La casa verde*. Barcelona: Seix Barral, 1965.

———. *La tía Julia y el escribidor/ Aunt Julia and the Scriptwriter*. Translated by Helen R. Lane. New York: Farrar/Straus/Giroux, 1982.

Veyne, Paul. *Writing History*. Translated by Mina Moore-Rinvolucri. Middletown, CT: Wesleyan University Press, 1984.

Vico, Giambattista. *New Science: Principles of the New Science Concerning the Common Nature of Nations*. Translated by David Marsh. New York: Penguin Books, 1999.

Villaverde, Cirilio. *Cecilia Valdés*. Caracas, Ven: Biblioteca Ayacucho, 1981.

Vitier, Cintio. *Crítica cubana*. Havana: Editorial Letras Cubanas, 1988.

———. *Lo cubano en la poesía*. 1958. Reprint. La Habana: Instituto Cubano del Libro, 1970.

Warhol, Robyn R., and Diane Price Herndl, eds. *Feminisms: An Anthology of Literary Theory and Criticism*. New Brunswick, NJ: Rutgers University Press, 1993.

Watt, Ian. *The Rise of the Novel: Studies in Defoe, Richardson, and Fielding*. Berkeley: University of California Press, 1957.

Waugh, Patricia, ed. *Postmodernism: A Reader*. New York: Routledge, Chapman and Hall, 1992.

Weiss, Judith A. *"Casa de las Americas": An Intellectual Review in the Cuban Revolution*. Chapel Hill, NC: Estudios de Hispanófila, 1977.

West, Alan. "Inscribing the Body of Perfection: Adorned with Signs and Graces: Thoughts on Severo Sarduy's *Maitreya*." In *Lo que no se ha dicho*, edited by Pedro R. Monge Rafuls, 115–24. New York: OLLANTAY Center for the Arts, 1994.

———. *Tropics of History: Cuba Imagined*. Westport, CT: Bergin & Garvey, 1997.

White, Rob. "Archive Power." *Oxford Literary Review* 21 (1999): 161–80.

Winks, Cathy, and Anne Semans. *The Good Vibrations Guide to Sex: The Most Complete Sex Manual Ever Written*. 3rd ed. San Francisco: Cleis Press, Inc., 2002.

Yúdice, George. "For a Practical Aesthetics." In *The Phantom Public Sphere*, edited by Bruce Robbins, 209–23. Minneapolis: University of Minnesota Press, 1993.

Yun, Lisa. *The Coolie Speaks: Chinese Indetured Laborers and African Slaves in Cuba*. Philadelphia, PA: Temple University Press, 2008.

Zagat Survey 1998, 2008: New York City Restaurants. New York: Zagat Survey LLC, 1998, 2008.

Zamora, Margarita. "Language and Authority in the *Comentarios reales*." *Modern Language Quarterly* 43, no. 3 (1982): 228–41.

Index

Aguilar Mora, Jorge, 157, 206n95, 206n97
Alonso, Carlos J.: on González Echevarría, 25–26, 187; *The Spanish American Regional Novel,* 192n61
Althusser, Louis, 151
Anderson, Benedict: *Imagined Communities,* 112–13
antislavery novels, 138, 203, 204
archive: defined, 37; destruction of, 52; etymology of, 47, 55; location of, 48; as pre-text, 67–68; purity of, 41; Spanish, 196n68, 196n74; universal, 63–66. *See also* Borges; Derrida; Foucault; González Echevarría; Guillory
Archivo de Indias, Seville, 57, 196
archons, 47–48, 72
Arenas, Reinaldo, 27
Argentina: cultural mythology of, and Puig, 73; literary traditions, 102
Aristotle: *Metaphysics,* 39
Arrom, José Juan: and the Latin American novel, 58–61
Auerbach, Erich: and *figura,* 195n45

Bakhtin, Mikhail, 98; "Discourse in the Novel," 59
Balboa, Silvestre de, 141; *Espejo de paciencia,* 136–37
Baroque, the: and Latin American literature, 144–45. *See also* Lezama Lima; Sarduy
Barroco de Indias, 144, 145
Barthes, Roland, 151
Benjamin, Walter, 130; "The Work of Art in the Age of Mechanical Reproduction," 64–65
Bennett, Tony, 151

Berelowitz, JoAnne, 151
bildungsroman, 106
Bloom, Harold, 65; and anxiety of influence, 195n45
body, the: as signifier, 129–30; and the text, 127
Boom novels, 21, 27, 29, 31, 58, 60, 73–75, 85, 102–3, 120, 158, 163; and García Márquez, 171; and language of authority, 72, 172; and phallogocentrism, 171; post-Boom, 103, 200n13; Puig and Sarduy and post-Boom, 26, 74, 93, 103, 133, 169, 171, 190n3, 191n49, 191n52, 198n27; reflexivity of, 125; search for authority, 172
Borges, Jorge Luis, 37; "The Analytical Language of John Wilkins," 38, 42; on the archive, 39–43; Chinese encyclopedia of, 43, 148; and Foucault, 42; *Historia universal de la infamia,* 145; library of, 164; "The Library of Babel," 38, 40, 60; "Tlön, Uqbar, Orbis Tertius," 148; "The Total Library," 38–40, 52, 97, 193–94n6; use of footnotes, 131
Bourdieu, Pierre, 38, 61 62, 150; and class distinction, 24; *champ,* 101; *La Distinction,* 94, 100–1; field, 24
Butler, Judith, 153

Cabrera Infante, Guillermo, 27
Calderón de la Barca, Pedro, 146; *La vida es sueño,* 144
canon/canonicity, 11, 13, 16–20, 22, 24, 26, 28, 56, 62, 67, 76, 78, 81, 97, 103, 124, 125, 127, 138, 140, 141, 144, 146, 147, 152, 163, 165, 175, 178, 193n4

227

canonical, 11, 30, 36, 38, 61, 63, 67, 70, 88, 99, 127, 159, 161, 162
captive tradition, 199n9
Cárdenás, Lázaro, 112
Carpentier, Alejo, 132; "El barroco y lo real maravilloso," 145; *Los pasos perdidos*, 184; *Lost Steps*, 74
censorship, 116–17
Cervantes, Miguel de, 113, 120, and censorship, 117; "El coloquio de los perros," 119; *Don Quixote*, 32, 112, 115–16, 119; *Novelas Ejemplares*, 115–16, 119; use of dialogue, 118–19
Charles V/Charles I in Spain, 56, 168, 196n68, 198n27
choteo: and Sarduy, 127–29, 137
Cicero: *De natura deorum*, 39
Cid, El, 140–41
Clarín: *La regenta*, 184
Columbus, Christopher, 144; *Diario de bitácora*, 126, 141, 155
contingency: value of, 34, 134
Corominas, Joan, 55, 196n70
Cortázar, Julio, 28
Cuba: revolution in, 126, 157, 174; literature/culture, 126, 129, 134–35, 138, 140, 143, 144, Curtius, Ernst Robert, 19; and González Echevarría, 59
cultural capital, 16, 24, 34, 61, 62, 90, 100, 190n30
cultural studies, 16, 17, 62, 67, 130
Curtius, Ernst Robert: and González Echevarría, 59

Derrida, Jacques, 37, 40, 44, 66, 195n45; archive of, 46–54, 71, 72, 115; *Archive Fever: A Freudian Impression*, 38, 39, 46–49, 71–72, 112, 164; and consignation, 48, 50; and Freud, 89; *Memoirs of the Blind*, 38, 53, 196n65; and phallogocentrism, 190–91n39, 201n2
detective novels, 199n6. See also Puig: *Buenos Aires Affair*
dictator novel, 181, 188, 207n22
discursive formations, 11–14, 24–26, 28, 33, 34, 43–45, 54, 55, 58, 60, 68–70, 73–77, 80, 86, 88, 91–94, 97–99, 102, 111, 112, 121, 125, 126, 133, 135, 137, 138, 145, 149, 152, 156, 189n3, 192n61, 195n24, 198n25

Donoso, José, 28
Dopico Black, Georgina, 116–17
Duguid, Paul, 65

Echevarren, Roberto, 27, 191n51
Elliott, J. H., 56
encyclopedia, 148, 149, 181
épistémès, 19, 43, 60–61
Escorial, El, 56, 57, 115, 147, 150, 159, 165, 168, 172, 179, 196n68, 198n27

Fechner, Gustav Theodor, 39
Fernández Moreno, César, 146
films, 117–19
fisting, 167–69, 171, 172
folletín, 25, 32, 77, 78
Foucault, Michel, 37, 38, 90, 140, 151; *The Archaeology of Knowledge*, 38, 43, 46, 195n24; and the archival process, 20; archive of, 43–46, 54; and Borges, 42; defines archaeology, 45; defines archive, 69; defines discourse, 44–45; defines heterotopia, 46, 113–15, 148, 200n25; and desexualizing practices, 171; *épistémès*, 19; *Les Mots et les choses*, 43, 148; and institutions, 151; *The Order of Things*, 38, 43; "Of Other Spaces," 38, 46; and utopia, 114
Franco, Jean, 191n41
Freud, Sigmund, 195n45; archives of, 47; and archiving, 89; *Beyond the Pleasure Principle*, 46; *Civilization and its Discontents*, 46; death drive, 39, 46, 52, 164; *Moses and Monotheism*, 46; and the psyche, 48
Frost, Derek, 82
Fuentes, Carlos: *La muerte de Artemio Cruz*, 158

Gallegos, Rómulo: *Doña Bárbara*, 184, 185
Garber, Marjorie: *Vested Interests: Cross-Dressing and Cultural Anxiety*, 153
García Canclini, Néstor, 70, 150
García Gómez, Emilio, 141
García Márquez, Gabriel: *One Hundred Years of Solitude*, 35, 74, 158, 169–71, 173
Garcilaso de la Vega (el Inca), 69; *Comentarios reales*, 71
Genette, Gérard, 197n4

Gilligan, Carol, 79, 111, 200n14, 200n15; *In a Different Voice,* 144
Góngora, Luis de, 146
González Echevarría, Roberto, 22, 37, 67, 70, 98, 172, 183, 187, 106n70; and the Baroque, 204n58; on *Boquitas pintadas: Folletín,* 73–74; and discursive forms, 25; on Foucault, 60; and master-narratives, 43, 59; *Myth and Archive,* 38, 54, 58, 124, 196n31; on the novel, 35, 59–60; and origins of Latin American literature, 25, 60; on Sarduy, 33, 125; and the subaltern, 24–25, 69; theory of the archive, 12, 15, 19, 21, 24, 54–57, 69, 74, 88, 122; *The Voice of the Masters,* 60, 191n42, 191–92n34, 192n60
Google (Google Book Project, Google Library Project), 38, 63
Grafton, Anthony, 65
Greenblatt, Stephen, 17
Guillén, Nicolás: "Balada de los dos abuelos," 138
Guillory, John, 37, 62, 193n4; archive of, 61–63; and Bourdieu, 61–62; on canonicity, 19, 24; *Cultural Capital: The Problem of Literary Canon Formation,* 38

Habsburgs, 168, 180; colonial archives of, 11, 55–57, 60; as information collectors, 56, 74
hegemonic discourse, 25, 54, 60, 69, 76, 98, 132
hegemonic master-stories, 183
hegemony, 12, 17, 18, 20, 21, 27, 70, 151, 188
Herrero-Olaizola, Alejandro: on archival research, 194n19
heterosexual/heterosexuality/heterosexist, 109, 113, 118, 161, 185, 187
Higgins, Antony, 60; *Constructing the Criollo Archive,* 70
high culture, 13, 25, 59, 70, 189n4. *See also* low culture
homosexuality, 112, 120, 121, 151, 182, 201n9
horror vacui, 172
Human Genome Project, 66, 37

impurity, 22, 42, 43, 102, 154

jade, 177–79, 207n25
Jameson, Fredric, 151

Kant, Immanuel, 94
kitsch, 20, 30, 153, 199n53, 205n89, 206n59

Lacan, Jacques, 190–91n39
Las Casas, Fray Bartolomé de, 141
Lasswirtz, Kurd, 39
Latin American narrative, 76; archival origins of, 11–12; archival traditions, 163; literature of, 154; and modernity, 29; and positivism, 29
letrados, 21
Levine, Suzanne Jill, 173
Lezama Lima, José, 127, 131, 141, 202n14, 202n15; *Las eras imaginarias,* 134; *La expresión americana,* 134; and the Latin American Baroque, 145; *Paradiso,* 126, 129, 158
library, the, 147–49, 151
literary canon, the, 18–20
lo cubano/la cubanidad, 126–29, 132, 134, 136–38, 141, 142, 143, 156, 157
low culture, 25, 73. *See also* high culture
Lugones, Maria, 12, 29, 154; on the hybrid, 22; "Purity, Impurity, and Separation," 22, 102; and subversion, 22–23

Machover, Jacobo, 188
Mañach, Jorge: *Indagación del choteo,* 126, 127
Manoff, Marlene, 193n3, 193n5, 194n18
marginalized groups, 26, 28. *See also* Puig: *géneros menores*
Martí, José: *Diary,* 127
mass culture, 189n4
mass media, 112. *See also* Franco; García Canclini; Santos
mestiza, 183, 184
mestizaje, 23
mestizo, 73, 117, 185, 186
monster, 19, 143, 146, 204n57
monstrosity/monstruos, 151, 167, 168, 170, 173, 186
Montero, Oscar: on *modernismo,* 127, 201n9
Möbius strip, 68, 126, 132, 141, 175

Moreiras, Alberto: "Mentoring Past the Ruins," 15–16; and the subaltern, 17
museum, the, 149–51
Mutanabbí, 141

Nebrija, Antonio de, 142
Neobaroque, the, 20, 28, 144. *See also* Sarduy
New Critics, 67
newspapers: and subaltern groups, 181
noncanonical, 28, 59, 78, 80, 84, 86, 146
novel of the self, 28, 35
novela de la selva, 35, 175, 181, 183, 207n21. *See also* Sarduy
novela de la tierra, 35, 175, 181, 183, 207n30. *See also* Sarduy
Núñez Cabeza de Vaca, Alvar: *Naufragios*, 126

Ochoa, John: "The Uses of Literary History: Some Recent Titles," 16–17
Ortiz, Fernando: *Contrapunteo cubano del tabaco y el azúcar*, 126; *La cubanidad y los negros*, 134; and "transculturación," 135
Other, the, 42, 43; Sarduy's use of, 155–57

pacotilla, 153, 155. *See also* kitsch
Pascal, Blaise, 39
patriarchal discourse, 27
Pérez Firmat, Gustavo, 134
Perón, Eva, 112
Perón, Juan Domingo, 32, 112
phallogocentrism, 190–91n39, 201n2. *See also* Sarduy
Philip II, 56, 57, 116, 147, 168, 179, 198n68
philology, 29, 43
popular culture, 12–14, 20, 27, 29, 30, 33, 61, 67, 69–71, 73–76, 80, 84, 89–91, 94, 100, 103–5, 107, 112, 118–20, 122–24, 138, 145, 191n51, 201n54
post-Boom, 26, 67, 74, 93, 103, 200n13. *See also* Boom novels
postmodernism, 200n13
post-structuralism: and Sarduy, 27
procuradores, 21
Puig, Manuel: and alternative archives, 72–73, 84, 90, 96; and archival contamination, 20–21; and the archive, 169; and archives of spurious culture, 102; *El beso de la mujer araña*, 28, 31, 46, 112–23; *Boquitas pintadas: Folletín*, 25, 28, 31, 32, 69, 73, 75–91, 99, 100, 117, 121; *The Buenos Aires Affair*, 28, 32, 69, 91–99, 111, 117, 121; and *cabecitas negras*, 73, 98; and canonicity, 26; characters of, 13–14; and Cervantes, 119; and detective novels, 69, 70, 91, 98, 117; and enfranchising the subaltern, 16; and *el folletín*, 25, 32; *géneros menores* (marginalized characters) 26, 27, 70–72, 76–80, 94, 100, 102, 104, 110, 113, 125; as hybrid author, 28, 78; novels of, 26–30; *Pubis angelical*, 30; and the serial novel, 69, 70, 73, 76–79, 99–123; *La traición de Rita Hayworth*, 28, 31, 33, 99, 103–11; use of letters, 76, 83, 84, 89, 80; use of the vernacular, 71
purity, 22, 23, 41, 42, 154

Rama, Ángel: *La ciudad letrada*, 21
Read, Malcolm, 19
relación, 74
Richard, Nelly, 100
Riobó, Carlos, 204n54, 204n56
Rivera, José Eustasio: *La vorágine*, 175, 183–87
Roa Bastos, Augusto: *I, the Supreme*, 74
Rodríguez Monegal, Emir, 93, 157, 205n89
Rojas, Fernando de: *La Celestina*, 125, 161
romanische philologie, 29

Said, Edward W.: and Orientalism, 173–74
Sánchez, Luis Rafael, 27
Santos, Lidia, 30, 72–73, 101, 112 201n54
Sapir, Edward: on spurious culture, 101
Sarduy, Severo: and archival contamination, 20–21; and the archive, 72, 169; and archive of spurious culture, 101; and the Baroque, 143–47; 151–52, 156, 192; *Barroco*, 144, 146; "El Barroco y el Neobarroco," 146; on *Boquitas pintadas*, 78–79; and canonicity, 26; characters of, 13–14; *Cobra*, 28, 33, 125, 127, 144–62, 182;

INDEX

Colibrí, 28, 33–35, 163, 175–88; and *lo cubano*, 127, 132, 141, 156, 157; on Dadaist collages, 130; *De donde son los cantantes*, 27, 28, 33, 34, 125, 127, 131–43, 157, 172, 203n36; "Dispersión: Falsas Notas/Homenaje a Lezama," 128; and enfranchising the subaltern, 16; *Escrito sobre un cuerpo: Ensayos de crítica*, 127, 130; and gender roles, 130–31; *Gestos*, 27, 30, 192n69; and homoeroticism, 166–69, 171, 172182, 183, 186, 187; as hybrid author, 28; and intertextuality, 141; on Lezama, 128, 133; *Maitreya*, 28, 33, 35, 163–75, 182; and marginalized characters, 26–27, 70–72, 125; and the Neobaroque, 35, 125, 144–45; novels of, 26–30, 101; and Orientalism, 35; and *la novela de la selva*, 35, 175, 181–83, 207n21; and *la novela de la tierra*, 35, 175, 181–83; and *pacotilla*, 155; and paradigm shift, 126; and patriarchy, 124–25, 127; *La simulación*, 130, 153; and the subaltern, 124; transvestism, 152–54, 157; use of Chinese boxes, 126, 131; and women, 130
Scheherazade, 113, 193n73
Self, the, 42, 43
serial novels, 198n25. *See also* Puig
Simancas (Spanish State Archive), 37, 56, 57, 196n58, 198n27

Spivak, Gayatri, 36, 69
subaltern, the: defined, 189n3. *See also* Sarduy
subversion, 22–23, 127
sub-versions, 20, 68, 184
Swartz, David, 101
Swift, Jonathan: "museum of commonplaces," 39

Thiebaut, Guy, 119
Thousand and One Nights, 14, 113, 193n73
Tittler, Jonathan, 79; on *The Buenos Aires Affair*, 95

ur text, 18, 65, 154, 155

Vargas Llosa, Mario, 28; *La casa verde*, 183, 184
Vico, Giambattista, 205n81
Vitier, Cintio, 128, 131; *Lo cubano en la poesía*, 126, 129, 134, 136

Weber, Max: analysis of status, 24
West, Alan, 171, 172

Yerushalmi, Yosef Hayim, 49, 52, 195n45

Zamora, Margarita: "Language and Authority in the *Comentarios reales*," 71